GLOBAL MARKET BRIEFINGS

# Doing Business with India
## Third Edition

Consultant Editor: Roderick Millar

Foreword from Dr Amit Mitra,
Secretary-General of the
Federation of Indian Chambers of Commerce and Industry

GMB

GMB Publishing Ltd.
Hereford House
23-24 Smithfield Street
London EC1A 9LF
United Kingdom
www.globalmarketbriefings.com

525 South 4th Street, #241
Philadelphia, PA 19147
United States of America

This edition first published 2009 by GMB Publishing Ltd.



ISBN-13 978-1-84673-113-6
E-ISBN-13 978-1-84673-114-3

**British Library Cataloguing in Publication Data**
A CIP record for this book is available from the British Library

Library of Congress Cataloguing-in Publication Data

Typeset by David Lewis XML Associates Ltd.

# Contents

2.7 Analysing the Indian Market 85
*Karthik Ramamurthy, Synovate Business Consulting*

2.8 Marketing 93
*Darrell Kofkin, Global Marketing Network*

**Part 3 Finance, Tax and Accounting** 99

3.1 Direct Taxation Issues 101
*KPMG India*

3.2 Indirect Taxation Issues 117
*KPMG India*

3.3 Accounting and Audit Requirements 125
*KPMG India*

**Part 4 Legal and Regulatory Framework** 129

4.1 Administrative Barriers to Entry 131
*Diljeet Titus and Pragya Dhamija, Titus & Co. Advocates*

4.2 Business Structures 139
*Diljeet Titus and Garima Bhagat, Titus & Co. Advocates*

4.3 Investment Facilities for NRIs / PIOs and Other Foreign Investors 147
*Diljeet Titus and Pragya Dhamija, Titus & Co. Advocates*

4.4 Mergers and Acquisitions 155
*Diljeet Titus and Monica Arora, Titus & Co. Advocates*

4.5 Employment Issues 163
*Diljeet Titus and Nishant Malhotra, Titus & Co. Advocates*

4.6 Export and Import Issues 171
*Diljeet Titus and Achint Singh Gyani, Titus & Co. Advocates*

4.7 Intellectual Property Law 179
*Diljeet Titus and Manish Gupta, Titus & Co. Advocates*

4.8 Company Dissolution and Liquidation 187
*Diljeet Titus and Sushmita Ganguly, Titus & Co. Advocates*

4.9 Dispute Resolution 195
*Diljeet Titus and Manish Gupta, Titus & Co. Advocates*

4.10 Contract Issues, Consumer Protection and Property Issues 201
*Diljeet Titus and Garima Bhagat, Titus & Co. Advocates*

4.11 Competition Law 209
*Diljeet Titus and Shamik Narain, Titus & Co. Advocates*

4.12 Corporate Governance 217
*Diljeet Titus and Raghav Handa, Titus & Co. Advocates*

# About the Contributors

The **Confederation of Indian Industry** has established a specialized **Institute of Logistics** – to become a centre of excellence in logistics and supply chain management. The principal objectives of the CII Institute of Logistics are to enhance the competitiveness of Indian industry and all the key sectors of the economy which impact India's growth through integrated initiatives in supply chain management and logistics domain area and meet the latent need of the industry for specialized services in logistics and supply chain management, ranging from education to research to consultancy, information services, etc.

**DTZ Debenham Tie Leung** is one of the world's leading property advisory groups with a strong presence in Europe, the Middle East and Africa, the Asia-Pacific region and is in partnership with the Staubach Company in the Americas.
**Vivek Dahiya** is an associate director of DTZ India, with over eight years' experience in real estate. He is a town planner and an MBNA (finance).

**Global HR** is an international human resources consulting firm that helps organizations stay competitive by providing assistance around the following:

- human resources (HR) strategy and planning around organic and inorganic growth;
- talent management and succession planning;
- improving the effectiveness of the HR organization.

A specialist focus of the firm is the emerging markets.
Having been responsible for human resources for international blue-chip companies across 40 different countries, **Devyani Vaishampayan** is a specialist in facilitating, managing and anticipating HR issues and talent management. She specializes in helping organizations design and implement HR solutions across an international base, particularly between Asia Pacific and Europe.

Her educational background includes a degree in Electronics and an MBA, in addition to being a trained behavioural scientist. She is an engaging speaker and has been invited to speak at various global forums by *The Economist*, London Business School, Executive Grapevine, ORC and CIPD.

**Global Marketing Network** is a professional body for marketing and marketing professionals. With profound changes now occurring in the global economy, and with businesses under increasing pressures to retain existing clients, attract new clients and create new, profitable and less risky business models, more and more individuals and organisations are committing to the GMN vision worldwide.

Global Marketing Network's vision is to be the world's professional body for marketing professionals by:

- supporting today's global marketer, wherever they live in the world, at whatever stage of their career they are;
- putting marketing and marketers back in the boardroom though a structured continuing professional development programme;
- raising standards in marketing practice to help businesses achieve greater profitability and Return on Investment (ROI);
- supporting aspirations and rewarding and recognising professional achievements;
- enabling marketers to be more employable, knowledgeable, promotable, capable, better networked and better rewarded.

**Darrell Kofkin** is Chief Executive of Global Marketing Network. Darrell commenced his career in marketing management with London Underground in 1990 before joining InterCity Midland Mainline as its Marketing Planning Manager in 1995. In 1997 Darrell entered academia and in 2002 he founded the premier private marketing training college, London School of Marketing. He subsequently sold his stake in the company in 2005 to establish Global Marketing Network, the global professional body for marketing and marketing professionals worldwide. Darrell currently sits on the Business Superbrands Council, was a senior judge and keynote speaker of the 2007 Marketing Week Effectiveness Awards, speaks at conferences and business schools around the world and writes regularly in the media on marketing issues. He also sits on the Advisory Council of the University of Hertfordshire Alumni Association.

**C. Jayanthi** has been working as a print journalist for over 18 years in leading English-language dailies in India and also with Gulf News, Dubai. He launched the Education Times supplement for the leading English daily in India, *The Times of India*, in 1998 and was its editor until 2005. Since then he has worked with *The Financial Express* as deputy features editor, corporate news features. He has written a couple of novels, *English Journalistic Quiche*, and *A Reporter's Journey*, published by the Writers Workshop, India.

**KPMG India:** KPMG is the global network of professional services firms of KPMG International. KPMG member firms provide audit, tax and advisory services through industry focused, talented professionals who deliver value for the benefit of their clients and communities.

The member firms of KPMG International in India were established in September 1993. As members of the cohesive business unit that serves the Middle East and South Asia (KPMG's MESA business unit), they respond to a client service environment by leveraging the resources of a globally aligned organization and providing detailed knowledge of local laws, regulations, markets and competition.

KPMG has offices in India in Mumbai, Delhi, Bangalore, Chennai, Hyderabad, Kolkata and Pune and services over 2,000 international and national clients. The firms in India have access to more than 1,500 Indian and expatriate professionals, many of whom are internationally trained.

**Management Development Institute** is a pioneer and market leader in executive education in India. Their educational programmes help executives in broadening their understanding and improving their skills to prepare them to face challenges at higher positions. MDI conducts more than 100 management development programmes every year. Programmes of varying duration and structure focus on the current areas of interest to executives at the senior, middle or junior management levels. Set in a verdant campus over 37 acres in Gurgaon, it is located about one hour from downtown New Delhi.

**Dr Amit Kapoor** is a PhD in Industrial Economics and Business Strategy. He has led several well-respected consultancy projects with the government, Bharti Televentures, Spice Telecom and NAFED amongst others. He is an affiliate faculty of the Institute of Strategy and Competitiveness, Harvard Business School. He also jointly offers the course with Professor Michael Porter at the Management Development Institute, India. Amit is also the Chairman of the Institute for Competitiveness in India. Under this initiative he compiled the India Competitiveness Report in 2006. He is also a member of the Sub Committee on Manufacturing Competitiveness of CII.

**Dr Arun Sahay**, Professor of Strategic Management, a hard core business executive turned academician, has been successful in both the corporate and academic world. He was Chairman and Managing Director of Scooters India Limited, a company which had been declared a "mortuary case" until his turnaround of it. In recognition of this, he was made the founder President of the Strategic Management Forum of India. He has been invited to serve on many corporate boards as well as those of the technical and management institutions. He represents the government on task forces in companies like Nuclear Power Corporation Of India, Power Grid Corporation of India, National Thermal Power Corporation and National Hydro Power Corporation. A mechanical engineer by training he also studied management at the University of Madras and the Advanced Management Course at Henley College of Management (UK). He is a ferocious reader and writer and presently contributes in the fields of business strategy, innovation & technology and entrepreneurship.

**Roderick Millar** is an experienced editor and has overseen this guide since 1999. He has an MBA from the University of Houston and an MA in Economic and Social History from St Andrews University, Scotland. He has written several books about finance and business and been a consultant editor for eight GMB Publishing titles. He also is managing editor of IEDP.info, a business that monitors the executive education sector. Currently he is Executive Editor for magazines at GMB Publishing.

**The National Association of Software and Service Companies (NASSCOM)** is the premier organization that represents and sets the tone for public policy for the Indian software industry. It is a not-for-profit global trade body with over 1200 members, of which over 250 are global companies from the US, UK, EU, Japan and China. NASSCOM's member companies are in the business of software development, software services, software products, IT-enabled/business process outsourcing (BPO) services and e-commerce. It was set up in 1988 to facilitate business and trade in software and services and to encourage advancement of research in software technology. Currently, NASSCOM is headquartered in New Delhi, India, with regional offices in the cities of Mumbai, Chennai, Hyderabad, Bangalore, Pune and Kolkata.
**Rajdeep Sahrawat** is a Vice President and part of the leadership team at NASSCOM and he is responsible for accelerating the growth of the domestic IT market and increasing innovation and research and development (R&D) within the IT industry. He started his career in 1990 with Tata Consultancy Services (TCS) and worked with TCS for 15 years in various roles. Rajdeep has a Masters degree in Business Administration (Finance) from the Faculty of Management Studies, University of Delhi (1990).

**Shilputsi Consultants** is a leading Indian consulting firm specialising in strategic human resource development solutions. Shilputsi provides strategic HR advisory, executive development and search and selection services.

Shilputsi has a global presence and reach with a wide range of multinational and Indian clients. They work in a variety of industries to offer valuable guidance for strategic business, HR and leadership issues.
**Purvi Sheth** is Vice President at Shilputsi Consultants, India and the USA. Purvi has a first class BA from St Xavier's College, Bombay University, and has completed the Leadership & Strategy Program at Wharton Business School. In addition to her work at Shilputsi she is an advisor to the Entrepreneurship Cells at the Indian Institute of Technology, Mumbai, and the Jamnalal Baj Institute of Management, Mumbai. She has been a member of the jury panel to judge "India's Under 40 Hot Executives" for three years.

**Synovate Business Consulting** is the market strategy consulting arm of Synovate, a leading market research firm. Synovate India is headquartered in Mumbai with a pan-India presence. Synovate is a group company of global media communications specialist Aegis Group plc.

**Karthik Ramamurthy** heads the business consulting operations of Synovate in Mumbai.

Headquartered in New Delhi, **Titus & Co. Advocates** has associate offices in Bangalore, Mumbai, Kolkata, Chennai, Hyderabad, Jalandhar and Jabalpur. Managed by a team of 36 professionals, Titus & Co. have authored/co-authored works on a diverse range of topics and issues in the field including: corporate and commercial; infrastructure projects; project finance; banking and finance; capital markets; commercial property; dispute resolution; information, communication and entertainment; intellectual property; and labour. The firm is a member of the Indo-American Chamber of Commerce, Confederation of Indian Industries (CII), Federation of Indian Chambers of Commerce and Industry (FICCI), Assosiated Chambers of Commerce and Industry of India (ASSOCHAM), the Supreme Court Bar Association, Delhi High Court Bar Association, Company Law Board, Bar Association, Joint Business Councils, Indian Council of Arbitration, the Society of Indian Law Firms, and the International Chamber of Commerce (ICC).

**Diljeet Titus** is Managing Partner of law firm Titus & Co. He holds a BA from St Stephen's College, University of Delhi, and an LLB from the University of Jabalpur, Madhya Pradesh. He is a member of the Supreme Court Bar Association and the Bar Council of Delhi. His main practice areas include project finance, mergers and acquisitions, capital markets and debt restructuring.

**Raghav Handa** is an Associate Advocate with law firm Titus & Co. He holds a BS LLB from the University of Pune. He is a member of the Bar Council of Punjab and Haryana. He has co-authored articles on various legal subjects. His main practice areas include: corporate and commercial; infrastructure; corporate investment; structuring and restructuring in the areas of power; project finance; joint ventures and collaborations; cross-border mergers and acquisitions; securities regulations; commercial and financial transactions; energy; communications; information technology; real estate; direct and indirect taxes; double taxation; intellectual property; labour and employment.

**Manish Gupta** is an Associate Advocate with law firm Titus & Co. He holds a BA LLB (Hons) from the National Law Institute University, Bhopal. He is a member of the Bar Council of Madhya Pradesh. He has co-authored articles on various legal subjects. His main practice areas include corporate laws including commercial litigation.

**Sushmita Ganguly** is a Company Secretary with law firm Titus & Co. She holds a B.Com from Allahabad University, Uttar Pradesh, and is a member of the Institute of Company Secretaries of India. Her main practice areas include regulatory compliances for corporate transactions, mergers and acquisitions, capital markets, venture capital funds, joint ventures and foreign investments.

**Monica Arora** is a Company Secretary with law firm Titus & Co. She holds a B.Com from University of Delhi and is a member of the Institute of Company Secretaries of India. Her main practice areas include regulatory compliances for corporate transactions, private equity investments, mergers and acquisitions.

**Pragya Dhamija** is an Associate Advocate with law firm Titus & Co. She holds a BSL LLB from the University of Pune. She is a member of the Bar Council of Madhya Pradesh. Her main practice areas include banking, corporate, mergers and acquisitions.

**Durgesh Singh** is an Associate Advocate with law firm Titus & Co. He holds a BSc. from St Stephen's College, University of Delhi, and an LLB from the University of Delhi. He is a member of the Bar Council of Delhi. He has co-authored articles on various legal subjects. His main practice areas include project finance and infrastructure, venture capital and private equity investments, mergers and acquisitions.

**Jasman Boparai** is an Associate Advocate with law firm Titus & Co. She holds a BS LLB from the University of Pune and an LLM from Boston University. She has co-authored articles on various legal subjects. Her main practice areas include corporate laws, mergers and acquisitions and inbound investments.

**Kanwalvir Kang** is an Associate Advocate with law firm Titus & Co. He holds a BA from Punjab University and an LLB from Barkatullah University. He has co-authored articles on various legal subjects. His main practice areas include general corporate matters; mergers and acquisitions; labour and employment.

**Ramandeep Kaur Arora** is an Associate Advocate with law firm Titus & Co. She holds an LLB from the Indraprastha University, Delhi. She is a member of the Bar Council of Delhi. She has co-authored articles on various legal subjects. Her main practice areas include mergers and acquisitions, joint ventures, inbound investments and intellectual property.

**Shamik Narain** is an Associate Advocate with law firm Titus & Co. He holds a BSL LLB from the Symbiosis International University. His main practice areas include dispute resolution, corporate litigation and taxation.

**Ratnika Sehgal** is an Associate Advocate with law firm Titus & Co. She holds an LLB (Hons.) from the Indraprastha University, Delhi. She is a member of the Bar Council of Delhi. She has co-authored articles on various legal subjects. Her main practice areas include corporate laws including intellectual property rights.

**Achint Singh Gyani** is an Associate Advocate with law firm Titus & Co. He holds a BSL LLB from the University of Pune. He is a member of the Bar Council of Punjab and Haryana. His main practice areas include dispute resolution, corporate litigation and taxation.

**Nishant Malhotra** is an Associate Advocate with law firm Titus & Co. He holds an LLB from the Indraprastha University. His main practice areas include corporate law, taxation and dispute resolution.

**Garima Bhagat** is an Associate Advocate with law firm Titus & Co. She holds a BS LLB from the Symbiosis International Law University, Pune. She is a member of the Bar Council of Delhi. Her main practice areas include corporate and intellectual property.

**Winning Communications Partnership Ltd** is a leading international consultancy offering tailor-made pragmatic solutions to assist organizations to develop appropriate strategies to compete globally. Its consultants have lived and worked abroad and are uniquely capable to help organizations align themselves to the changes in both the global and local marketplace. It works in partnership with its clients to create communities of best practice where the highest value organizational learning and transformational change maximize individual potential and organizational growth. WCP develop leaders at all levels of the organization who are committed to clear value sets about: who they are and what they stand for; the bigger global potential and opportunities; creating a working environment where quality is not just the end product, but the way they do business. The profits of the company are wholly dedicated to charitable use.

**Deepak Mahtani**, BA, MIMC, FRSA has a business degree from Sophia University in Tokyo, Japan, and the American College, Switzerland. Deepak is of Indian origin, lived in the Far East for 14 years and Switzerland for 14 years, and speaks English, French, Spanish, Japanese, and two Indian languages.

He is currently a management training consultant, specializing in understanding and working with different cultures, especially in India, Japan, and China.

He has coached and trained hundreds of senior managers who are involved in offshore developments and outsourcing to Indian companies, and in remote team management around the globe. Most of his clients are FTSE100 or Fortune 500 companies.

# Foreword

In the midst of the current global meltdown, India, along with China, is still presenting a strong growth performance. The economy had been growing above 9 per cent a year for the past three years and is widely estimated to show 8.5 per cent growth during the present fiscal year. That is a major milestone when the rest of the world is staring at the prospect of even negative growth. But analysts are increasingly asking the question whether a deepening crisis in the global markets will leave its mark on the Indian economy. Obviously, it will have some impact, hence, the slowing down from a +9 per cent record to a slightly lower level.

The fact of the matter is that the Indian economy is driven by domestic consumption and investment. Going by the latest figures, consumption accounts for 60 per cent of gross domestic product (GDP), and of total investments only 8 per cent originates from overseas. The growth of the economy in the last few years has further strengthened the demand factors and international slackness should not ordinarily affect that. Hence, the growth drivers will retain their strength even when the global economy slows down. Had it been otherwise, that is, had the India story been led by export linkages with the outside world, the Indian growth story would have been adversely affected by the global turmoil. There are several countries that have shown very strong growth performance on the basis of their exports that are more prone to the global meltdown viruses.

While consumption demand has gone up sharply, the investment rate has also increased in the post-reforms era. Overall savings have increased to 34.8 per cent of GDP and investments to 35.9 per cent of GDP. This trend is likely to maintained in the current phase. Along with this, the authorities have liberalized the foreign direct investment (FDI) regime since the middle of the 1990s and India's FDI rules can now be termed one of the most liberal. In step with the liberalization drive, we have noticed a quantum jump in FDI into India. The latest figures indicate that FDI flows into India have increased to as much as $22 billion in 2006–2007, from about $5 billion just about three years back. Given the current interest in India, there is no doubt that the FDI levels will increase further in the medium to long term.

It is in this context that a business guide is all the more welcome. As outsiders come in larger numbers to invest in India, they will demand ready-made guides for their entry into and for carrying on their day-to-day operations in the country. This 3rd edition of ***Doing Business with India*** is therefore timely and should be a great help to those who want to come into India. This guide is welcome for another reason: the remaining complexities of registering a business in India or for carrying on operations appear somewhat intimidating to those coming from outside. These are much more manageable for those who are already in the country.

In fact, an annual survey conducted by Federation of Indian Chambers of Commerce and Industry (FICCI) confirms this trend. While companies already in India are doing fine business and contemplating further investment to expand their Indian operations, those yet to enter the market show considerable anxiety about committing their funds in India. The FICCI survey points out that most of the FDI firms have been earning profit within five–six years of starting their operations. Again, most of the FDI firms are coming in to cash in on the domestic market and not expressly to cater to export markets. And yet, many of them have started using India as an export hub after successfully establishing themselves in the Indian market and enjoying substantial economies of scale from their Indian operations. A business guide could surely help those firms who are sitting on the fence and are somewhat undecided whether to enter or not.

I welcome your effort to bring out your publication. It will complement the FICCI's own efforts to lend a helping hand to those foreign direct investors who want to come into the country. FICCI has already a fully fledged set-up for providing hand-holding services to prospective investors. Together, we can convert many of the proposals into real-time investments. Good luck, God speed.

**Dr Amit Mitra**
**Secretary-General**
**Federation of Indian Chambers of Commerce and Industry**
**New Delhi**

# Country Map

India: states and union territories

Source: www.mapsofindia.com

# Part 1

# Background to the Market

# 1.1

# India at a Glance

| | |
|---|---|
| Government: | Democratic Federal Republic, gained independence in 1947 |
| Political Structure: | Head of State: President (Shrimati Pratibha Devisingh Patil, elected 2007)<br>Head of Government: Prime Minister (Manmohan Singh, since 2004)<br>Bicameral Parliament (Sansad) comprising the Council of States (Rajya Sabha) and the People's Assembly (Lok Sabha) |
| Current Government: | A coalition headed by Congress. There are 675 million registered voters. Over 387 million votes were cast at the last federal election in April/May 2004. The next elections must be before 2009. |
| Main Parties: | There are many regionally significant political parties. Below are the five largest parties in the Federal parliament, with the number of seats won in 2004 (272 seats are required for a majority):<br>• India National Congress (known as "Congress") – 145<br>• Bharatiya Janata Party (known as "BJP") – 138<br>• Communist Party of India (Marxist) (not to be confused with the Communist Party of India) – 43<br>• Samajwadi Party (a democratic socialist party based in Uttar Pradesh) – 36<br>• Rashtriya Janata Dal (Hindu/Muslim based democratic party based in Bihar) – 24 |
| Currency: | Indian Rupee (Rs or INR) Aug 08 $1 = 43 Rs; €1 = 63 Rs; £1 = 80 Rs* |
| GDP: | $2.989 trillion at PPP; $1.099 trillion at official exchange rate (Sept 07 est)** |
| GDP Growth Rate: | 7.5% to 8% for 2008/09*** |
| GDP per Capita: | $2,700 (2007 est)** |
| GDP by Sector: | Agriculture – 17.2% (2007 est)**<br>Industry – 29.4%<br>Services – 52.9% |
| Exports: | 2002 – $44 billion<br>2005 – $76 billion<br>2007 – $150 billion (est) |
| Imports: | 2002 – $52 billion<br>2005 – $113 billion<br>2007 – $230 billion (est) |
| Labour Force: | 516 million (2007 est)**<br><br>Agriculture – 60%<br>Industry – 12%<br>Services – 28% |
| Inflation Rate: | 12% (year to Jul 26, 2008)**** |
| Area: | 3.29 million square kilometres (approx 1/3 the size of the USA)** |
| Population: | 1.147 billion (July 2008)** |
| Population Structure**: | 31.5% under the age of 15 years<br>63.3% between 15-64 years<br>5.2% 65 years and over |
| Literacy**†: | Male – 73%<br>Female – 48% |
| Below Poverty Line: | 25% (people living on less than $1 per day)** |

Main Holidays: 1st January (New Years Day)
26th January (Republic Day)
15th August (Independence Day)
2nd October (Mahatma Gandhi's Birthday)
25th December (Christmas Day)

Some Religious Holidays/Festivals††: Al Hijra / Muharram (Islamic New Year) (29th December, 2008)
Holi (Last day of) (11th March 2009)
Mahavir Jayanthi (7th April, 2009)
Sri Rama Navami (Birthday of Sri Rama) (3rd April, 2009)
Milad-Un-Nabi (Birth of the Prophet) (9th March, 2009)
Good Friday (10th April, 2009)
Baisakhi, Vishu/Bahag, (13th April, 2009)
Buddha Purnima (8th May, 2009)
Mesadi (14th August, 2009)
Ramadan (Starts) (22nd August, 2009)
Eid al-Fitr (End of Ramadan) (21st September, 2009)
Vijaya Dasami (Dasera) (28th September, 2009)
Diwali (Festival of Lights) (17th October, 2009)
Eid al Adha (Feast of the Sacrifice) (27th November, 2009)
Bakrid (21st December, 2009)
Al Hijra / Muharram (Islamic New Year) (18th December, 2009)

Languages Spoken: English is the principal business language.
Hindi is the first language of approx 38% of the population
There are 16 further principal languages and hundreds of regional dialects.

International Airports: New Delhi – Indira Gandhi International, www.newdelhiairport.in
Mumbai (Bombay) – Chattrapathi Shivaji International Airport, www.csia.in
Chennai (Madras), www.chennaiairport.com (unofficial site)
Kolkata (Calcutta) – Netaji Subhash Airport (Dum Dum), www.calcuttaairport.com (unofficial site)
Kochi (Cochin), www.cochin-airport.com
Hyderabad, www.newhyderabadairport.com
Bengaluru (formerly Bangalore), www.bengaluruairport.com

Major Ports: Kolkata (Calcutta) – www.kolkataporttrust.gov.in
Chennai (Madras) – www.chennaiport.gov.in
Kandla – Gujarat, www.kandlaport.gov.in
Kochi (Cochin) – Kerala, www.cochinport.com
Mormugao – Goa, www.mormugaoport.gov.in
Mumbai (Bombay) – www.mumbaiport.gov.in
New Mangalore – Karnataka, www.newmangalore-port.com
Paradip – Orissa, www.paradipport.gov.in
Tuticorin – Tamil Nadhu, www.tuticorinport.gov.in
Vishakapatnam – Andhra Pradesh, www.vizagport.com

## Climate (average monthly minimum/maximum temperatures and average monthly rainfall)

| | January | | April | | July | | October | |
|---|---|---|---|---|---|---|---|---|
| | Temp | *Rain* | Temp | *Rain* | Temp | *Rain* | Temp | *Rain* |
| **Bengaluru** | 14/27 °C | *6 mm* | 21/34 °C | *41 mm* | 19/27 °C | *100 mm* | 18/28 °C | *149 mm* |
| **Hyderabad** | 15/29 °C | *11 mm* | 24/38 °C | *19 mm* | 22/31 °C | *160 mm* | 20/31 °C | *72 mm* |
| **Kochi** | 23/30 °C | *23 mm* | 26/37 °C | *125 mm* | 24/28 °C | *592 mm* | 24/29 °C | *340 mm* |
| **Kolkata** | 13/26 °C | *9 mm* | 24/36 °C | *44 mm* | 26/32 °C | *125 mm* | 23/32 °C | *114 mm* |
| **Mumbai** | 19/28 °C | *4 mm* | 24/32 °C | *4 mm* | 25/30 °C | *165 mm* | 24/32 °C | *64 mm* |
| **New Delhi** | 6/21 °C | *25 mm* | 20/36 °C | *8 mm* | 25/30 °C | *179 mm* | 18/34 °C | *10 mm* |

* OANDA.com
** CIA Factbook
*** FICCI
**** Centre for Monitoring the Indian Economy, CMIE
† ie. able to read and write at age 15 years and over.
†† These festivals/holidays change date each year, and are not necessarily observed nationally.

# 1.2

# Political Background and Overview

*Dr Arun Sahay, Centre for Entrepreneurship, Management Development Institute*

India has long been a nation of philosophers with a well-developed and peaceful society. One of the oldest scriptures in the world is the four-volume *Vedas,* which many regard as the thought repository of 'Indic culture' that projected some of the modern scientific discoveries. There have been many major ruling dynasties, for example the Maurayas, Guptas, the Shakas and the Kushans. Chanakya (350 BC–275 BC) is known for his political and economic astuteness and is still quoted in management institutes whilst teaching strategy or policy. John D. Barrow's book *The Book of Nothing* credits the Indian astronomer Brahmagupta (628 AD) for defining zero, whilst Aryabhata (476 BC) is credited for inventing zero, without which today's progress in science and technology would not have been possible. Nearly every major religion in the world is represented in India. It is also the land of Lord Buddha, Lord Mahavira and Guru Nanak Dev, the founders of Buddhism, Jainism and Sikhism.

Despite formidable barriers in the form of the mighty Himalayas to the north and oceans to the east, south and west, India has also received a succession of foreigners, many of them carrying swords, guns and dynamite. The Aryans were among the first to arrive in India, which was, until then, inhabited by the Dravidians. Others who came later included Greeks, Persians, Mughals and latterly the British, Portuguese and French. Among them, the British gained supremacy and ruled India for centuries.

Out of these waves of immigration, a composite culture has emerged. Thus India has become a land of unity in diversity – a land of integration, adoption and learning, a land of change and continuity.

Mahatma Gandhi, a British-educated lawyer, mobilized the Indians and through his Satyagraha (Quest for Truth), a unique non-violent campaign, India threw off the bondage of British rule on 15 August 1947. Free India's first prime minister, Pandit Jawaharlal Nehru, described the moment as a 'tryst with destiny'. In less than three years of attaining freedom, India had framed a Constitution and declared itself a Republic on 26 January 1950. The constitution was given shape by some of the finest minds of the country, who ensured the trinity of justice, liberty and equality for the citizens of India. The Constitution was made flexible enough to adjust to the demands of social and economic changes within a democratic framework.

India, a union of states, is a sovereign, secular, democratic Republic with a parliamentary system of government. The Indian polity is governed in terms of the Constitution, which was adopted by the Constituent Assembly on 26 November 1949 and came into force on 26 January 1950. The president is the constitutional head of the Executive of the Union. Real executive power, however, vests in a Council of Ministers with the prime minister as head. Article 74(1) of the Constitution provides that the Council of Ministers headed by the prime minister shall aid and advise the president who shall, in exercise of his/her functions, act in accordance with such advice. The Council of Ministers is collectively responsible to the Lok Sabha – the House of the People.

India's bicameral parliament consists of the Rajya Sabha (Council of States) and the aforementioned Lok Sabha. The legislatures of the states and union territories elect 233 members to the Rajya Sabha, and the president appoints another 12. The elected members of the Rajya Sabha serve six-year terms, with one-third up for election every two years. The Lok Sabha consists of 545 members: 543 are directly elected to five-year terms; the other two are appointed.

It is generally believed that states are represented in the Rajya Sabha and the people in the Lok Sabha but with so many regional parties springing up, the roles of the Rajya Sabha and the Lok Sabha seem to have become inverted. After 1996, due to the pre-eminence of regional parties in the Lok Sabha, for all practical purposes, it is the Lower House (Lok Sabha) that represents states' interests. Thus the importance of the Upper House (Rajya Sabha) has been declining. Given the scheme and design of the Indian Constitution, the federalism has been weak because it flows downwards from the centre, rather than upwards from the states. The political scenario has been changing and presently an era of coalition government at the centre has emerged, due to the following four developments:

1. Formal regional parties – 'regional' meaning confined to one state (or at best extended to the neighbouring states) – now account for around half the seats in the Lok Sabha. This proportion is likely to increase in future elections.
2. Even the so-called national parties have now become regional in terms of the interests they represent. This is partly due to the aggregative definition of 'national' that is used in the electoral context. A party needs to win only more than 5 per cent of the total votes polled to become national, regardless of the distribution of those votes. Hence, the Communist Party of India-Marxist is a 'national' party, even though it is concentrated in just two-and-a-half states.

3. Due to criteria used for candidate selection by political parties – caste, money and muscle, in that order – there is lesser talent available in the Lok Sabha for ministerial posts than in the Rajya Sabha. However, partly, it is compensated for by the generally rising level of education. Nonetheless, the best ministers are from the Rajya Sabha, which also provides a way of bringing new folk into politics. Thus the quality of parliamentary debate, which should form an essential element of governance and legislation, is better in Rajya Sabha compared to that in Lok Sabha.
4. The balance between Rajya Sabha and Lok Sabha has been changing. The bill that should be thoroughly debated in Lok Sabha and should pass through Rajya Sabha in reality is debated in Rajya Sabha before being sent for presidential assent.

There are 26 states and six union territories in the country. The system of governance in the states closely resembles that of the Union. In the states, the governor, as the representative of the president, is the Head of State, but real executive power rests with the Chief Minister, who heads the Council of Ministers. The Council of Ministers of a state is collectively responsible to the elected legislative assembly of the state.

The Constitution governs the sharing of legislative power between Parliament and the State Legislatures, and provides for the vesting of residual powers in Parliament. The power to amend the Constitution is also vested in Parliament.

## Government and its role

According to its constitution, India is a 'sovereign, socialist, secular, democratic republic.' Like the United States, India has a federal form of government. However, the central government in India has greater power in relation to its states, and its central government is patterned after the British parliamentary system. Subjects like defence, foreign policy and atomic energy are dealt with by the central government, whilst law and order is dealt with by the state governments. Certain subjects like science and technology, education and environment are concurrent and dealt with by both the governments.

In 1948, immediately after independence, the governments introduced the Industrial Policy Resolution. This outlined the approach to industrial growth and development. To meet new challenges, from time to time, it was modified – in 1973, 1977 and 1980. The Industrial Policy Statement of 1980 focused attention on the need for promoting competition in the domestic market, technological upgrading and modernization. The policy laid the foundation for the change of attitude from import substitution to export promotion which encouraged foreign investment, especially in high-technology areas. A number of policy and procedural changes were introduced in 1985 and

1986 under the leadership of the then Prime Minister Shri Rajiv Gandhi. These policy initiatives aimed at increasing productivity, reducing costs and improving quality. The emphasis was on opening the domestic market to increased competition and readying the domestic industry to stand on its own in the face of international competition. The public sector was freed from a number of constraints and given a larger measure of autonomy. The technological and managerial modernization of industry was pursued as the key instrument for increasing productivity and improving global competition. The net result of all these changes was that Indian industry grew by an impressive average annual growth rate of 8.5 per cent.

However, India's 1991 debt crisis provided the opportunity for major economic reforms to deregulate the private sector and liberalize trade and investment. A new industrial policy was initiated in 1991. This led to the drastic cut-back of compulsory licensing of private sector industries and by 1997 applied only to nine industries. Restrictions on foreign companies and foreign financial institutions wishing to enter the Indian market were later lifted and presently 100 per cent investment is allowed in most industrial sectors.

With the creation of the World Trade Organization (WTO) in 1995 (of which India was an original signatory), a steady process of removing quantitative quotas and reducing tariff rates on imports created a more favourable environment for export-oriented production. The recovery from the initial shock of structural adjustment, buffered by a massive infusion of International Monetary Fund (IMF) loans, has generally been considered remarkable. Initially, the politicians of the opposition parties resisted the reforms tooth and nail, but when they came to power, they found no alternative but to proceed with the reform.

When the present United Progressive Alliance (UPA) government was formed, backed by the support of communist parties, the general expectation was that the reforms undertaken by earlier governments would be made redundant and the economy would not be able to maintain its growth targets. The UPA government's parliamentary majority was challenged in mid-2008 due to opposition to the proposed US-India nuclear agreement. While the UPA lost the support of the communist parties, it gained the support of the Samajwadi Party, allowing the UPA to continue to pursue its policies of liberalization, privatization and globalization. Implementation of these policies resulted in improved educational and job opportunities, brought about a reduction in the balance of payments deficit, and increased foreign exchange reserves.

## Indian judiciary

India's present judicial system came to life under the British. Thus its concepts and procedures resemble those of Anglo-Saxon countries. The Supreme Court consists of a chief justice and 25 other justices, all appointed by the president on the advice of the prime minister. The active role of the Indian judiciary, particularly the Supreme Court of India, has been widely appreciated both within and outside India. The Indian judicial system proved its mettle in handling the Bhopal gas leak case, which was unique for the whole world. The independence of the judiciary, ensured through the constitutional provisions and subsequent strengthening by judicial interpretation, has definitely contributed to the present status of the Indian judiciary.

## Judicial framework

- The judiciary is independent with minimal interference from the government.
- The Supreme Court, the apex judicial authority, is vested with powers to enforce fundamental rights and act as a guardian of the Constitution.
- Apart from the Supreme Court, the Indian judicial system has High Courts in every state, and lower courts at town level.
- In addition, there are alternative dispute resolution mechanisms to help liquidate pending cases in the various courts, either through arbitration or conciliation.

# Change in attitude of Indian policy

As the fourth-largest economy in the world, India is undoubtedly one of the most preferred destinations for FDI (foreign direct investment). The country has strength in IT (information technology) and other significant areas such as auto components, chemicals, apparels, pharmaceuticals and jewellery. India has always held promise for global investors, but its rigid FDI policies have proved a significant hindrance in this regard. However, as a result of a series of ambitious and positive reforms aimed at deregulating the economy and stimulating FDI, India has positioned itself as one of the front-runners of the rapidly growing Asia Pacific Region. India has a large pool of skilled managerial and technical expertise. The size of the middle class population, at 300 million, exceeds the population of both the US and the EU, and represents a powerful consumer market.

Since its liberalization in mid-1991, India has become a magnet for FDI. A noteworthy feature is the dramatic speed of approvals, some taking only a week. Automatic approval of projects in 34 industrial sectors is permitted. The constraint that FDI should reach only 40 per cent has been relaxed to 51 per cent. In certain sectors, such as infrastructure and computer software, foreign ownership can also be as high as 74 per cent and in some other sectors ownership can be 100 per cent.

As a result of these policy initiatives, FDI rose from $170 million in 1991–1992 to $1.3 billion in 1994–1995. It attracted a total of $2.4 billion in 1996–

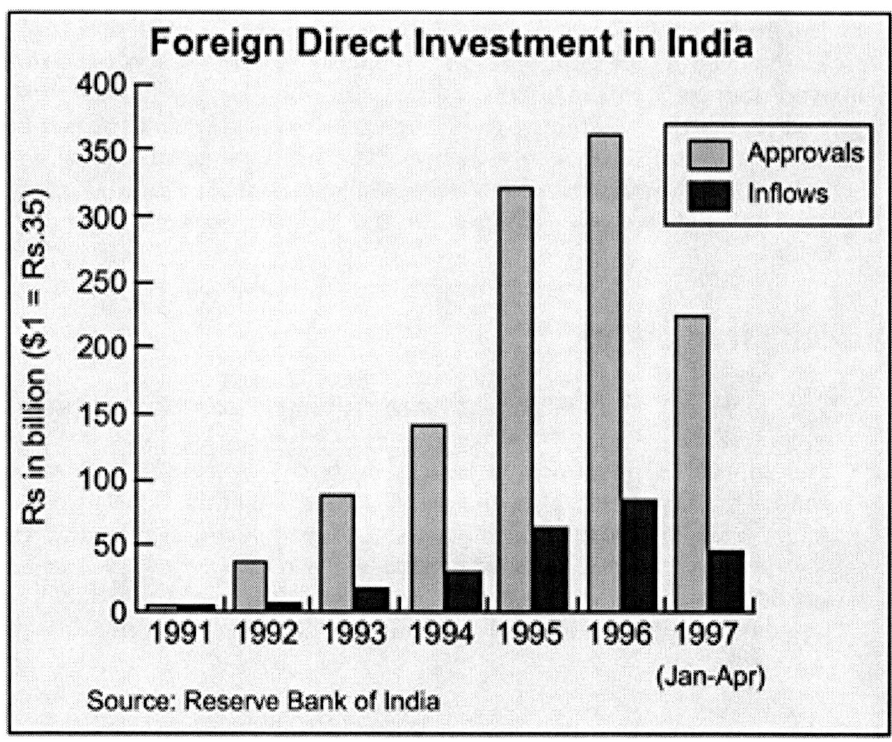


*Source:* Reserve Bank of India

Figure 1. Foreign direct investment in India

1997, and $3.4 billion in 1997–1998. FDI is nearly 25 times higher than it was before the economy was liberalized. FDI into India has surged to over $25 billion in 2007–2008, and the country's foreign exchange reserves crossed $341 billion.

The recently liberalized FDI policy (2005) allows up to a 100 per cent FDI stake in ventures. The upward moving growth curve of the real-estate sector owes some credit to a booming economy and liberalized FDI regime. In March 2005, the government amended the rules to allow 100 per cent FDI in the construction business. This automatic route has been permitted in townships, housing, built-up infrastructure and construction development projects, including housing, commercial premises, hotels, resorts, hospitals, educational institutions, recreational facilities, and city- and regional-level infrastructure.

## From licence raj to the era of innovation and entrepreneurship

After independence in 1947, India embarked on a period of centrally planned industrialization. The centrepiece of the planning regime was the Industries

(Development and Regulation) Act of 1951, which states that 'it is expedient in the public interest that the Union should take under its control the industries in the First Schedule', which included metallurgical industries, fuels, boilers and steam-generating plants, prime movers, electrical equipment, telecommunications and transportation. This Act introduced a system of industrial licensing to control the pace and pattern of industrial development across the country, which became known as the ' licence raj'. Licensing became the key means of allocating production targets set out in the five-year plans to firms. Both state and private firms in the registered manufacturing sector were covered under the licensing regime. State control over industrial development via licensing was intended to accelerate industrialization and economic growth, and to reduce regional disparities in income and wealth. However, the policy encouraged the industries to pursue licences rather than serve consumers.

The bureaucratic nature of the licensing process imposed a substantial administrative burden on firms. There was also considerable uncertainty as to whether licence applications would be approved and within what time frame. For example, 35 per cent of licence applications in 1959 and 1960 were rejected, with the rejected applicants accounting for around 50 per cent of the investment value of all applications. Recognition of these problems led to various reforms in the 1970s, which attempted to streamline the application process, raise exemption and expansion limits and exempt specific product lines from the provisions of the 1951 Industries Act. By this time it had become apparent that industrial licensing had failed to bring about the rapid industrial development that had been anticipated in the 1950s. The heightened political competition that followed led to pressure to dismantle government controls, including the industrial licensing system. The Congress leader Indira Gandhi responded via the 1980 Statement on Industrial Policy, which signalled a renewed emphasis on economic growth (government of India, 1980). Large-scale de-licensing, however, did not occur until her son Rajiv Gandhi unexpectedly came to power following his mother's assassination in 1984. Some 25 broad categories of industry were entirely exempted from industrial licensing in March 1985. In late 1985 and 1986, further relaxations of the industrial licensing system followed.

In response to external pressures, Rajiv Gandhi's successors implemented a large-scale liberalization of the Indian economy. Such reformist tendencies of Narasimha Rao's government were unexpected. Perhaps then finance minister Manmohan Singh saw the possibilities in reform. In 1991, industrial licensing was abolished, except for a small number of industries where it was retained 'for reasons related to security and strategic concerns, social reasons, problems related to safety and overriding environmental issues, manufacture of products of hazardous nature and articles of elitist consumption'. Additional industries were removed from the provisions of the 1951 Industries Act in the post-1991 period. With the advent of WTO, in which India plays a key role, non-tariff barriers were removed and tariff rates slashed. The stated rationale for the liberalization of industrial policy

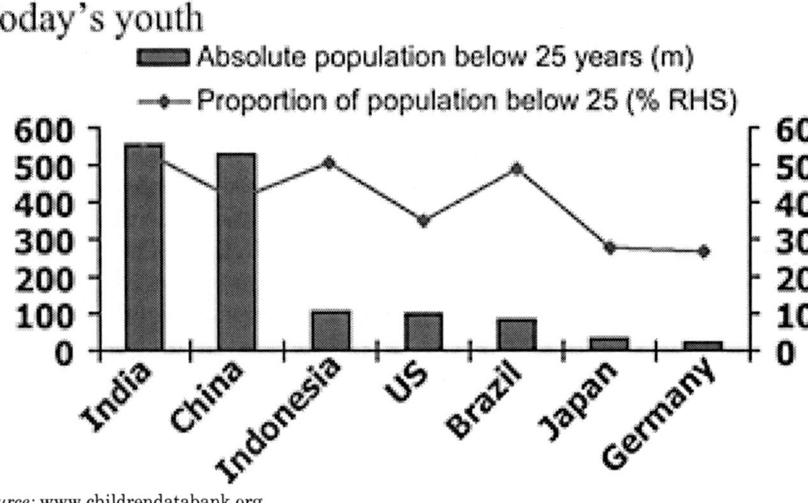


*Source:* www.childrendatabank.org

Figure 2. Today's youth (2001 census)

was to actively encourage and assist Indian entrepreneurs to exploit and meet the emerging domestic and global opportunities and challenges.

## Growing youth population

In the 1990s, the population growth rate came down from 2.1 per cent (recorded in the previous decade) to 1.9 per cent. Population control is a legitimate economic agenda item but is shunned by political parties due to election pressures and the voting game. India is the second most populous country in the world, with a higher population growth rate than China. India's population has crossed the billion mark and will soon exceed that of China. Some 68 per cent of the population still live in rural areas yet to witness the benefits of the reform process. However, there is a silver lining in this population growth. A total of 550 million Indians are under the age of 25, and 350 million under 15 years (source: India Brand Equity Foundation, 2006). By 2013, the net addition to the productive population (aged 25–44 years) will be 91 million, or 33 per cent. The biggest benefit of this demography is the high consumer base. They will also form an educated labour force, trained in technology and aware of the forces of globalization.

The youth brings with it newer and more advanced knowledge, technological know-how, and an assertiveness that was not encouraged by earlier, more sober and rigid social and governmental systems. The manufacturing industry is on a roll once again, banks have improved their efficiency to cater for demanding customers, and private entrepreneurship has found a new lease of life from the government's policies. A new trend of shifting from job-seeking to searching for self-employment opportunities is also taking place.

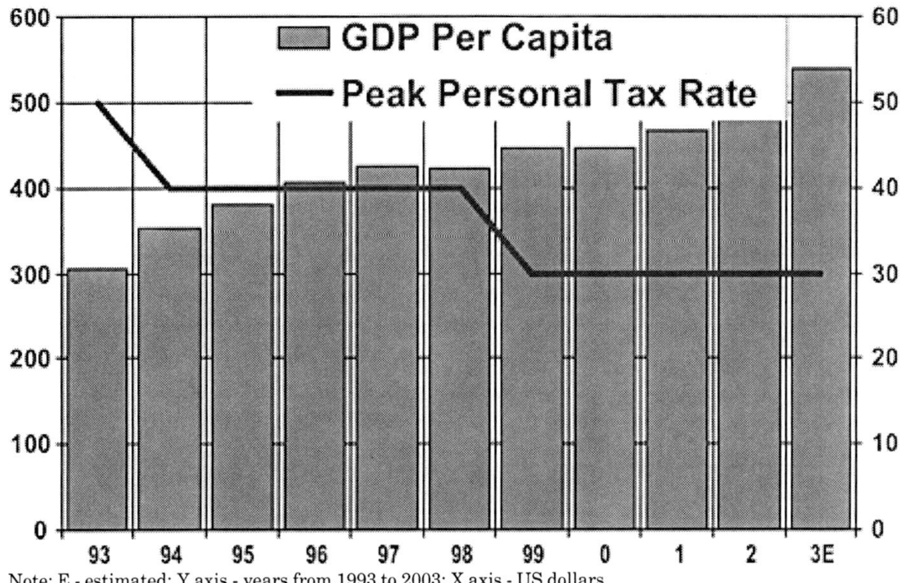


Note: E - estimated; Y axis - years from 1993 to 2003; X axis - US dollars.

Figure 3. Indian consumer purchasing power

## The new face of the Indian consumers

Indian consumers are increasingly exposed to the latest products and technologies available in different sectors. Exposure occurs not only through international media, including the Internet and satellite television but also through travel. With more Indians travelling to foreign countries for business or holiday, purchasing opportunities are also increasing. Around 5.5 million Indians travelled abroad in 2004, representing a rise of 25 per cent compared to 2003. Indian shoppers spent $100 million during the Dubai Shopping Festival in 2003, with a large part dedicated to luxury goods such as fragrances, cosmetics, watches and jewellery (Source: 2006 – www.beauty-on-line.com).

## Reforms and results during the last 15 years

- **1991**: Economic liberalization initiated by Indian Prime Minister PV Narasimha Rao and his Finance Minister Manmohan Singh in response to a macroeconomic crisis;
- **1998**: India's economy was $1702.7 billion, which accounted for a 5 per cent share of world income;
- **2005**: India's economy was worth $3319 billion (Purchasing Power Parity) which accounted for a 6 per cent share of world income, the fourth largest in the world in terms of purchasing power parity.

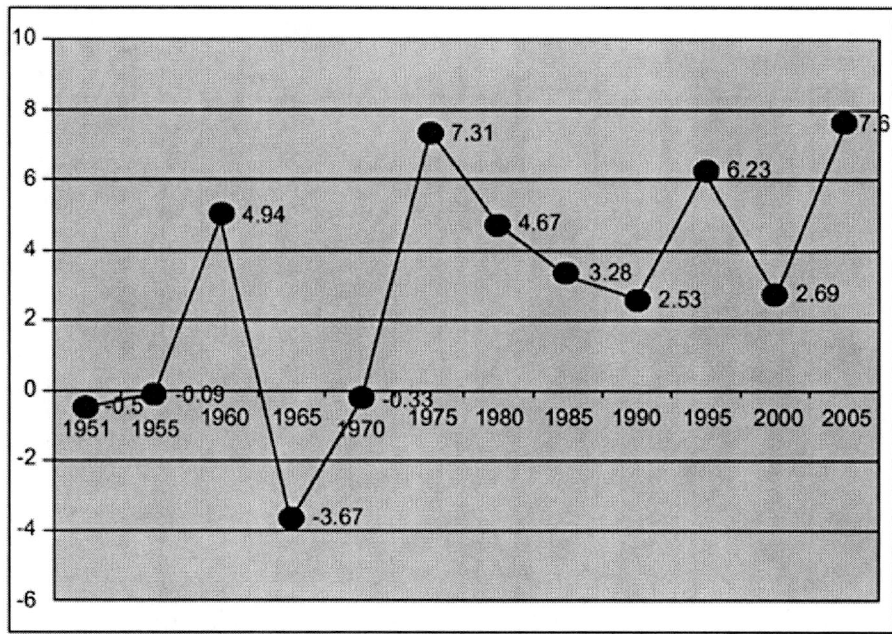


Note: *Constant Prices: Chain series
*Source:* Penn World tables

Figure 4. Percentage growth rate of India's real GDP per capita, 1950–2006*

# 1.3

# An Economic Overview

*Dr Amit Kapoor, Centre for Entrepreneurship, Management Development Institute*

## Introduction

In a global context, India is the seventh largest country by land mass, the fourth largest economy on a purchasing power parity basis and the tenth largest economy in GDP (gross domestic product) terms. Some 1.1 billion people inhabit the country across a diverse regional, ethnic, social and wealth base. India has 35 cities with a population of over 1 million inhabitants. Economics experts and various studies conducted across the globe envisage India and China to rule the world in the 21st century. For over a century the United States has been the largest economy in the world but major developments have taken place in the world economy since then, leading to the shift of focus from the United States and the rich countries of Europe to the two Asian giants – India and China.

But then India is a study in contrasts. It is undeniable that India is one of the fastest growing economies in the world, but stark issues stare it in the face, such as: low GDP per capita; a lowly rank on the HDI (Human Development Index); abject poverty with 26 per cent of its people living under the poverty line (in fact 86 per cent if the poverty line is taken as 2 cents a day; 40 cents PPP – purchasing power parity); the growing economic disparity, still a large part of the population deriving income from agriculture; a mere 2 per cent of world land accommodating nearly 17 per cent of the world population; a dismal state of health care and nutrition; crumbling infrastructure with projects that are delayed for years; a power situation that is appalling; an all pervasive corruption that is a menace; interfering polity and bureaucracy, very parochial in planning; an FDI (foreign direct investment) that is smaller than that received by Hong Kong; a long list indeed, and by no means exhaustive.

This paints a fairly gloomy picture for India as a country. Then what makes it tick? Why is it that every economist talks about India and each multinational company has an India strategy? Lying under this dismal picture is the opportunity that presents itself, the opportunity to change, contribute and grow. Even though India has a low GDP per capita, it has one of the highest saving rates in the world. It is this base of GDP per capita that is about to explode and present to the world the largest middle class market in the world, which is standing at 50 million today and is projected to be 590 million by 2020. At present, it is estimated that the urban and the rural middle class homes in the country total around 40 million. The opportunities that await are highly alluring:

- the telecom market sensing an exploding market that is growing exponentially at 30 million connections a year;
- the opportunities in the health care industry;
- the growing tourism industry;
- the opportunities in infrastructure projects;
- the growing airline industry;
- the coming of age of Indian manufacturing;
- the talented workforce that India presents to the world; and
- the dynamic Indian IT (information technology) and ITES (IT-enabled services) industry.

India is sitting on the cusp of change, the change that will transform the very structure and nature of the world economy in the coming five decades. India, which is now the fourth largest economy in terms of PPP, will overtake Japan and become the third major economic power within 10 years. This is what Toshihiko Fukui, governor of the Bank of Japan, states, 'At the current growth rate, India's purchasing power parity (PPP) is set to overtake Japan by 2025 to rank third only after the US and China.' By 2025 India's economy is projected to be about 60 per cent the size of the US economy. According to some experts, the share of the United States in the world GDP is expected to fall (from 21 to 18 per cent) and that of India's GDP to rise (from 6 to 11 per cent in 2025), and hence the latter will emerge as the third pole in the global economy after the United States and China. The transformation into a tri-polar economy will be complete by 2035, with the Indian economy only a little smaller than the US economy but larger than that of Western Europe. By 2035, India is likely to be a larger growth driver than the six largest countries in the European Union.

## The Indian economic history

India has housed a 5,000-year-old civilization but has a legacy of long-term colonial stagnation and economic backwardness. It was in 1947 that India regained independence from British rule and started a journey towards self-reliance. The aspiration of the leaders during independence was to turn India into a vibrant, self-reliant national economy and do away with the vagaries of abject poverty. India had negatives, in the form of a limited entrepreneurial class and non-functional capital markets. The permit system further swung the preponderance of family-owned businesses, as only they could seek licences to do business. Looking at this, the state, ie. the government, had to fulfil the role of capital accumulation and act as an entrepreneur. This gave rise to public sector units which ended up becoming the agents for growth and industrialization. The strategy gave results as it accelerated the pace of growth and moved India out of the stagnancy of the pre-independence era.

As India continued to pursue these goals, the policies ended up being more inward looking and protectionist. A huge bureaucracy was put in place to monitor and govern the permits designed to stimulate and control the industry while limiting foreign trade and investment. The 'licence Raj' created high barriers through tariffs and quantitative restrictions on imports. This disincentivized domestic Indian industry from innovating and improving its manufacturing quality. The licence Raj administered almost all aspects of business, limiting the capability of business to expand and improve its productivity. The government interfered in the proper functioning of the markets by setting prices in many industries, regulating transport costs and regulating the labour markets.

Due to these interventionist and isolationist policies, the economy started to suffer. Exports declined from 6.5 per cent of GDP in 1969 to 3.6 per cent in 1970. The pride of the country, the public sector units, came to be known as white elephants, sucking resources under their protected and inefficient business policies. The trend continued and India ended up facing the worst economic crisis since its existence as an independent nation. India faced a severe BOP (balance of payments) crisis in 1991 when it had just a few days of liquidity (foreign currency reserves). The crisis was exacerbated by the collapse of the Soviet Union in the same year. The collapse of the Soviet Union (USSR) depicted the final blow to the ideals of a centrally controlled economy, against which India had modelled itself. The collapse of the USSR crippled India's most significant export market and struck a mortal blow to its primary source of economic aid.

This crisis created a situation severe enough for the government to re-examine the approach to development that India had had since independence. It was in July 1991 that the government embarked on a new approach to economic development. It was clearly recognized that correcting the macroeconomic imbalances, and replacing oppressive control of managing the entry of firms and competition, would help in overcoming the BOP crisis. India started taking serious steps towards making a systematic shift towards a more open economy. The move was meant to reflect the need for a greater reliance on market forces and a larger role for the private sector within the country, as well as to highlight the changing role of the government.

Today's positive outlook for investment in India owes its roots to a period of reform which began with a change of government in 1991, opening the Indian economy over time to foreign investment and liberating a new entrepreneurial business environment. The key features in India's economic reforms were related to fiscal and monetary tightening, overhaul of foreign trade and investment regulation, reduced state control of industry, financial sector liberalization and elimination of microeconomic regulation.

# The present economic situation

In real terms, the size of the Indian economy has more than doubled since 1991, a clincher in favour of reforms. Over 100 Indian corporations now have a stock market value of $1 billion or more and well over 200 of the Fortune 500 companies have a presence in India.

The rich countries of Europe have seen the greatest decline in global GDP share by 4.9 percentage points, followed by the United States and Japan with a decline of about 1 percentage point each. Within Asia, the rising share of China and India has more than made up the declining global share of Japan since 1990. During the 1970s and 1980s, ASEAN (Association of South East Asian Nations) countries and during the 1980s South Korea, along with China and India, contributed to the rising share of Asia in the world GDP.

Table 1. Economic indicators

| | 2002-2006 avg. | 2007 | 2008* | 2009* |
|---|---|---|---|---|
| GDP (% growth, real) | 7.8 | 8.9 | 8.3 | 7.9 |
| Inflation (%, year-end) | 4.5 | 6.4 | 7.1 | 6.2 |
| Fiscal balance (% of GDP) | –4.4 | –3.1 | –3.0 | –2.5 |
| Exports (% growth) | 22.4 | 20.5 | 15.9 | 12.3 |
| Imports (% growth) | 26.6 | 20.2 | 17.1 | 9.3 |
| Current account (% of GDP) | 0.1 | –1.3 | –2.3 | –1.5 |
| Reserves (month of imports) | 9.8 | 11.0 | 10.4 | 10.4 |
| External debt (% of GDP) | 17.5 | 13.0 | 11.8 | 10.6 |
| Debt service ratio | 12.5 | 7.2 | 6.7 | 6.4 |
| Currency (per $, year-end) | 45.3 | 39.4 | 37.3 | 35.9 |

Source: EIU, EDC Economics
* Forecast

The present economic situation in India looks promising, with a GDP growth rate around 8.4 per cent. The economy is being propelled upwards with the increase in domestic demand. The service sector contributes 54 per cent of economic output and is growing at a rate of nearly 10.4 per cent. Business services, communication services, financial services, community services, hotels and restaurants and trade services are among the fastest growing sectors. The Indian IT and BPO (business process outsourcing) sectors are continuing to grow and perform, driven by international demand and the low-cost labour that India has in quantity. This sector, though, has a limited impact on employment generation as at present it employs around 1 million people which is insignificant looking at the base of 1.1 billion population of the country. In fact, this is a characteristic common to China and India – that the growth in economic terms has not been significantly reflected in proportionate enhancement in employment figures; and that whatever employment has ensued has been primarily towards lower levels of productivity ladder.

The industry or the manufacturing sector accounts for about 26 per cent of GDP. The sectors that contribute to the success are textiles, metals and alloys and transport equipment. The index of industrial production, which measures the overall industrial growth rate, is growing at 9 per cent. The largest sector here is the textile industry. The automobile sector has also demonstrated the inherent strength of Indian labour and capital. The three main sub-sectors of industry, ie. mining and quarrying, manufacturing, and electricity, gas and water supply, have recorded growths of 5–9 per cent.

Agriculture (as well as allied sectors like forestry, logging and fishing) accounts for 20 per cent of GDP, a cause for concern. It employs almost 58 per cent of the total workforce. It is the largest economic sector and plays a significant role in the overall socio-economic development of India. Due to the steady improvement in irrigation, technology and modern agricultural practices, the yield per unit area of all crops has increased tremendously. However, even though India has had favourable monsoons in the last few years, the growth rate for the sector has been a meagre 2.3 per cent. This reflects the difficulties the agriculture sector faces in the country especially in raising productivity. The sector is beginning to face an acute water crisis with problems further accentuated through mismanagement of irrigation and surface water management.

Table 2. Rate of growth of GDP at factor cost at 1999–2000 prices (per cent)

| | IX Plan | 2002–2003 | 2003–2004 | 2004–2005 | 2005–2006 | 2006–2007 | X Plan | 2007–2008 |
|---|---|---|---|---|---|---|---|---|
| Agriculture and allied | 2.5 | –7.2 | 10.0 | 0.0 | 5.9 | 3.8 | 2.5 | 2.6 |
| mining | 4.0 | 8.8 | 3.1 | 8.2 | 4.9 | 5.7 | 6.1 | 3.4 |
| Manufacturing | 3.3 | 6.8 | 6.6 | 8.7 | 9.0 | 12.0 | 8.6 | 9.4 |
| Electricity | 4.8 | 4.7 | 4.8 | 7.9 | 4.7 | 6.0 | 5.6 | 7.8 |
| Construction | 7.1 | 7.9 | 12.0 | 16.1 | 16.5 | 12.0 | 12.9 | 9.6 |
| Trade and hotels | 7.5 | 6.9 | 10.1 | 7.7 | 9.4 | 8.5 | 8.5 | 12.1 |
| Transport and communication | 8.9 | 14.1 | 15.3 | 15.6 | 14.6 | 16.6 | 15.3 | |
| Financing, real estate, housing | 8.0 | 8.0 | 5.6 | 8.7 | 11.4 | 13.9 | 9.5 | 11.7 |
| Community services | 7.7 | 3.9 | 5.4 | 6.9 | 7.2 | 6.9 | 6.1 | 7.0 |
| GDP | 5.5 | 3.8 | 8.5 | 7.5 | 9.4 | 9.6 | 7.8 | 8.7 |

Note: Plan period is simple average
IX Plan - government five-year plan for the period of 1997–2002
X Plan - government five-year plan for the period of 2002–2007

The Indian Economic Survey of 2007–2008 underlines that the congenial environment for investment still continues in India and the future of investments in the country is encouraging. The survey suggested that the XIth plan (government five-year plan for the period of 2007–2012) can attain an average of 9 per cent GDP growth. Some of the Indian states are expected to generate surplus revenue from this financial year onwards. The employment sector took a beating and unemployment in India rose by 1 per cent against the last financial year. Lowering of the fiscal deficit to below 3 per cent should be targeted in the coming years. A zero revenue deficit has been targeted for the next financial year. The report suggested increased growth of the Indian farm sector is essential and important. A proposal to allow 5–10 per cent of disinvestment in the Indian non-Navratna companies was suggested and a proposal for private sector involvement in the coal mining sector was also tabled. The report also suggested that licensing procedures be eased in the coming years. FDI in the Indian retail sector has been proposed to help this sector grow to its full potential. Moreover, to boost the rural health insurance sector of India, 51 per cent FDI has been proposed. Around 26 per cent FDI in the Indian insurance industry has also been proposed in the economic survey report.

## NAVRATNA COMPANIES

In 1997, the government created nine public sector undertakings (PSUs or state owned companies) as "Navratnas". So named after the traditional Indian lucky charm set with nine gem stones – the navaratna.

They were given greater autonomy of management and expenditure without recourse to central government approval. They can also enter into joint ventures, form alliances and sell subsidiaries abroad.

The composition of the list of Navratnas has changed over time – and a further three were added in June 2007.

Two lesser grades of autonomy also exist – "the Miniratnas" – of which there are 54 in total.

A list of the companies can be found at http://dpe.nic.in/newsite/navmini.htm

The budgetary deficit is assessed at 3.1 per cent for the current year and forecast to be 2.5 per cent in 2009, but this cleverly excludes the deficit at states' level, besides camouflaging some 3.5 per cent of GDP in the form of fertilizer and oil subsidies. The government lacks funds to fuel infrastructure growth and is holding fast onto banks and pension funds, lest its economic muscle atrophy.

## External trade

India's greater integration with the world economy was reflected by the trade openness indicator, the trade to GDP ratio, which increased from 22.5 per cent of GDP in 2000–2001, to 34.8 per cent of GDP in 2006–2007. If services trade is included, the increase is higher at 48 per cent of GDP in 2006–2007, from 29.2 per cent of GDP in 2000–2001, reflecting a greater degree of openness. India's merchandise exports and imports (in US dollars, on customs basis) grew by 22.6 per cent and 24.5 per cent, respectively, in 2006–2007, recording the lowest gap between growth rates after 2002–2003. Petroleum products (59.3 per cent) and engineering goods (38.1 per cent) were the fastest growing exports. The notable increase in the share of petroleum products in total exports reflected India's enhanced refining capacity and higher POL (petroleum, oil, lubricants) prices. The rising share of engineering goods reflected improved competitiveness. The value of POL imports increased by 30 per cent, with volume increasing by 13.8 per cent and prices by 12.1 per cent in 2006–2007. Non-POL import growth at 22.2 per cent was due to the 29.4 per cent growth of gold and silver and 21.4 per cent growth of non-POL non-bullion imports needed to meet industrial demand. While exports grew by 21.76 per cent during April–December 2007, imports increased by 25.97 per cent in the same period. Money supply (M3) has grown by a robust 22.8 per cent (year-on-year) as of 21 December 2007, compared to 19.3 per cent last year. The fiscal and revenue deficits decreased by 11 per cent and 17.2 per cent, respectively, during April–November 2007 over the corresponding period in 2006.

With the central bank tightening monetary policy on numerous occasions in 2007, economic growth has slowed in each of the past three quarters. Tighter monetary policy resulted in weaker credit conditions and consumer durable demand, while the rising rupee is affecting export earnings. This also affected the manufacturing sector, where output growth has markedly slowed in the second half of 2007. Real GDP growth will ease further in 2008 to 8.3 per cent and to 7.9 per cent in 2009 from 8.9 per cent in 2007.

## Fiscal policy

The budget for fiscal year (FY) 2008–2009 projects continued improvements for the deficit to 2.5 per cent of GDP and tax revenues to 13 per cent of GDP. As in the past, however, the budget omits large subsidies for food, oil and fertilizers, which will probably bring the actual deficit closer to 4 per cent of GDP. With the upcoming elections, the government used the budget to introduce a number of populist measures, including expanding the inefficient and corruption-prone National Rural Employment Guarantee Scheme and a $15 billion debt forgiveness to small farmers. IR (Indian Railways) plans reduced fares and much higher infrastructure spending in its budget, although IR is on sound financial footing, having recorded a $6.3-billion surplus last year. Infrastructure spending will see some improvements, with an increase of 20 per cent for power, road and rail and 50 per cent for ports. A key downside risk to the outlook will be the impact of the Sixth Pay Commission, which has revised the salary structure of government employees and pensioners. Nonetheless, the debt to GDP ratio is expected to continue to improve but remain high reaching 70 per cent by the end of next fiscal year.

## Monetary policy

The different measures of consumer inflation continue to decline after peaking in August at 6.5–8.0 per cent, suggesting that the tightening measures of RBI (Reserve Bank of India, the central bank) are having the desired impact. However, the wholesale price index, the RBI's target indicator for inflation, has been strengthening recently, rising above the RBI ceiling of 5 per cent early in March. With rising food prices and greater oil products price pass-through in 2008, inflation will continue to gain in the coming months. The RBI has held off on further tightening recently as the slowing economy, the US rate cuts and the rising rupee are expected to ease inflation pressures, currently hovering at 7 per cent.

## The external sector

After letting the rupee appreciate by 11 per cent in 2007, the rupee has started to depreciate early in 2008, losing 2.3 per cent against the US dollar and trading above 40 Indian rupees (INR) to the dollar. Nonetheless, exports have continued to expand rapidly in recent months, expanding 20.5 per cent year-on-year in January. With rising energy prices however, the trade deficit has ballooned since the second half of 2007, reaching $9.4 billion in January. The latest BOP figures (July–September 2007) still show a sizeable surplus, with the trade deficit largely offset by growing remittances from abroad (India has the world's largest remittances inflows) and surging capital inflows. External debt ratios are favourable and continue to improve, supporting solvency. The external debt represents 13 per cent of GDP and foreign exchange reserves, at $301.2 billion, representing almost 12 months of import cover and 16 times short-term external debt.

## Matching up with China

The development that India sees today seems outstanding when compared to its own historical data. If we look at the data in comparison to China the sheen seems to tarnish a little. India grows at 8.4 per cent whereas China grows at 10 per cent; India contributes 6.2 per cent of world GDP as against China's 14 per cent; 44 per cent of India live in extreme poverty against that of 39 per cent in China; China has a literacy rate of 95 per cent, compared with India's 68 per cent; manufacturing is 16 per cent of India's GDP, 37 per cent of GDP in China; Indian exports are $71 billion, which are just 10 per cent of China's exports which amount to $713 billion.

Moving further on, we notice that China commands 25,000 kilometres of four-lane highways against 3,000 kilometres in India; China has 375 million mobile phone subscribers to that of 100 million in India; 73 per cent of Chinese access the Internet, whereas only 23 per cent of Indians access the Internet; it takes 71 days to start a business in India compared to 48 days in China; 49.5 per cent of per capita income is required to start a business in India compared to 14 per cent in China; enforcing contracts can be a problem in comparison to China; India received around $8 billion of FDI against $70 billion in China, etc. Although India's FDI rules have progressively been reformed to facilitate foreign investment into various sectors, the signs depict an ad hoc non-transparent strategy. There remain sections of the economy where FDI is either not permitted or limited. But China has had the twin advantages of having triggered reforms almost two decades along with a centralized – almost totalitarian – governance. Of course, the maturing of India's political landscape and the country's uninterrupted endeavours towards democracy building might prove to be decisive winners in the very long run.

These statistics may seem to dim the picture for India, but they also provide indications as to what India needs to do to have a more resilient model for growth. India needs to invest in infrastructure, focus on manufacturing, improve legal procedures, etc. India is also a nascent market which is ready to explode as it would foresee 'hockey stick' growth in sectors like telecoms, Internet, infrastructure, hospitality and health care. It is beyond doubt that if India starts looking at infrastructure alone, not only will it propel sectors like aviation, etc., the infrastructure sector has the potential to move India out of its dangerous levels of unemployment, which today stands at about 42 million unemployed graduates. If India focuses on improving its governance and its legal frameworks, then it has the potential to become one of the most attractive FDI destinations amongst the emerging economies.

# 1.4

# Country Competitiveness

*Dr Amit Kapoor, Centre for Entrepreneurship, Management Development Institute*

According to the acclaimed Harvard academic Professor Michael E. Porter, competitiveness is the fundamental underpinning of prosperity. While macroeconomic shifts, political development, resource price swings and spurs of trade can all move GDP per capita, the only reliable basis for true prosperity is the productive capacity of a nation's economy. He further maintains that productivity sets a nation's standard of living. Productivity supports high wages, strong currency and attractive returns to capital inducing a high standard of living. Going further, Porter explains that productivity improves when a country can mobilize its human resources to generate value within the economy. According to Porter, it is the innovative capacity of an economy that will be the cornerstone of productivity in the long run. In the context of economic development, innovation refers to a country's ability to upgrade its business environment. The aspects that reflect the microeconomic business environment are:

- factor conditions;
- demand conditions;
- related and supporting industries; and
- context for firm strategy and rivalry.

It is eventually the management of these four determinants that will increase levels of competitiveness of an economy.

Analysing these aspects of the microeconomic business environment further, we can look at factors that have an impact on growth of the Indian economy and further its competitiveness and economic prowess internationally. The aspects that are driving India's growth are basically the factor conditions and the demand conditions.

'Factor conditions' refer to the situation in a country regarding production factors, like skilled labour, infrastructure, etc., which are relevant for competition in particular industries. India's factor conditions are mixed with contradictions across categories. India has one of the largest pool of engineers and scientists, but concurrently there is an abysmal rate of patenting within the country. It is perceived that India has a large English-speaking population, but according to some estimates it is just around 2 per cent of the population. The infrastructure in the country is improving, but not at the rate which is required to sustain growth rates of greater than 8 per cent. India faces huge problems in its transport infrastructure including rail, road and air. Today the infrastructure bottlenecks have started hindering the growth of sectors within the country.

A major driver of economic growth in India is a growing and aspirational young middle class workforce. Some 70 per cent of India's population is less than 36 years of age. Moreover, India is home to some 20 per cent of the world's population under the age of 24 years. This position contrasts greatly with most of the developed world, which faces a shortage of working age inhabitants and the growing social cost of an ageing population. As of today, 33 per cent of India's population is below the age of 15 years. In the next 10–15 years, it is estimated that 250 million workers will be added to the labour pool, who, when gainfully employed, will create a consumption class that will be parallel to none. The Indian population may be divided into a number of economic groups for present purposes:

- The most affluent group, 'Global India', comprises approximately 1.2 million people inhabiting the major cities. Whilst this segment is fast growing, it is too small to be a major consumer force in the Indian economy as a whole.
- The most influential group is 'Aspiring India', the 40 million middle income households. This group is thought to be growing at 10 per cent per annum through to 2010, by which time it would constitute some 65 million households. The emerging purchasing power of this group can be evidenced by some simple statistics: passenger car sales of $5 billion in 2004 were more than double the level five years earlier.

Table 1. Population of seven big cities

| No. | City | Population (millions) |
|---|---|---|
| 1 | Greater Mumbai | 16.4 |
| 2 | Kolkata | 13.2 |
| 3 | Delhi NCR | 12.9 |
| 4 | Chennai | 6.6 |
| 5 | Hyderabad | 5.8 |
| 6 | Bengaluru | 5.7 |
| 7 | Pune | 3.8 |

Note: Compare with global cities (in millions): Tokyo 12.4; New York 8.1; London 7.4.
Source: India Census 2001, Tokyo Metropolitan Government, US Census Bureau, Greater London Authority.

Furthering the concept of competitiveness, we see that successful economic development is a process of successive upgrading, in which the nation's business environment evolves to support increasingly sophisticated and productive ways of competing by firms. Nations evolve through various stages of competitive development. The growth strategy currently followed by India focuses primarily on exploiting its factor inputs. The boom in IT and BPO (business process outsourcing) is driven by the availability of low-cost labour, commonly called labour arbitrage. The focus and growth has been to lead in work which is not high in value added. The growth in the software sector is not driven by innovation; rather it is the availability of cheap technical human resources which is driving the industry's growth. When comparing the productivity of an Indian IT professional *vis-à-vis* an Israeli professional, the results are surprising. Per employee, wealth addition for Infosys, India's leading IT firm, is $42,000 compared to $320,000 for Adobe and $640,000 for Microsoft. Low-cost labour does not necessarily provide competitive advantage to the nation as it is always in a precarious position and in danger of being overtaken by another low-cost provider of human capital. In the long run, it is not the low cost of factor inputs that drives the economy; rather it is the innovative capacity and capability that makes the difference. Innovation in all likelihood increases trade, helps in maintaining market share, improves processes and offers high-quality products. India is clearly lagging behind in producing products efficiently. It is the long-term orientation and outlook which would make a difference and not the policy initiatives that are incomplete and in bursts. India as a country has been driven by inherited prosperity, ie. focusing on population, low cost of labour, etc. India will have to move ahead, wake up and take action. To say the least, India is gaining advantage because of labour arbitrage. In the future, it will have to focus more on manufacturing and innovation. At this juncture, India's economic situation is full of promise as it has nowhere else to go except upwards.

Table 2. Per capita income and consumption (in 1999–2000 prices)

| | Income | | Consumption | |
|---|---|---|---|---|
| | Rupees | Growth % | Rupees | Growth % |
| IX plan avg. | 19,245 | 3.4 | 12,392 | 3.0 |
| X plan avg. | 24,156 | 6.2 | 14,677 | 4.3 |
| 2002–03 | 20,996 | 2.2 | 13,352 | 1.1 |
| 2003–04 | 22,413 | 6.8 | 13,918 | 4.2 |
| 2004–05 | 23,890 | 6.6 | 14,413 | 3.6 |
| 2005–06 | 25,696 | 7.6 | 15,422 | 7.0 |
| 2006–07 | 27,784 | 8.1 | 16,279 | 5.6 |
| 2007–08 | 29,786 | 7.2 | 17,145 | 5.3 |

Note: Income is taken as GDP at market prices. Consumption is PFCE (private final consumption expenditure). Per capita is obtained by dividing these by population.
IX Plan - government five-year plan for the period 1997–2002
X Plan - government five-year plan for the period 2002–2007

Table 3. Private final consumption – annual growth and share (in per cent)

| | 2000–2001 | 2001–2002 | 2002–2003 | 2003–;2004 | 2004–;2005 | 2005–;2006 | 2006–2007 |
|---|---|---|---|---|---|---|---|
| Food and beverages | –3.4 | 5.9 | –1.9 | 4.5 | 1.0 | 7.5 | 4.8 |
| Clothing and footwear | 16.8 | –2.9 | 4.5 | –2.4 | 4.7 | 12.0 | 3.7 |
| Rent, fuel, power | 2.8 | 2.6 | 2.9 | 3.3 | 7.4 | 3.0 | 3.0 |
| Appliances | 7.2 | 3.5 | 4.0 | 8.1 | 12.2 | 11.6 | 13.5 |
| Medical and health care | 11.6 | 14.2 | 5.3 | 3.3 | 3.4 | 2.0 | 0.7 |
| Transport | 14.3 | 6.6 | 10.6 | 11.4 | 10.2 | 10.4 | 12.2 |
| Education and recreation | 11.8 | 7.3 | 4.5 | 12.0 | 13.9 | 12.4 | 15.8 |
| Others | 12.2 | 11.4 | 9.8 | 9.5 | 12.4 | 11.7 | 11.3 |
| Total private consumption | 3.4 | 5.9 | 2.6 | 5.9 | 5.5 | 8.3 | 7.2 |
| Share of total | | | | | | | |
| Food and beverages | 48.1 | 48.1 | 45.9 | 45.3 | 43.4 | 43.1 | 42.1 |
| Clothing and footwear | 6.0 | 5.5 | 5.6 | 5.1 | 5.1 | 5.3 | 5.1 |
| Rent, fuel, power | 11.4 | 11.0 | 11.0 | 10.8 | 11.0 | 10.4 | 10.0 |
| Appliances | 3.4 | 3.3 | 3.3 | 3.4 | 3.6 | 3.7 | 4.0 |
| Medical and health care | 4.7 | 5.1 | 5.2 | 5.1 | 5.0 | 4.7 | 4.4 |
| Transport | 14.5 | 14.5 | 15.7 | 16.5 | 17.2 | 17.5 | 18.4 |
| Education and recreation | 3.7 | 3.7 | 3.8 | 4.0 | 4.3 | 4.5 | 4.9 |
| Others | 8.4 | 8.9 | 9.5 | 9.8 | 10.4 | 10.8 | 11.2 |

## Social sectors

As per the Human Development Report 2007 of the UNDP (United Nations Development Programme), in spite of the absolute value of the HDI (Human Development Index) for India improving from 0.577 in 2000 to 0.611 in 2004 and further to 0.619 in 2005, the relative ranking of India has not changed much. India's economy and business has played a significant role. But India's 10-million-strong bureaucracy needs to be reformed to foster efficiencies in business. Only then would India's growth become inclusive and not meet the harsh resistance it has begun to face of late, in the hands of regional political forces.

The 'demographic dividend' will manifest itself as a rise in the working age population aged 15–64 years, from 62.9 per cent in 2006 to 68.4 per cent in 2026. To tap into this dividend, the 11th Five-Year Plan focuses on ensuring better delivery of health care, skill development and encouragement of labour intensive industries.

Global citizenry demands respect and provision for global issues. Issues like global warming and the resultant climate change have gained importance in international discussions. Globally, carbon trading has grown rapidly in recent years. There is, however, a need to balance the harmful effects of human activity on global warming against the need for poverty reduction and economic growth in developing and least developed countries. The issue of global social justice cannot be detached from the issue of global public goods like the environment. The costs and benefits to the people living in different countries and their respective contributions must be dealt with in an integrated way. India is actively lobbying for positive changes, without compromising its sovereignty and without succumbing to US pressures.

The Indian economy now comprises a strong base of international and domestic corporations. Well over 200 of the Fortune 500 companies have a presence in India. This has not only been important in establishing India's new commercial base but has contributed to growing bilateral trade between India and these companies' home nations. Investments in India by Fortune 500 companies span a number of industry sectors, including consumer goods, automotives, computer and software, petrochemicals and food and beverages. There are 23 stock exchanges in India with a total market capitalization of over $700 billion. Over 100 Indian corporations now have a stock market value of $1 billion or more. India's large and diverse industrial base is predicted to be one of the drivers for growth in the real estate infrastructure required to support the commercial development of the economy. Key sectors driving this predicted growth are discussed in the following sections.

## IT and business services offshoring

India has emerged as the fastest growing and fourth largest IT market in Asia. Outsourcing and ITES (IT-enabled services) are major drivers in this growth pattern, particularly contributing to exports. India has an estimated share of 65 per cent of the global IT services offshoring market and approximately 46 per cent of the global BPO market. The IT and BPO sectors are driving white collar employment by domestic and international companies. With a large English-speaking workforce, India is well placed to see further growth in this segment. India remains the preferred offshore location for sourcing a broad range of business services, including call centre help-desks, industry-specific research and development, and human resources for the telemarketing and financial sectors. Industry experts believe that India can sustain its global leadership position and grow its offshore IT and BPO industries at an annual rate in excess of 25 per cent over the medium term. The government has established a National Task Force on IT and software development and has set a policy target of $50 billion in exports from IT software and services by 2008. India's offshoring industry is predicted to be at the centre of this growth. The industry currently accounts for as much as 3.3 per cent of GDP and is seeking to take advantage of the continued global trend towards offshoring. It is estimated that 80 per cent of Fortune 500 companies are currently considering offshoring most of their non-strategic processes and that 46 per cent have stated they will consider India as their preferred location. Relocating work from the United Kingdom to cities such as Delhi and Bangalore can cut costs by up to 40 per cent for British firms.

## Retail

In India, the retail sector is the largest provider of jobs after the agriculture sector, and accounts for 6 to 7 per cent of employment and 10 per cent of national GDP. Most Indian retail outlets consist of small, family-owned mom-and-pop stores, with 'organized' retailing accounting for only 2 per cent of the total retail industry. However, organized retailing is projected to grow to a market share of between 8 and 10 per cent by 2010. By 2010, organized retailing sales by multiple store groups are expected to grow to $15 billion. Consumer spending accounts for a large proportion of the Indian economy, with recent growth being assisted by the availability of credit and higher disposable incomes. The Indian government recently relaxed the rules regarding FDI in the Indian retail sector. The changes include allowing foreign firms to own up to 51 per cent of 'single-brand' retail outlets and permitting overseas firms to invest in Indian wholesale retailers. Based on PPP (purchasing power parity), India is the fourth largest economy in the world and currently offers a significant opportunity for retailers. Furthermore, urbanization is expected to result in 30 per cent of the total population residing in cities by 2010, as against nearly 28 per cent today, representing an increase of over 20 million people. The Indian retail sector is estimated to have a value of $330 billion based on sales. There is evidence of increasing consumer demand for large format malls inclusive of entertainment, retail and leisure components, with several having been built in tier I and II cities in India. However, the major obstacle for many international retailers is the limited access to suitable space.

## Mobile technology

Mobile telephony is now the first choice of connection for new telecom subscribers. Overall connection levels at end-2007 stand at nearly 136 million, having grown from just over 65 million in 2006. Part of the growth comes from the migration of fixed-line consumers to mobile connections. National and international long-distance services have been opened to non-state competition and a number of new entrants have now entered the fixed-line markets. India has registered a total telecom subscriber base of 272.87 million for the quarter ending December 2007, as against 248.65 million for the quarter ending September 2007, according to data released by the sector regulator. India, which is the world's fastest growing market for wireless subscribers, also recorded 233.62 million users in the segment during the quarter October–December 2007 from 209.67 million in the quarter ending September 2007. India is expected to surpass the United States as the world's second biggest market, led by China. This has, however, negatively impacted the growth of wireline users, which decreased from 39.58 million during the quarter ending September 2007 to 39.25 million in the quarter ending December 2007, according to data released by TRAI (Telecom Regulatory Authority of India). Similarly, in rural areas, the growth of wireless subscribers reached 52.52 million users as opposed to 43.98 million, while in the case of wireline subscribers it declined from 11.99 million in the quarter ending September 2007 to 11.75 million in the quarter ending December 2007. The teledensity for the October–December 2007 quarter reached 23.87 compared to 21.87 for the previous quarter, the authority said. The number of broadband subscribers was 3.13 million for the quarter ending December 2007, as against 2.67 million for the previous quarter. The Indian government has set a target of 500 million telecom connections by 2010, half of which was reached in 2007. It also has a target of 20 million broadband connections within the next three years.

## Health care

As the population ages and as wealth per capita rises, India's health care infrastructure may be expected to grow correspondingly. Total health care spending is expected to double to close to $50 billion by 2012, amounting to some 8.5 per cent of GDP. The number of patients visiting Indian hospitals from overseas has risen 10-fold to 100,000 in the last five years, closing the gap on Singapore as the current pre-eminent health care provider to visitors with 150,000 patients per year. Health care tourism, as it has become known, is estimated to generate an additional $2 billion of revenue for the economy by 2012. With over 4 million people employed in the industry, health care is one of the largest service sectors in the overall economy.

## Pharmaceuticals

The Indian pharmaceutical industry has the highest number of plants approved by the US Food and Drug Administration anywhere in the world outside the United States. As the generic drugs market continues to grow, the Indian pharmaceutical industry will be able to leverage its strength in research and development and its sizeable skilled workforce. Low-cost production combined with international standard manufacturing and distribution facilities will be important to the success of the industry, which comprises a growing number of large domestic participants as well as a number of multinationals.

## Infrastructure and real estate

As India prepares herself for becoming an economic superpower, it must expedite socio-economic reforms and take steps to overcome institutional and infrastructure bottlenecks inherent in the system. Availability of both physical and social infrastructure is central to sustainable economic growth. The finance ministry talks of a need for $400 billion investments in this sector alone. Estimates from leading market analysts suggest that the commercial real estate sector is expanding by 30 per cent per annum. Should the sector maintain this momentum, the market could potentially be worth $45–50 billion within five years and in excess of $90 billion in less than 10 years. Real estate markets are expected to capture approximately 18–20 per cent of total FDI. Another factor that fuels the growth of the Indian residential property market is the housing shortage, estimated at between 20 million and 30 million homes. It is predicted that by 2030, India will be dealing with a demand for 10 million housing units per year in addition to the existing shortage. By then, it will have overtaken China as the most populous country in the world. Moody's reports that the average age of the home buyer has decreased from 45 to 32 in one decade as the country's professional youth embraces the Western philosophy on owning property.

## Special economic zones

An SEZ (special economic zone) is a geographical region that has economic laws that are more liberal than a country's typical economic laws. Usually the goal is an increase in foreign investment. One of the earliest and the most famous SEZs were founded by the government of the People's Republic of China under Deng Xiaoping in the early 1980s. The most successful SEZ in China, Shenzhen, has developed from a small village into a city with a population of over 10 million within 20 years. The SEZs in India were established with a view to bringing in expertise for the country's exports sector. For this a policy was introduced on 1 April 2006. The policy provides for the setting up of SEZs in the public, private or joint sectors or by state governments. It was also envisaged that some of the existing EPZs (export processing zones) would be converted into SEZs. Accordingly, the government has converted the EPZs located at Kandla and Surat (Gujarat), Cochin (Kerala), Santa Cruz (Mumbai, Maharashtra), Falta (West Bengal), Chennai (Tamil Nadu), Visakhapatnam (Andhra Pradesh), NOIDA (Uttar Pradesh), Nanguneri and Tirunelveli (Tamil Nadu). Currently, India has 811 units in operation in eight functional SEZs, each an average size of 200 acres. Eight EPZs have been converted into SEZs. These are fully functional. All these SEZs are in various parts of the country and are held by the private/joint sectors or by the state governments. But this process of planning and development is under question, as the states in which the SEZs have been approved are facing intense protests from the farming community, accusing the government of forcibly snatching fertile land from them at heavily discounted prices as against the prevailing prices in the commercial real estate industry. In addition, well-known companies such as Bajaj and others have also commented against this policy and have suggested using barren and wasteland for setting up SEZs.

## Regulation

The RBI (Reserve Bank of India) is the national central bank and was established in 1935. It has regulatory and supervisory powers within the Indian financial system while also playing a direct role in the formulation and implementation of monetary policy. The RBI is credited with a number of major contributions to India's economic success; whereas inflation regularly stood above 9 per cent per annum in the 1990s, it has averaged less than 5 per cent in the period from 2000 to 2007, growing to 7+ levels in early 2008; a growing young, educated and aspiring middle class workforce has been able to access banking products. Because of the weakening of the US dollar for the last two years (caused mainly by widening US deficits), the Indian rupee has steadily appreciated *vis-à-vis* the US dollar.

Looking at regulation becomes important as it sets the tone for entry of firms and how a business conducts itself in the country. India has an exhaustive legal framework governing all aspects of business. Some of the important ones that have implications for a foreign investor are:

- Companies Act, 1956, governing corporate bodies;
- Competition Act, 2002, ensuring competitive spirit in the market;
- Consumer Protection Act, 1986, protecting consumers;
- Factories Act, 1948, regulating labour in factories;

- Foreign Exchange Management Act, 1999, providing a framework regulating foreign exchange transactions;
- Industries Disputes Act and Workmen Compensation Act, 1951, dealing with labour disputes;
- IT Act, 1999, regulating Internet commerce activities;
- Sales Tax Act, 1948, governing the levy of tax on sales.

Various regulatory bodies act as points of contact between investors and the Indian government. Some of the significant regulatory authorities are the FIPB (Foreign Investment Promotion Board), Registrar of Companies, SEBI (Securities and Exchange Board of India), CBDT (Central Board of Direct Taxes), etc.

Since India is moving on the path of economic deregulation, there has been substantial removal of bureaucratic controls and hurdles on the industry. Licensing has been abolished in most sectors except atomic energy and railways. Certain industries where licensing is still mandatory are alcohol, cigarettes and tobacco, electronics, aerospace and defence equipment, industrial explosives and hazardous chemicals. With the new Industrial Policy of 1991, the regulatory environment for foreign investment has been eased consistently, which has made the policy much more investor friendly. FDI is permitted in most sectors apart from atomic energy, lottery and gambling businesses, plantations, retail trading and agriculture (excluding floriculture, horticulture, seed development, animal husbandry, pisciculture and cultivation of vegetables and mushrooms).

## Challenges that India faces

Without a doubt, India, with its massive pool of humanity and resources, is expected to play a significant role in world development,and its own development in the coming years. But this requires the country to mature and rise to the challenge it faces; if not, the country could face severe problems which will also impact on the rest of the world. William Baumol, professor of economics and entrepreneurship at New York University, talks of 'the use of imagination, boldness, ingenuity, leadership, persistence and determination' as relevant characteristics of those who go for entrepreneurship, a useful inventory of attributes to be applied to any assessment of an investor in the current and continuously changing India. But a better connected global economy has brought greater risks of chaos; to quote Martin Sorrell, chief executive of WPP Group, 'the 21st century is not for tidy minds.' India's population is likely to reach around 1.5 billion by 2025, according to a UN ESCAP (Economic and Social Commission for Asia and the Pacific) projection carrying concomitant perils. ESCAP also estimated that about half of population will live in cities and urban centres by this time, further burdening urban settlements.

The authorities are trying to weaken inflationary pressures without sacrificing economic growth, but the cumulative monetary tightening, appreciating rupee and weaker global economy will slow down Indian expansion in 2008. One main growth challenge in India and, by the same token, a significant investment opportunity in the coming years will be infrastructure investments, as the rapid pace of expansion is constrained by infrastructure shortcomings in power and transportation. Nonetheless, growth will remain healthy at 8.3 per cent in 2008, and 7.9 per cent in 2009. Overall, the medium-term outlook remains favourable. FDI will continue to pour into the country, while infrastructure investment will benefit the burgeoning manufacturing sector.

Though huge strides seem to have been made in the economic and social environment, the momentum is now flagging. The initial exuberance is dwindling and policy framers are at the mercy of parochial, sectarian and regionally obsessed politicians. The disparities have grown. Report after report by global agencies rank the country relatively low on positive attributes such as per capita income and ease of doing business in India while shamefully high on negative traits such as corruption and infant mortality. Resilience to internal disturbances at the hands of terrorists and a successful combating of the Indo-Pakistan border conflict along the way is praiseworthy. Sadly, this resilience is due more to the apathy and ineffectiveness of peace ensuring mechanisms than rooting out the fundamental drivers of disruptive vectors. The population is yet to invoke truly mature democratic practices to ensure accountability by the ruling elite. If India is to give to its people a country that commands respect all across the world in the coming years, it will certainly have to respond to and tackle the issues it faces. Even though the negatives that India faces can be burdensome and may disrupt the growth that India has today, they are greatly outnumbered by the positives.

Surely India's economy is on the fulcrum of an ever-increasing growth curve. With positive indicators such as a stable 8–9 per cent annual growth, rising foreign exchange reserves, a booming capital market and rapidly expanding FDI inflows, India has emerged as the second fastest growing major economy in the world. Another significant feature of the growth process has been the consistently increasing savings and investment rate. While the gross savings rate as a proportion of GDP has increased from 23.5 per cent in 2001–2002 to 34.8 per cent in 2006–2007, the investment rate – reflected as the gross capital formation as a proportion of GDP – has increased from 22.8 per cent in 2001–2002 to 35.9 per cent in 2006–2007. The rupee has already appreciated 12 per cent against the US dollar over the last year, enabling it to join the elite club of 12 countries with a trillion dollar economy. Global CEOs see 5 per cent share of world trade for India by 2020. The government continues to develop the mortgage market. However, mortgages in India still only account for 2 per cent of the country's GDP as compared to 54 per cent in the United States.

Finally, let it be said that it is a mistake to analyse India as a monolithic nation or one nation: its cultural diversity and economic disparities coupled with its geographical-people-economic size make it an equivalent in complexity to all of Europe and Africa. Accordingly, its 29 states need to be studied as unique entities. In fact, it could be said that there are two Indias, with nearly 28 per cent living in urbanized locations and the major part in rural areas. The sensibilities, mindsets and priorities are dramatically different across these two Indias. Accordingly, all policymaking that employs scale neutral techniques and harnesses the tremendous human resources, in addition to exploiting the country's diversity, shall yield better and longer-term results. This mandates evolving economic models best suited to these realities rather than mindless aping of models which have worked in the past for the United States or Europe or South Asian tigers. If India can successfully implement indigenous development models, it can become a role model for the next round of economic growth countries of Africa.

# Part 2

# Mechanics of Business Engagement

# 2.1

# Labour, Skills and Training

*C. Jayanthi*

As is widely acknowledged, India's economic growth has been nothing short of inspiring, and the country's growth – at 8.4 per cent – is among the highest in the world. As a result, the country's education system has been turned upside down. From a population of approximately 300 million at the time of independence, the country is now 1 billion people strong. However, a fast growing economy needs people with skills. The first prime minister of the nation, Jawaharlal Nehru, built excellent institutions of higher education, such as the IITs (Indian Institutions of Technology) and the IIMs (Indian Institutions of Management), which have benefited the country greatly. Some 80 per cent of India is still rural and primary education has been in a state of neglect. To set right this anomaly, the government has attacked the problem with renewed vigour through the EFA (Education for All) or the SSA (Sarva Shiksha Abhiyan) programmes.

The SSA, the flagship programme of the UPA government – that the central government launched in partnership with the state governments, is expected to be instrumental in attaining the goal of UEE (Universal Elementary Education) in the country. The prime minister heads the National Mission for the SSA, which monitors the progress made under the scheme. The SSA is expected to provide relevant elementary education for children in the country aged between six and 14 years old by 2010. The goal of the SSA is consistent with the Constitution (86th) Amendment Act, 2002, which makes elementary education a fundamental right of every child living in the country.

The performance audit of the SSA, carried out by the CAG (Comptroller and Auditor General) of India (March 2005) mentions specifically the aim of the SSA:

> to ensure that all children complete five years of primary schooling by 2007; to ensure that all children complete eight years of elementary schooling by 2010; bridge all gender and social category gaps at the primary stage by 2007 and at the elementary educational level by 2010 and achieve universal retention by 2010.

Covering the period from 2003–2004 to 2007, the SSA has received external funding to the tune of $1 billion from the World Bank's IDA (International Development Association), the UK's Department for International Development, and the European Commission. The SSA is an ambitious programme, meant to cover 19.2 million children in the country. It evolved from the recommendations of the state education ministers' conference held in October 1998 to kick-start UEE. The programme was launched in 2001–2002. Since its inception, allocation of funds under the SSA has shown high growth from $77,467,906 in 2000–2001 to $1.6 billion in 2005–2006, and to $2.4 billion in 2006–2007, representing an increase of 41 per cent over the previous year (2005–2006).

The World Bank Aide-Memoire (January 2006) on the third joint-review mission of the SSA mentions that the target of reducing out-of-school children by 3 million per year is being exceeded. It mentions that the number of out-of-school children has fallen from 25 million in 2003 to 13.5 million as on March 2005 and that 'the positive trend will continue in 2006'.

Clearly, a great deal needs to be done. There are 48 districts in the country where more than 50,000 children are out of school, according to the World Bank report. According to the CAG of India's report on the SSA (March 2005), nationally, there were 71 children out-of-school per thousand. Therefore efforts need to be speeded up in this direction. Gender parity continues to improve, almost within reach at the primary level, according to the World Bank report. The girls to boys ratio at the primary level has increased from 0.90 in 2003–2004 to 0.91 in 2004–2005.

Another key component of the flagship programme of the UPA government has been the midday meal scheme that is seen as key to retaining children at school. The scheme was launched as a centrally sponsored scheme in August 1995. Central assistance comprised free food grain via the Food Corporation of India and an admissible transport subsidy. Initially, most states received a dry ration of 3 kilogrammes per person. The centre earlier provided a cooking cost of 1 Indian rupee (INR) per day, which has now been increased to INR 1.50 per day, with 0.50 paise contributed by the state – the bare minimum by any country's standards.

Under the scheme, a cooked meal of a minimum of 300 calories is made available to 12 crore children in over 950,000 schools. The allocation for the midday meal scheme has gone up from $2.7 billion in 2005–2006 to $3.7 billion in 2006–2007, signalling a rise of over 37 per cent, according to a parliamentary standing committee report (2006) on the scheme.

The 2 per cent education cess (tax) levied through the Finance Act 2004 yielded $1.08 billion in FY (financial year) 2004–2005: in FY 2005–2006 it rose to to $1.5 billion and in 2006–2007 it amounted to $1.9 billion, according to the ministry of human resource development (MHRD). The cess is used exclusively to finance the SSA and the government's midday meal scheme. During 2006–2007, funds amounting to $1.6 billion would have been required to construct 500,000 much-needed classrooms, according to the World Bank.

As far as secondary education is concerned, the age of 14–17 years is crucial. It encompasses classes nine to 12. According to figures available from the 2001 census, there are 91.7 million children eligible for secondary education in India. This segment is expected to grow to 98.2 million by 2011. In the 1990s, the enrolment in secondary schools increased at a rate of 2.83 per cent per annum, whereas in the early 2000s, the rate of growth was 7.4 per cent. According to government statistics, enrolment in secondary schools is expected to reach 26.4 million by 2006–2007. This will mean an additional $1 billion investment just for secondary education. There is a government proposal to expand the level of skills taught through industrial training institutes, which is expected to be considered. Industrial training institutes prepare students to become technicians, for example, electricians or plumbers. The government's aim is also make sure that students who do not want to study beyond class X and instead join vocational courses should be able to do so. The Planning Commission (determines government priorities for balanced use of the country's resources) wishes to place vocational training on a par with secondary, in terms of resources and status, within the next five years.

India has progressed in the realm of higher education from having 30 universities in 1950–1951 to 324 in 2006. The number of colleges is up from 750 in 1950–1951 to 16,000 in 2006. Enrolment has risen from 263,000 in 1950–1951 to 9.23 million in 2004–2005 and the number of teachers has gone up from 24,000 to 436,000 in the same period. There is also the UGC (University Grants Committee), an autonomous body that disburses grants to recognized institutions of higher learning. There are institutions of higher learning too – the aforementioned IITs (seven) and IIMs (eight), granted autonomy through Acts of Parliament. The number of students enrolled in universities and colleges in 2005 was 9.28 million, of which 3.6 million – 40 per cent – are women.

The percentage of young people (18–23 years) who are eligible for higher education form 7 per cent of the population; unlike in Organization for Economic Co-operation and Development (OECD) where it is as high as 40–50 per cent. The government's aim, therefore, is to increase the access ratio by 20 per cent by 2015.

There are discrepancies, for example: only 16 out of 1,000 young people are graduates in rural areas, whereas the number of urban graduates is higher in number – 111 out of 1,000. Most colleges and universities are located in urban areas.

The five southern states, Tamil Nadu, Karnataka, Kerala, Andhra Pradesh and the western state of Maharashtra have 32 per cent of the population, whereas they have 46 per cent of the total general colleges and almost 60 per cent of the professional institutions.

The IGNOU (Indira Gandhi National Open University) was set up in 1985 under the IGNOU Act. According to the annual report 2005–2006 of the MHRD, 'The total number of students registered in IGNOU during 2005 was 460,807.' The open or distance learning university offers a range of general and professional degrees, including Bachelors', Masters' and PhDs in general. It also offers professional courses, with the exception of medical degrees. This particular university was intended to reach the most remote corner of India. Although IGNOU has established centres all over the country, the courses and skill sets that they offer in areas such as management, health and computer sciences are more popular in urban areas.

The University Grants Commission, which disburses grants to various universities in the country and coordinates between the Union and state governments and the various institutions of higher learning, has set up a National Accreditation Council for periodic assessment of quality and standards in universities and colleges throughout India. Enrolment of women in higher education has increased from 10 per cent of the total population to 40 per cent in 2004–2005. According to a government estimate, $774 million is required to upgrade existing universities, filling vacancies of teachers, upgrading libraries etc.

Given the dire need for universities and colleges, the government is considering whether to allow 100 per cent foreign direct investment (FDI). This is, however, expected to be subject to the law of the land, which would mean allowing a certain percentage of reservations for disadvantaged castes (backward classes). Foreign universities that want to set up campuses in India still have to wait a while, as the law has yet to be enacted by the Indian Parliament. Currently, although FDI is allowed through the automatic route, a foreign institution must have an Indian partner – and the stake must be equal, ie. 50:50. If the foreign institution wants to increase the stake, it has to apply to the Foreign Investment Promotion Board (FIPB).

A consultative paper entitled *Higher Education in India and GATS: an opportunity*, brought out by the ministry of commerce and industry, makes out a case for foreign participation in Indian higher education. It says,

> General Agreement on Trade and Tariffs could provide an opportunity to put together a mechanism whereby private and foreign investment in higher education can be encouraged subject to high quality standards and efficient regulation.

Although India may be far from treating education as a service that can be traded internationally, rather than a fundamental right, the higher education system in the country is characterized by scarcity of resources. However, despite all this, India's growth has been tremendous in knowledge-based sectors, such as IT and ITES (IT-enabled services) and traditional sectors such as manufacturing. IT is expected to need approximately 5 million skilled workers within the next few years, according to Nandan Nilekani, CEO of Infosys, one of the top Indian ITcompanies, who spoke at a Confederation of Indian Industries seminar. Manufacturing in the next decade or so will create 25 million jobs and this will clearly require a skilled workforce. Will India be able to produce the jobs? In the first half of 2006, 52 per cent of Indian companies increased their workforce.

The IITs currently have 15,000 undergraduate and approximately 12,000 postgraduate students. These institutes provide top-class engineering education in virtually every field of engineering. There are 19 National Institutes of Technology that are next only to the IITs (Indian Institutes of Technology) in education. India's IT revolution no doubt has its roots firmly attached to the attention and support that science and technology has got from the forefathers of the nation, when it attained independence from British rule in 1947.

There are also private engineering colleges. Tamil Nadu has witnessed a big leap in the number of private engineering, medical and paramedical colleges since the mid-1980s, when the central government was looking for private investment in higher education. Now, the state has 254 engineering colleges offering over 80,000 seats in undergraduate courses and accounts for approximately 20 per cent of the 1,346 engineering institutions in the country. The government now runs only nine engineering colleges in the state. However, the quality of education offered by the private engineering colleges, which give courses in a range of engineering subjects such as civil, electrical, mechanical and chemical just like the IITs, is open to question. The National Accreditation Council, which follows stringent parameters to assess the quality of education offered by various institutes of higher learning, does not make it mandatory for institutions to seek accreditation.

Every university offers a legal degree and there are specialized law schools in Bangalore, Hyderabad, Bhopal and Pune. However, legal literacy in India still has a long way to go. To some extent this inevitably delays law enforcement within the country. In terms of legal specializations, cyber law is still at a nascent stage in India. It tends to be offered more as a course module than a fully fledged degree course. Civil and criminal law specializations are still popular.

Some 81 per cent of Indian companies, according to a McKinsey survey, believe that the lack of human resources will be the single largest deterrent to speedy development. The fact remains that nearly 50 per cent of students drop out of school at secondary levels, with another 75 per cent dropping out at the higher secondary level. Of the 3 million who then make it to graduation, only 15–20 per cent can be given a job or be hired. Only 10 per cent look into research – a primary need for all industries for their future growth.

Hewitt India has painted two scenarios of India – the present one with enrolment increases at the historical 2–5 per cent levels, low quality of educational inputs and low rate of conversion to employment for a student. The other scenario sees enrolments growing exponentially, with improvement in education quality and conversion to employment increasing with most graduates being employed. This leads to higher national income, increased consumption, increased knowledge employment and high economic growth, whilst the former leads to high rates of unemployment, social unrest, rapid wage inflation and economic non-competitiveness.

Whilst IT and ITES professionals have the biggest chances of being hired (companies forming the sector hired at an aggressive 11.9 per cent, with the benchmark 30 hiring at even more aggressive rate of 16.1 per cent), those from sectors like construction and manufacturing are also seeing an increase in demand at 6.43 per cent and 1.9 per cent, respectively. The increase in hiring in these two sectors corresponds to a 10.6 per cent increase in industrial output over the first five months of fiscal year 2006. Manufacturing accounts for approximately 15 per cent of India's gross domestic product.

A Ma Foi survey (Global Search Services) predicts that 10,30,040 jobs will be created this year. The sectors expected to drive job demand in India are IT and ITES, manufacturing, retail, communication and transport. Looking at business education in India, it is largely driven by the IIM. The IITs have also started their own school of management, and there are also some private management schools, such as the Indian School of Business, Hyderabad and the Management Development Institute, Gurgaon. The IIMs are government-funded and offer a range of courses in all areas of management. However, typically, a student who goes to study in the IIM – after passing a nationwide competitive test – does not have work experience. The ideal top qualification in India would be an IIT–IIM combination.

In conclusion, skilled human resource will be a critical issue in the years to come in India. It is still necessary for it to keep pace with fast-moving economic development. Despite India's 1 billion people, imparting the right skills for a rapidly developing job market will test its institutions of learning.

# 2.2

# Real Estate Sector

*Vivek Dahiya, DTZ Debenham Tie Leung*

Real estate is one of the fastest growing sectors in India. Market analysis pegs returns from realty in India at an average of 12–14 per cent per annum with a tremendous upsurge in commercial real estate on account of the Indian BPO (business process outsourcing) boom.

Lease rentals and occupancies have been picking up steadily, and there is a gaping demand for quality infrastructure. A significant demand is also likely to be generated as the outsourcing boom moves into the manufacturing sector. Further, the housing sector has been growing at an average of 34 per cent annually, while the hospitality industry witnessed a growth of 10–15 per cent last year.

Apart from the huge demand, India also scores on the construction front. A McKinsey report reveals that the average profit from construction in India is 18 per cent, which is approximately double the profitability for a construction project undertaken in the United States. Aided and abetted by a bullish economy, strong demand from domestic and foreign sources and proactive policy initiatives like relaxation of FDI (foreign direct investment) in construction, rationalization of stamp duty and repeal of the urban land ceiling act, Indian realty over the past two years has seen unprecedented investment.

The fundamental demand drivers of real estate remain strong. The sub-prime crises could result in marginally reduced demand for commercial office space over the next 12 months, but even that is expected to have a positive impact in the medium term.

Improved economic growth and availability of finance (institutional and retail) had resulted in surging needs for commercial and residential space over the past five years. However, the hardening of interest rates in the past few quarters has impacted on the retail buyer in urban areas, and developers also are witnessing reduced availability of construction finance from banks. The government took action on interest rate because of a significant increase in values across all markets and product types, with the aim of reducing speculative price rises.

The Indian economy has steadily moved away from its overdependence on agriculture to services and more recently to manufacturing, the latter two being significant drivers of real estate demand. The last few years have seen Indian market mature through regulatory reforms (rationalization of stamp duties, reform of urban land ceilings), improving products in terms of quality and technology, changing tenant profile (multinational companies, and respect for tenancy laws) and improving management and maintenance models.

## IT/ITES demand

Indian real estate can be characterized by a few key demand drivers – commercial, retail, residential and hospitality. Fuelled by demand from these sectors all over India, real estate is experiencing a boom. The IT-ITES (information information-IT-enabled services) industry, the main driver for commercial real estate demand all over India, has grown at a 36 per cent CAGR (compound annual growth rate) over the last decade. In 2008, it is expected to account for over 7 per cent of India's GDP (gross domestic product) and 30 per cent of foreign exchange inflows, creating over 2 million jobs. In 2006 alone, the IT-ITES sector absorbed a total of approximately 46 million square feet across India. This sector is expected to continue with its robust growth at least for the foreseeable future.

If an IT-ITES company is considering starting operations in India, it has building options available across multiple cities. Most large cities like Bangalore, Delhi, Mumbai, Chennai, Pune, Hyderabad and Kolkata (Calcutta) have several operational IT park projects and many SEZs (special economic zones) in the pipeline which are dedicated to the IT-ITES companies. Based on the skill set of the human resources, infrastructure at city level, scalability options to cater to future expansion and cost requirements of the company, it is usually advisable to select the ideal location in one of these cities. Many international property consultants with operations in India can assist all such companies in their city evaluation, site selection and project management needs.

## Retail market

The retail sector is also growing at a robust rate with continuing investment from domestic retail companies. With the opening up of high-end retail to FDI, this sector is set to experience a further boost. Recent surveys have repeatedly shown India as an attractive destination among emerging markets for retailers to enter. With organized retail still at a minuscule 3 per cent of the total market, the potential for growth is not lost on any investor. In fact, the growth rate of organized retail is anywhere between 25 and 30 per cent per annum, and a McKinsey and CII (Confederation of Indian Industry) economic review (2003) estimated that organized retail would grow to 10 per cent of the retail market or $30 billion by 2007. The sector is seeing increased focus on the development of integrated retail cum entertainment centres (malls) as opposed to stand-alone formats. The number of malls is scheduled to increase from the current 100 to almost 350 by 2010 providing increased opportunities to investors. With a shift in the mindset of the Indian middle class consumer and a substantial increase in the 'young' consuming class population, India is slowly emerging as a consumption led economy.

Most large cities in India now provide options in the mall formats. The reach of these formats are now spreading in the smaller cities as well. Some micro markets in various cities are currently witnessing a situation where retailers are unable to sustain profitable businesses. This is because of very high rents and limited professional management. Most mall projects in India, so far, have concerns with regard to strata titles which are detrimental to the mall's financial health in the long run. Retailers have also been affected by delayed delivery/construction schedules in malls, which in turn slow their expansion plans.

Some of the key points to be considered while taking up space in a mall in India are:

- profile of the developer;
- emphasis being given to trade and tenant mix in the design; and
- whether a mall manager is appointed for the project.

It is also important to understand from the developer the process of calculating CAM (common area maintenance) charges. CAM charges in some small malls are a very large percentage of the total outflow.

## Residential market

Increasing urbanization and higher aspiration needs (better quality real estate) are fuelling the demand for residential real estate. Low per capita housing stock, higher disposable income, falling age of first-time home buyers and low interest rates coupled with surging home loans have also contributed significantly to this phenomenon. The housing sector is currently growing at 30–35 per cent per annum. A lot of demand is also coming from investors who view housing as a safer investment option as compared to shares and mutual funds. The decision to liberalize FDI norms in the construction development sector is perhaps the most significant economic policy decision taken by the government last year. Many developers now feel the need to focus on *affordable housing* as due to recent price hikes the end users have been pushed out of the market.

## Hospitality sector

Another key sector for growth is hospitality. India's keen interest to leverage its tourism potential to attract a significant flow of high-spending foreign tourists has resulted in renewed interest in the hospitality sector with established foreign brands entering the market. On one account, the five-star room capacity in India needs to double in the next five years from the current paltry 96,000 beds, giving a potentially golden opportunity for investors. It has been noticed that almost all the large hotel developers and operators have over a dozen projects under construction across India.

## Industrial property

Finally, interesting changes are taking place even for industrial properties. So far, most industrial options have been available as land in industrial parks developed and promoted by state-promoted industrial development corporations. However, the government has now enacted a policy allowing the establishment of SEZs in India, even by private developers. This has resulted in very high interest from various Indian and international developers to undertake development at scales (over 25,000 acres) not seen in India. SEZs would also benefit the IT-ITES companies, as mentioned earlier, wherein all new businesses they bring to India will benefit from tax incentives for a 10-year period, if they operate in an SEZ. It should be noted here that the current tax exemptions given to IT-ITES companies under the Software Technology Parks of India policy has a sunset clause which the government has now pushed to March 2009.

## Real estate investment vehicles

A more recent phenomenon in the real estate industry in India has been that of REMFs (real estate mutual funds). REITs (real estate investment trusts) are currently non-existent in India. Over the last few years, there have been several representations by the real estate industry and mutual funds to permit the establishment of REITs in India to the SEBI (Securities Exchange Board of India), the agency which regulates mutual funds and stock markets in India.

In response, the SEBI, in consultation with the Association of Mutual Funds of India, appointed a committee to study the feasibility of REITs in India. The committee has now recommended that REMFs should be implemented in India through the mutual fund schemes. Under this scheme, an existing mutual fund with an adequate number of personnel and directors with real estate experience, with a positive net worth for the five preceding years and other similar regulations would be allowed to float REMFs. All

Table 1. Occupancy levels

| Sector | Commercial | Retail | Residential |
|---|---|---|---|
| Occupancy levels | 85–90% in Delhi NCR | Varies across India. Metro cities have seen almost no availability of high-end retail space. Occupancies are quite low in malls. NCR region has on average approximately 20–25% vacancy. Similar situations across India. | Still high investment demand. Thus end-users are relatively low, anywhere between 60 and 70%. |
| | 90% in Mumbai<br>95% in Bengaluru<br>90–95% in Chennai<br>90–95% in Hyderabad<br>85–90% in Kolkata | | |

REMFs would be close ended and would be listed in a recognized stock exchange.

While this demand was being met, in April 2004, SEBI had opened a small window for real estate investments under the VCF (venture capital fund) and FVCI (foreign venture capital investor) regime. Pursuant to that, Fire Capital, IREO, HDFC, SBI and ICICI Ventures have already announced their foray in this space and more are scheduled to enter.

# Geographic spread

Although the initial real estate boom was concentrated in places like Bangalore and the NCR (National Capital Region) of Delhi including Gurgaon, more recently the geographical spread has been substantial. Southern states and the NCR continue to attract the majority share of the IT/ITES and BPO investment; however, secondary cities, like Chandigarh, Indore, Kochi and Kolkata, are now emerging as destinations due to cost and infrastructure advantages. Retail is again an India-wide phenomenon with retail chains targeting Tier II and III cities. The demand for housing is widespread with townships being built in metros and Tier II and III cities as well. In a nutshell, investment opportunities are increasingly being offered in various parts of the country.

# Future outlook

The Indian real estate sector promises to be a big draw for foreign investments into the country. The continued growth of the Indian outsourcing industry provides excellent opportunities for real estate investors. The booming middle class will result in a continued demand for housing and retail space. The fact that foreign investors are willing to commit billions of dollars in this sector, coupled with their understanding that real estate investment requires a longer term commitment, demonstrates the growing confidence of investors in the Indian economy. Also if channelled properly, the Indian realty sector could spur the growth of several other sectors in India through its backward and forward linkages.

# 2.3

# Inward Investment

*Roderick Millar*

As Minister of Commerce and Industry Shri Kamal Nath has noted, '...during the last 14 years there has been a sea change not only in the world's perception about India's future, but in our own perception about ourselves. The world has acknowledged the "arrival of India". We no longer discuss the future of India, we say "the future India".'

This is well expressed by examining the foreign direct investment (FDI) statistics over those 14 years since the 1991 reforms came into effect (1992–2006). The first 12 years showed inward investment to India rising from $393 million in 1992–1993 and growing steadily to $3.62 billion in 1997–1998. There was a noticeable lull in the trend over the millennial period, but FDI was up again in 2001–2002, and following some retrenchment during the global downturn it has continued upward vigorously in the last three years.

Mauritius continues to head the list of originating FDI countries throughout the period by a considerable margin. This is due to the Double

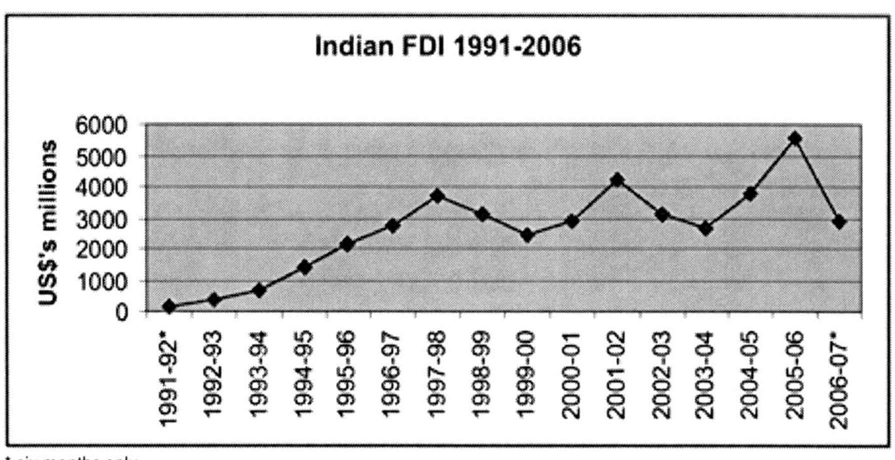


* six months only
Source: Department of Commerce, Ministry of Commerce and Industry

Figure 1. Indian FDI, 1991–2006

Table 1. Top Indian FDI countries, 2005–2006

| *Rank* | *Country* | *2004-05 (Apr-Mar)* | *2005-06 (Apr-Mar)* | *2006 (Apr-Jul only)* | *Totals 2004-06* |
|---|---|---|---|---|---|
| 1 | Mauritius | $1129m | $2570m | $1506m | $5205m |
| 2 | USA | $669m | $502m | $263m | $1434m |
| 3 | Singapore | $184m | $275m | $432m | $891m |
| 4 | Germany | $145m | $303m | $28m | $476m |
| 5 | UK | $101m | $266m | $79m | $446m |
| 6 | Netherlands | $267m | $76m | $77m | $420m |
| 7 | Japan | $126m | $208m | $29m | $363m |
| 8 | Switzerland | $77m | $96m | $19m | $192m |
| 9 | France | $117m | $18m | $36m | $171m |
| 10 | South Korea | $35m | $60m | $20m | $115m |

Source: Govt of India, Dept of Commerce

Taxation Avoidance Treaty (DTAT) between India and Mauritius that has created a beneficial tax loophole through which vast amounts of FDI have been funnelled. This continues to be a sore point with India, and although Mauritius has tightened the tax residency certificate rules for overseas companies the Indian government would still like to see more done.

There are two popular avoidance schemes. In one, companies from high-tax, usually developing countries route their investments through Mauritius's low tax system and thus take advantage of the DTAT regime. This has come to be known as 'treaty shopping'. In the other scheme Indian domestic companies take advantage of the Mauritian tax regime by investing back in India via Mauritius, known as 'round-tripping'; clearly this loses the Indian government many millions in tax revenue – and distorts the FDI figures to the extent that some of the Mauritian FDI is, in fact, re-routed Indian domestic investments.

Recently Mauritius has tightened its rules requiring at least two *bona fide* directors to be resident in Mauritius for the DTAT to apply; in addition, all board meetings and bank transactions must occur on the islands. If these measures do not make a significant impact it is likely that India will put pressure for more to be done.

Ignoring the Mauritian anomaly the lead investing nations in India are more obvious (see Table 1). Below the level of the top five investors it should be noted that single large deals can significantly distort the order.

## Where the money is going?

Of more interest to the inward investor is where the investments are directed, both in terms of Indian geography and industrial sector.

By sectors, the technology area is drawing in by far the greatest financial input from outside the country. The electrical equipment and telecommuni-

Table 2. Main sectors attracting FDI, 2004–2006

| *Rank* | *Sector* | *2004-05 (Apr–Mar)* | *2005-06 (Apr–Mar)* | *2006 (Apr–Jul only)* | *Totals 2004–06* |
|---|---|---|---|---|---|
| 1 | Electrical equipment (incl software and electronics) | $721m | $1451m | $524m | $2696m |
| 2 | Telecommunications (radio, mobile and fixed line) | $129m | $680m | $854m | $1663m |
| 3 | Services (financial and non-financial) | $469m | $581m | $337m | $1387m |
| 4 | Chemicals (not fertilizer) | $198m | $447m | $86m | $731m |
| 5 | Transportation | $179m | $222m | $219m | $620m |
| 6 | Drugs and pharmaceutical | $292m | $172m | $45m | $509m |
| 7 | Cement and gypsum | $0m | $452m | $21m | $473m |
| 8 | Metallurgical Industries | $192m | $153m | $67m | $412m |
| 9 | Fuels (power and refining) | $166m | $94m | $106m | $366m |
| 10 | Food processing | $38m | $42m | $27m | $107m |

Table 3. RBI office areas attracting FDI, January 2000–July 2006

| *Rank* | *RBI – Regional Office* | *State Covered* | *US $ millions* |
|---|---|---|---|
| 1 | New Delhi | Delhi; part of Uttar Pradesh; Haryana | 5732.7 |
| 2 | Mumbai | Maharashtra, Dadra & Nagar; Haveli; Daman & Diu | 5239.0 |
| 3 | Bangalore | Karnataka | 1676.6 |
| 4 | Chennai | Tamil Nadu & Pondicherry | 1560.0 |
| 5 | Hyderabad | Andhra Pradesh | 849.7 |
| 6 | Ahmedabad | Gujarat | 826.1 |
| 7 | Chandigarh | Chandigarh; Punjab; Haryana; Himachal Pradesh | 328.3 |
| 8 | Kolkata | West Bengal; Sikkim; Andaman & Niocobar Islands | 311.1 |
| 9 | Panaji | Goa | 180.2 |
| 10 | Kochi | Kerala; Lakshadweep | 73.9 |

cations sectors account for over one-quarter of all FDI and the financial and non-financial services a further 11 per cent. This to some extent under-emphasises the role of services in FDI; the fact that services are less capital intensive than other sectors means they require less initial start-up investment than other areas for equally large potential returns.

The main regional beneficiaries of FDI are as obvious as the sectors that attract it.

This exemplifies one of the major issues facing the developing India: the great divide between the urban and rural areas. Some 70 per cent of the Indian population remains rurally based and to a large extent is missing out on the changes being brought by the FDI inflows. Nearly two-thirds of India's FDI inflows have been invested in the five city areas of New Delhi, Mumbai, Bangalore, Chennai and Hyderabad. These are the electronics, computer and financial service hubs of India and have left the old-economy powerhouses, such as Kolkata, far behind in terms of recent investment and development.

## State incentives, bureaucracy and the single window system

The liberalization process started in the 1990s has made India a much more plausible location to do business. However, as mentioned, the bureaucratic overlay is still a major obstacle. This is most prevalent at the state level.

Trying to identify which states offer the best environment for any particular project can be daunting. Each state has a website, although not all of them are very clear in their presentation of investment incentives. The federal government business website does a good job at listing all the various incentives.

In an attempt to make the process of application more streamlined the 'Single Window System' has been developed where a single agency coordinates all the necessary applications, approvals and regulations required in establishing new businesses. Not all states have yet implemented it, and it is not totally seamless even where implemented, but the Single Window System does offer a substantial step forward with this process.

## Infrastructure investment and incentives

The speed of development in India is such that enormous improvements in the country's infrastructure are required. The government has focused on these areas and makes special tax holidays and other incentives available to companies interested in developing these areas.

### Power

Non-atomic electricity generation, transmission and distribution can have 100 per cent FDI. The government offers a 10-year tax holiday on new development projects started before April 2010. Renovation and modernization projects will not be taxed on any profits prior to this date either. The 2005 Electricity Act enables easier private sector involvement; it is believed that 41000 MW of extra power are needed, requiring approximately $120 billion of investment.

### Telecommunications

One hundred per cent FDI in telecoms equipment and 100 per cent FDI in electronic and voice mail services are available, on condition that at least 26 per cent of shares are made available to the Indian public if the shares are publicly listed. Fixed and mobile services are subject to a 49 per cent FDI ownership cap. An initial five-year tax holiday followed by a 30 per cent tax reduction for five years is offered to telecoms service providers. Mobile and Internet usage in India is growing fast.

### Road

One hundred per cent FDI is available in road construction and maintenance, and in return a 10-year tax holiday is available. Capital gains tax exemption is also offered under certain rules. The National Highway Development Programme envisages over 24,000 kilometres of road construction and improvement.

### Civil Aviation

One hundred per cent FDI is available for greenfield airport construction and 49 per cent (100 per cent for for Non-Resident Indians (NRIs)) FDI for air transportation services as long as there is no foreign airline involvement. A 10-year tax holiday is available to airport operators. Airline usage is growing fast currently.

### Automobile

Car and other vehicle assembly and components are growth industries in India and 100 per cent FDI is available. Certain incentives exist on a state-by-state basis and further tax reductions are available on research and development investment.

## Technology transfer

Foreign Technology Transfer (or Foreign Technology Collaboration agreements, FTC) approvals are closely managed in India. The system is overseen by the Department of Industrial Policy & Promotion (D/o IPP) and non-automatic approvals are made through the Reserve Bank of India (RBI).

### Government assistance for FDI

Dealing with the Indian government is not always as straightforward as it might be. The Indian system is notoriously bureaucratic and the administrative procedures that are often required to be progressed through can appear over-complex to those more used to flatter government systems.

In addition to this background of bureaucracy the potential investor must also assure themselves that they have met all the requirements placed on them by both the federal and state levels of government. Checking for particular incentive schemes, again at either federal or state level, is recommended.

There are two main approaches: employ an advisor to help with this initial phase and guide you through the first steps or make the first round of investigation in-house. Sooner or later professional advisers will probably be necessary. However, if low-cost initial research is more appropriate, there are some useful agencies that will help and offer a wide range of data.

The D/o IPP within the ministry of commerce and industry has created a series of bodies that serve the inward investor and others that offer help to domestic entrepreneurs, to make the investment process as simple as possible.

The principal amongst these is the Secretariat for Industrial Assistance (SIA). Its stated remit is:

> to provide a single window for entrepreneurial assistance, investor facilitation, processing all applications which require Government approval, assisting entrepreneurs and investors in setting up projects (including liaison with other organisations and State Governments) and in monitoring the implementation of projects.

The SIA is best approached through its website (http://dipp.nic.in) where it presents a mass of information regarding specific industrial policies and licensing. Usefully, they have a 'bulletin board' where questions can be posted on technical questions relating to FDI and a department employee will respond to them. A further service is offered in the form of a 'chat room' where twice a day (11am to 12pm and 4pm to 5pm each working day, Indian time) questions can be sent for immediate responses in the form of online messages.

For more specific or sensitive enquiries the best route is through the 'Nodal Officer' whose contact details are available from the above webpage.

The SIA is also home to the officer in charge of dealing with grievances that businesses may have in the manner in which their applications are addressed. The Joint Secretary (Public Grievances) contact details are also to be found on this website.

Also within the D/o IPP–SIA structure is the Foreign Investment Implementation Authority (FIIA) set up to

> facilitate quick translation of FDI approvals into implementation, to provide a pro-active one stop after care service to foreign investors by helping them obtain necessary approvals, sort out operational problems and meet with various Government agencies to find solution to their problems.

The website allows for certain applications to be submitted online.

Under the auspices of the Department of Economic Affairs at the ministry of finance, but in close association with the D/o IPP is the Foreign Investment Promotion Board (FIPB) that 'provides a time bound, transparent and pro-active FDI regime for approval of FDI investment proposals'. All 'non-automatic route' FDI proposals have to go through the FIPB for approval. The FAQ page at http://siadipp.nic.in/publicat/most_frq.htm covers many basic application procedural questions.

Other potential sources of data and advice exist. One of the best is the Confederation of Indian Industry's associate organization the India Brand Equity Foundation (IBEF), which has a useful selection of resources at www.ibef.org.

The government directory (http://goidirectory.nic.in) is also useful in seeking the appropriate department or individual.

# 2.4

# ITES-BPO

*Rajdeep Sahrawat, National Association of Software and Service Companies (NASSCOM)*

Worldwide spending on IT (information technology) and related business services is estimated to exceed $1.7 trillion in 2007, growing at 7.3 per cent over the previous year. With outsourcing as the key growth driver, the IT-ITES (IT-enabled services) grew by 7.8 per cent and accounted for an increasing share of total technology spend. Worldwide IT services spending grew at 6 per cent in 2007, and IT outsourcing reported above average growth at 74 per cent. Worldwide BPO (business process outsourcing) spending growth was at nearly 10 per cent with a strong offshoring bias. While North America and Western Europe continue to lead in overall market share, BRIC (Brazil, Russia, India and China) nations are growing three to four times faster.

The Indian IT-ITES services industry continued to show a strong growth trajectory in FY 2007–2008 and grew by a CAGR (compound annual growth rate) of 28 per cent to reach an overall size of $64 billion. The export services (IT and ITES) grew by 32 per cent to reach an overall size of $40.8 billion. The IT-ITES industry contributes over 5 per cent to India's GDP (gross domestic product) and employs 2 million people directly, and for every one job in the Indian IT industry four additional jobs are created in other sectors of the Indian economy. The United States (61 per cent) continues to be the major market, followed by the United Kingdom (18 per cent), Continental Europe (12 per cent), Asia Pacific (6 per cent) and the rest of the world (2 per cent).

Driven by a fast growing economy, increased consumption of goods and services, ubiquitous and cheap connectivity and growth in technology spending, the domestic IT market in India complemented the growth in IT-ITES exports and reached a size of $23.6 billion in 2007, and has placed India amongst the fastest growing IT markets in the Asia-Pacific region. With spending on services and the outsourced model gaining noticeable traction in India, the domestic market is witnessing the signs of service line depth that characterizes maturing markets.

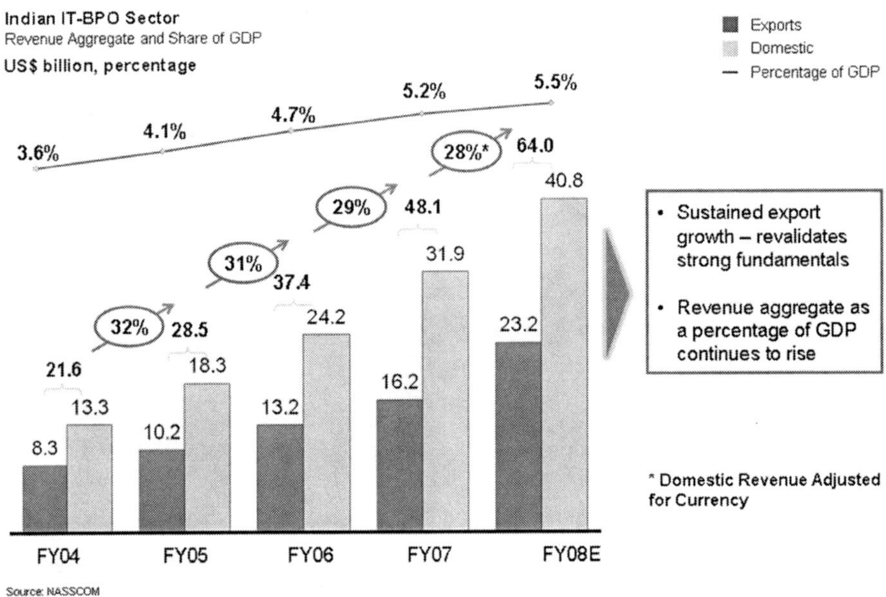


Figure 1. Overview of the Indian IT-ITES industry

Also in 2007 the Indian multinational IT firms came of age, with the traditionally India-centric firms beginning to build significant presence in other locations – through cross-border acquisitions, onshore contract wins and organic growth. This was complemented by global majors continuing to ramp up the offshore delivery capabilities – predominantly in India, vindicating the success of the global delivery model and highlighting India's important role in the new world IT order. The deal sizes in the Indian IT-ITES industry have grown significantly and many $100 million plus deals were awarded to Indian IT firms during 2007.

The leading publicly listed players[1] have reported a year-on-year top line growth of nearly 30 per cent. Additionally, MNC (multinational company)-owned captive units have been scaling up their operations steadily with the headcount forecast to grow by at least 30 per cent this year.

## IT services

IT services (excluding ITES) continue to lead Indian IT-ITES exports, accounting for about 57 per cent of the total. This segment is expected to grow by about 28 per cent and cross $23 billion in 2007. Project-based services, contributing about 53 per cent continues to be the largest segment of the IT exports. Higher value project-based services such as IT consulting,

[1] Comprising over 50 leading publicly listed companies, accounting for approximately two-third of the total revenues earned by Indian companies.

systems integration and testing services are seeing rapid growth as Indian IT firms strengthen their capabilities.

The growth in the IT services is broad based; while the traditional sectors like BFSI (banking, financial services and insurance) and telecom continue to lead the way, accounting for nearly 60 per cent of Indian IT services exports, other emerging sectors, such as airlines, media, healthcare and utilities, are expected to grow faster in the coming years.

Table 1. IT services revenue spread by sector

| Sector | Share of revenue (%) |
|---|---|
| BFSI | 40 |
| Hi-tech/telecoms | 19 |
| Manufacturing | 15 |
| Retail | 8 |
| Construction and utilities | 4 |
| Airlines and transportation | 3 |
| Healthcare | 3 |
| Media, publishing and entertainment | 3 |
| Other | 5 |

Outsourcing services gained share in FY 2007, contributing 37 per cent to exports. Application management and IS (infrastructure services) outsourcing both grew rapidly, clocking growth rates of over 60 per cent and 100 per cent, respectively. Support and training exports were estimated at about $1.5 billion.

The trend towards an increasing share of outsourcing services is likely to show a strong bias in FY 2008 with applications outsourcing estimated to grow at 40 per cent, while remote infrastructure services are expected to nearly double.

Buyers are readily acknowledging the increasing maturity of global sourcing and increasingly committing to longer-term annuity contracts. While application management outsourcing has led the way thus far, infrastructure services outsourcing is expected to grow faster as buyers increasingly shift to asset-light deals.

## ITES services

Growing at a CAGR of nearly 37 per cent over the last four years, the ITES sector is the fastest growing segment of the Indian IT-ITES industry, and Indian ITES exports are estimated to have grown to $8.4 billion, representing a CAGR of 36.9 per cent over the previous year in FY 2007. Direct employment in the ITES segment is estimated to have reached 553,000. Employee turnover/attrition levels appear to be stabilizing with the talent acquisition, development and retention initiatives being undertaken by the players beginning to deliver results.

The Indian ITES sector has undergone significant transformation since its inception over a decade ago. Starting out with basic data entry tasks, the industry has rapidly acquired a reputation as the primary low-cost destination for voice-based customer contact/support services, finance and accounting, and a range of back office processing activities. The ITES segment is currently in its third stage of evolution with rapid proliferation of players, service lines and sourcing destinations.

The structure of the Indian ITES services segment is relatively more fragmented, as compared to the IT services segment – with the top 10 third-party players accounting for a market share of approximately 30 per cent (the corresponding figure for IT services is over 50 per cent). Further, unlike in IT services where MNCs account for approximately 30 per cent of the exports, MNCs with captive BPO operations in India account for approximately two-thirds of the segment. Currently, over 1,500 firms provide services to clients across 120 countries.

In India, firms are expanding their operations within as well as beyond the existing ITES hubs into satellite towns and newer cities – the latter offering several incremental benefits such as access to different sources of talent, lower facility and administrative costs and distributed facilities for business continuity.

In addition to expanding operations at various locations within the country, Indian firms are also building capabilities – organically or through M&A (mergers and acquisitions) – in other countries to strengthen their global service delivery proposition and skill/service portfolio.

While offshore cost effectiveness continues to add pressure on the average billing rates, Indian service providers have managed to maintain relatively stable pricing across key categories. Mature customers are moving beyond purely cost-based negotiations to develop innovative deal structures that include pricing models in which the service providers assume greater risk by correlating revenue with outcomes of the engagement.

Horizontal ITES accounting for about 80 per cent of Indian BPO exports represents the larger and relatively more established set of services being delivered from India. Key categories within horizontal ITES services include:

- customer interaction and support;
- finance and accounting;
- knowledge services;
- human resource management; and
- procurement services.

Some of the key growth drivers of Indian ITES services industry are as follows:

| Phase I (1996–2000) | Phase II (2000–2003) | Phase III (2003–2008E) |
|---|---|---|
| • operational cultures previously seen only in western shared-service centres were developed;<br>• large operations and high-quality infrastructure were built;<br>• development of delivery processes – legalising shift work for men and women;<br>• low-resistance to off-shore outsourcing. | • improving risk profile of the business model – supply-side still perceived to be immature;<br>• early movers display advantage of scale;<br>• credibility of the business model reinforced – perceived risks dealt with satisfactorily;<br>• initiation of work on process and regulatory standards;<br>• rise in anti-off-shore backlash. | • widespread global acceptance of the economic imperative of global sourcing;<br>• proliferation of players service lines and sourcing destinations;<br>• changing cost of economics – decline in labour arbitrage offset by leveraging and SG&A (selling, general and administration expenses) efficiencies and scale;<br>• shift towards higher order, cost-plus benefits from global sourcing;<br>• maturity of process and regulatory standards in the industry. |
| • pioneers focus on building scale;<br>• absence of vendors with exhibited capabilities;<br>• preference for the captive model. | • early adopters sharpen outsourcing strategy;<br>• rise of the third party service provider. | • cautious followers embrace outsourcing unconditionally;<br>• higher degree of consolidation and shakeout. |

Source: IBM Consulting Services, NASSCOM

Figure 2. Phases of ITES-BPO evolution in India

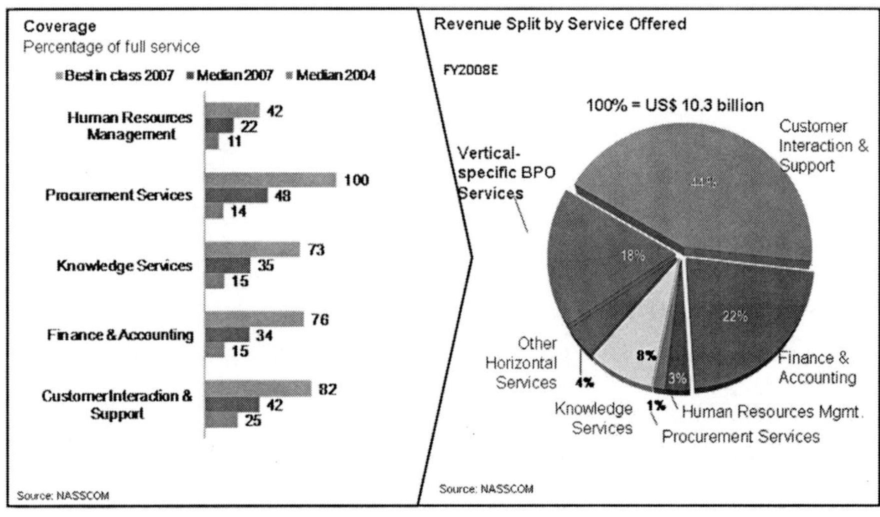


Figure 3. Services split of the ITES segment

Table 2. Indicative list of Fortune 1000 firms sourcing ITES services from India

| Vertical | Company |
|---|---|
| BFSI | Fidelity, JP Morgan, Bank of America, American Express, HSBC, Standard Chartered Bank, ABN AMRO, Goldman Sachs, Prudential, Morgan Stanley, Deutsche Bank, Lloyds TSB, Capital One, AXA, Winterthur, Lehman Brothers |
| Professional Services | McKinsey & Co., Deloitte Consulting, Accenture, Bain & Co., Ernst & Young, Reuters, Frost & Sullivan, Datamonitor |
| Technology and Telecom | Hewlett Packard, IBM, EDS, Dell, Samsung, Honeywell, Yahoo!, City of London Telecom (COLT), Alcatel, Accenture |
| Automotive and Heavy Machinery | General Motors, Hyundai, Ford, Daimler Chrysler, Caterpillar, Bechtel, Lear, Magna |
| Pharmaceuticals/ Biotechnology | Vision HealthSource (Perot Systems), Eli Lilly, Astra Zeneca, Pfizer |
| Others/Conglomerates | AOL, Tesco, Unilever, General Electric |

Source: NASSCOM

1. Rapid growth of globalization has added to competitive pressures across geographic markets that were previously relatively isolated from overseas competition. The resulting impact on growth and profitability continues to push organizations towards more cost efficient business models including IT-ITES outsourcing.
2. As a part of mainstream business strategies, offshore/outsourcing initiatives are being accorded significant senior leadership. There is increasing emphasis on leveraging the model for greater strategic business impact, not restricted to functional support (IT, HR, etc.).

3. Outsourcing to India has provided companies with significant benefits over and above cost arbitrage, through business process enhancements and improvements. In spite of the rising elements of cost, Indian offshore operations provide cost savings of 40–50 per cent; in spite of wage inflation averaging 10–15 per cent annually, companies are able to leverage declines in telecom and other overhead costs, and productivity gains and economies of scale to sustain the cost arbitrage.
4. Indian vendors are expanding their service offerings, enabling customers to deepen their offshore engagements; the shift from low-end business processes to higher value knowledge-based processes is having a positive impact on the overall industry growth.
5. India has the largest English-speaking talent pool in the world – over 440,000 engineering degree and diploma holders, approximately 2.3 million other (arts, commerce and science) graduates and 300,000 postgraduates are added each year. Three-fifths of the Indian technical workforce has more than four years of experience and an even higher proportion has an engineering degree.

## Selection of an ITES outsourcing model

'What is the most appropriate model for outsourcing ITES-BPO services to India?' is a question which often gets asked by prospective customers. While there is no 'one size fits all' engagement model and each customer has to select the outsourcing model based on its context, the following are some broad parameters to define the two components of any outsourcing model – engagement structure and pricing.

The selection of a suitable offshore outsourcing engagement model is governed by three primary factors:

1. nature of the process – degree of complexity, risk of IP (intellectual property) loss;
2. availability of 3PSPs (third-party service providers) with the requisite scope and scale to undertake the process; and
3. management capability to handle global operations.

Other factors include the desired level of control on operations, investment intent and capability, total cost economics and tax implications and the targeted transition time.

Based on their assessment, companies have traditionally chosen between captive and third-party vendor models. Some companies have formed joint ventures to spread the enterprise risk. The BOT (build–operate–transfer) model is a relatively newer model under which the client firm contracts with an independent vendor to undertake a process in a dedicated manner and acquire it once an agreed scale and scope has been achieved.

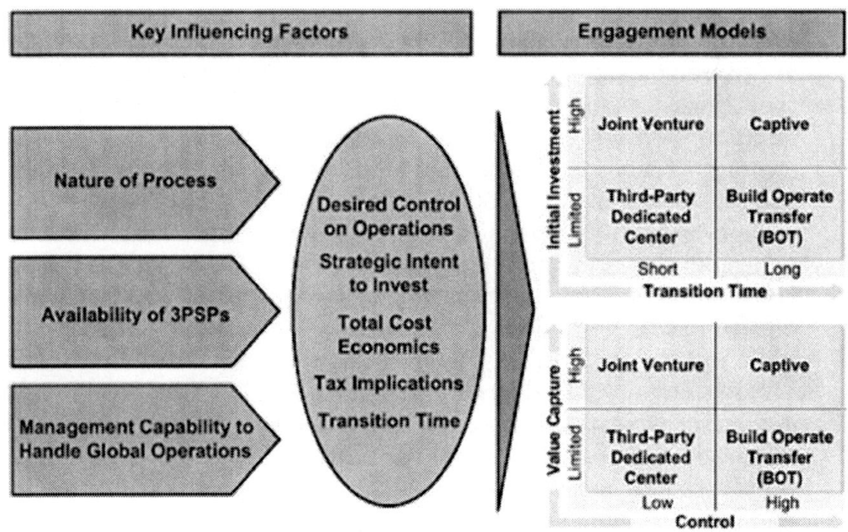


Source: NASSCOM, neoIT

Figure 4. Key influencing factors and engagement models

The following is a list of commonly used pricing models in the offshore ITES industry:

1. Per-unit time/variable pricing (per seat, per hour, etc.): This is the most common pricing model adopted by Indian ITES companies. The client guarantees a minimum amount of business and is billed on a per hour/seat basis.
2. Per seat or FTE (full-time employee) per month: The client guarantees a minimum amount of business for a number of FTEs on a monthly basis.
3. Activity-based billing: Billing is by the volume of activity (ie. per call, per statement, per line transcribed).
4. Gain-share models: Billing is based on quantifiable value delivered (ie. success rate, conversion ratio, etc.) – based on mutually agreed parameters.
5. Hybrid-pricing models: This combination of two or more models and typically incorporates a fixed volume rate plus a marginally higher rate for peak-load absorption.

# Sustaining competitiveness

For the Indian IT-ITES industry to fully capitalize on the available opportunity and sustain its leadership, the following are key focus areas:

(*a*) enhancing the talent pool advantage – focus on skill development to better leverage the world's largest working population;
(*b*) strengthening urban infrastructure in existing (Tier I) and emerging (Tiers II and III) cities and continued emphasis on proactive regulatory reform to facilitate greater ease of doing business;
(*c*) driving a philosophy of operational excellence amongst industry players (across the board) to ensure that India-based delivery sustains world-leading benchmarks in performance;
(*d*) catalysing domestic market development; and
(*e*) actively promoting an uncompromised agenda towards global free trade.

The large pool of skilled professionals has been a key driver of the rapid growth in Indian IT-ITES industry. There have been concerns that a part of the available pool is unsuitable for direct employment into the industry. However, recent research has proved that at current levels of suitability, India has the single largest pool of suitable offshore talent, accounting for 28 per cent of the total suitable pool available across all offshore destinations and outpacing the share of the next closest destination by at least a factor of 2.5.

NASSCOM (National Association of Software and Service Companies) is working with the academic institutes to encourage and facilitate greater industry interaction. The industry has initiated several initiatives to further enhance the availability of and access to suitable talent for IT-ITES services including a comprehensive skill assessment and certification programme for entry-level talent and executives (low–middle level) and an image enhancement programme to build greater awareness about the career opportunities in this segment. NASSCOM is also working with the government of India to establish 20 new Indian Institutes of Information Technology (IIIT) in Public Private Partnership.

There are increasing incidents involving loss or misuse of data across the world. A review of the Indian policy environment and company practices by independent authorities has revealed that the policy and practices in India match and often exceed those observed in the client countries. The positive evaluation of the policy environment is further complemented by the efficiency of the Indian law enforcement agencies to track down perpetrators in the few cases that occurred in India. NASSCOM has established the DSCI (Data Security Council of India) to act as a self-regulatory organization for data security in the Indian IT-ITES industry.

Indian policymakers are further strengthening the information security environment in India through key initiatives including enhancing the legal framework through proposed amendments to the IT Act 2000 – currently under review by the government – increasing interaction with the enforcement agencies to help create awareness about information security and provide any support they require.

Demonstrated process quality and service delivery expertise has been a key factor driving India's leadership in global service delivery. Today, India-based delivery centres constitute the largest number of quality certifications achieved by any single country. Further, several client organizations have acknowledged that superior process and project management capabilities at their India-based centres have helped deliver higher performance levels in comparison with their other sourcing locations.

The transition from discrete outsourcing to global sourcing of services is expected to drive the next phase of evolution in process quality frameworks and practices. With their experience of aligning internal processes and practices to international standards such as ISO, CMM, Six Sigma, etc., Indian firms will play an integral role in defining best practices, standards and global benchmarks.

## Policy reforms

Progressive policy reform in India's post-liberalization era has been a key contributor to the accelerated growth of the Indian economy and the IT-ITES sector is no exception.

In addition to the continuing policy reforms aimed at addressing the evolving needs of the industry and sustaining India's attractiveness as a sourcing destination, the Indian government continues to support the interests of the industry by being an active proponent of global free trade.

India's core proposition of talent, quality and cost advantage has been complemented by rapid scaling up of business infrastructure across the country. In addition to telecom links, most cities possess office facilities, hotels and other supporting business infrastructure matching global standards.

Physical connectivity, via road and air, has also improved significantly over the last few years. Further, the deregulation of the aviation sector and the recently enacted open-skies policy has enhanced availability and affordability of airline travel.

Notwithstanding these developments, certain elements of physical infrastructure – mainly in a few hubs – are beginning to show some signs of strain. Recognizing the imperatives of having adequate infrastructure for continued business growth, the central and state governments have initiated several efforts including expansion of existing airports and developing plans for the building of new airports, strengthening the highway networks in the country and scaling up public transport infrastructure within the cities.

While some imbalances may persist in a few areas over the short term, successful execution of the outlined programmes will address any concerns of infrastructure availability in the country. Further, the experience of developing initial hubs is helping urban planners to proactively manage infrastructure demand due to the rapid growth expected in this sector.

## Alternatives to India

Inspired by the Indian success story, several other locations are often presented as alternate options for offshore outsourcing. However, organizational experiences as well as syndicated analyses comparing the various sourcing locations has revealed that India continues to offer and deliver the best 'package' of benefits sought from global sourcing.

However, India's unparalleled attractiveness as an IT-ITES destination is not the only factor attracting international investors to the country. Strong economic prospects backed by sound fundamentals of favourable demographics and investment ratios, human capital, trade openness, increasing urbanization and rising consumption spending make India an attractive investment destination – as a sourcing base as well as a significant market.

## Future outlook

The future holds significant opportunity for India and the strong, consistent performance so far coupled with a positive outlook have put it well on track to achieve the targeted $60 billion in exports by FY 2010 and an overall industry size of over $80 billion. However, the opportunity for India is much larger. With less than 10 per cent of the current addressable (offshore) market captured to date, there is significant headroom for further growth.

Recognizing the potential of the sector and the opportunity it holds for the country, all key stakeholder groups including the government, industry and NASSCOM and the academic community are actively engaged in developing and implementing initiatives to strengthen India's bid for sustained leadership.

Clearly, the Indian growth story remains unchanged. In spite of sporadic scepticism and rhetoric observed in the media over the past few months, the Indian IT-ITES sector continues on its high-growth trajectory and is well on track to achieve the targets that the industry has set for itself by the end of the decade.

# 2.5

# Distribution

*Confederation of Indian Industry*

The trucking industry in India is a major contributor to the economy. It is run privately and is dominated by small road transport operators; the majority being single truck owners. In recent years, it has increased its share in the movement of goods within the country *vis-à-vis* other modes of transport, up from less than 20 per cent in 1951 to 70 per cent currently.

India has 3.4 million kilometres (km) of roads, comprised of national highways (65,569 km), state highways (1,28,000 km), major district roads (4,70,000 km) and rural and other district roads (2.65 million km). Road infrastructure increased significantly after independence, both in terms of spread and capacity. Road traffic has overtaken railways in both the passenger and freight segments.

At present, road transport accounts for 85 per cent and 70 per cent of total passenger and freight transport, respectively. The railway accounts for most of the remaining traffic, with a small percentage using the air transport sector.

## Structure of the trucking industry

At present, there are no regular arrangements for the collection of data relating to truck operation. The structure of the trucking industry can be studied as a system consisting of truck operators, intermediaries and users (see Figure 1).

The structure is adversely affected by factors such as nature, financing costs, vehicle technology, the absence of roadside amenities, the condition of the roads, the increased delays and waiting times of vehicles involving additional of fuel cost, the increase in turnaround time which leads to under utilization of vehicles, and the legal framework.

## Regulation

The road transport sectors are regulated by the Motor Vehicle Act (1988), the Motor Transport Workers Act (1961) and the Carriers Act (1865).

Table 1. Basic road statistics in India, 1991–2002*

| *Category* | *Total / Surfaced* | *1991* | *1995* | *2000* | *2001* | *2002(P)* |
|---|---|---|---|---|---|---|
| **All India** | T | 2327362 | 3057411 | 3316078 | 3346667 | 3383344 |
| | S | 1090167 | 1379300 | 1573800 | 1597749 | 1603691 |
| **National Highways** | T | 33650 | 34262 | 52010 | 57679 | 58006 |
| | S | 33399 | 34046 | 51952 | 57679 | 58006 |
| **State Highways** | T | 127311 | 134085 | 132797 | 132100 | 137711 |
| | S | 124847 | 131506 | 130592 | 129862 | 135546 |
| **Other PWD Roads** | T | 509435 | 511046 | 730680 | 736001 | 725425 |
| | S | 390931 | 414320 | 601512 | 610516 | 603358 |
| **Rural Roads** | T | 1260430 | 1949866 | 1938356 | 1945163 | 1986858 |
| | S | 373978 | 611304 | 545378 | 551354 | 561645 |
| **Other Roads** | T | 396536 | 428152 | 462235 | 475666 | 475238 |
| | S | 167012 | 188124 | 244366 | 248338 | 245136 |

Note: *most recent data available, taken from 2004 report (2002 figures projected)
*Source: Basic Road Statistics (2004)*, ministry of shipping, road transport and highways

Amongst others, the Motor Transport Workers Act regulates the hours of work of a person engaged in operating a transport vehicle.

The Motor Vehicle Act covers the legislation by which trucking is regulated and is, by and large, fairly comprehensive. However, it suffers from two lacunae:

- failure to keep pace with its small print, which involves the emerging changes in economic and technological parameters;
- enforcement difficult, owing to certain inherent contradictions in its overall design.

New provisions need to be incorporated in the Motor Vehicle Act relating to the issue of driving licences, inspection and maintenance of vehicles, registration of intermediaries and the insurance of goods. The most important part is the overloading of goods (new provisions include large fines for overloading).

The Carriers Act covers the loss or damage of the goods and other insurance aspects.

Regulation of these acts can be effective only:

- if the regulator makes a clear distinction between bilateral contracts between buyer and seller;
- if the larger, unwritten contract between the service providers and the public interest is better observed.

It is therefore necessary to make rules that are compatible with both these objectives.

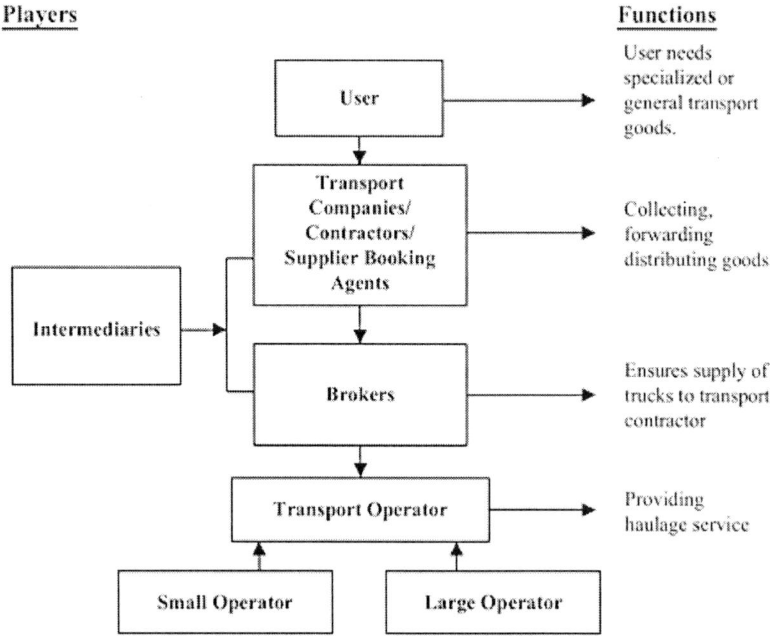


*Source:* CII Logistics

Figure 1. Players in the industry and their functions

The regulation of trucking also needs to be reoriented with a new perspective geared towards globalization, keeping in mind the fact that the maximization of private utilities may not lead to a socially optimal outcome. Entry regulation is a problem in India, where it involves determining important economic tradeoffs and managing the severe negative externalities. Achieving the right balance is an important goal in trucking.

In order to ensure smooth and consistent application of the laws, it is not only necessary to make those laws simple and enforceable, but it should also adopt the principle of third party regulation and adjudication. It is therefore recommended that a road transport regulatory system be set up.

Major problems with taxation are common regarding motor vehicles, with variation both in the basis of rates at which these taxes are levied, the high incidence of these taxes and also the absence of guidelines for tax authorities. The complexities increase in India's federal polity, where not only are there opportunities to levy taxes but the proceeds of the taxation have to be shared between the central and state government.

The present tax structure provides neither economic efficiency nor equity. It has no relationship with the cost of the vehicles operating on the roads. It is imperative to harmonize the basis and the rates at which different tax-entitled entities should levy taxes on road transportation. An important feature of the prevailing tax system is the existence of the number of check posts, which interfere with the free flow of traffic within the state and cause inconvenience to large sections of road users.

The existence of check posts does not contribute significantly to monitoring tax evasion. On the contrary, the more check posts, the higher the wastage resulting from stopping traffic.

Perhaps India should take a leaf out of the European Union's (EU's) book. If all the states come together and operate as a single market, it will be easier to maintain control without causing problems. In the EU, there are still spot checks for drugs or immigration issues, but routine internal border checks are now on a lesser scale.

## Road infrastructure

The existing road networks cannot handle the projected traffic. The vehicle traffic on inter-city routes is expected to grow four to six times over the next 20 years. To meet the growing demand, the Road Development Plan Vision: 2021 has estimated the requirement of the road sector in terms of augmentation, strengthening and expansion for the next 20 years.

Massive investments are being made to strengthen the road network. As the road infrastructure and its supporting services improve, there is likely to be a shift in the tonnage mix, from medium commercial vehicles to heavy commercial vehicles. This would reduce the cost of operations by carrying higher loads with minimum distress to the roads themselves.

In view of excessive overloading of vehicles, the latest guidelines of the Indian Road Congress provide for the designing of roads on the basis of prevailing standardized axle weight limits and for is uniformity in the design of roads across the network.

Building and maintaining good roads is a priority when it comes to improving trucking services. Many of the other corrective measures will follow automatically. Given the large financial requirement for improving the highway network and the government's constraints, there is a need for mobilizing all possible funding sources, private financing, multinational loans and assistance to meet the proposed target.

## Technology

In order to improve technology in the trucking industry, there are two important factors to be considered. First, the introduction of more truck manufacturers is necessary in order to increase competition and therefore general standards. Second, on the demand side, the cost structure of the industry has to change in such a way that trucking firms begin to work towards technological solutions, in order to gain maximum profit.

Table 2. Proposed development of highways

| Highway Category | 2001–11 | | 2011–21 | | 2001–21 | |
|---|---|---|---|---|---|---|
| | Length (km) | Amount (Rs. Crore) | Length | Amount (Rs. Crore) | Length | Amount (Rs. Crore) |
| National Highways | | | | | | |
| • Four–six laning | | | | | | |
| • Two–laning with hard shoulders | 16,000 | 64,000 | 19,000 | 76,000 | 35,000 | 140,000 |
| • Strengthening weak pavements | 15,000 | 18,750 | 7,000 | 8,750 | 22,000 | 27,500 |
| • Bypasses, over bridges, safety and drainage | 20,000 | 15,000 | 24,000 | 18,000 | 44,000 | 33,000 |
| measures | Lump sum 10,000 | 7,250 | Lump sum 5,000 | 9,250 | Lump sum 10,500 | 16,500 |
| • Expansion of NH system* | | | | | | |
| | | 15,000 | | 7,000 | | 25,500 |
| Total NHs | | 120,000 | | 130,000 | | 250,000 |
| Expressways | 3,000 | 30,000 | 7,000 | 70,000 | 10,000 | 100,000 |
| State Highways | | | | | | |
| • Four–six laning | 3,000 | 10,000 | 7,000 | 25,000 | 10,000 | 35,000 |
| • Two–laning with hard shoulders | 35,000 | 28,000 | 60,000 | 50,000 | 95,000 | 78,000 |
| • Strengthening weak pavements | 30,000 | 22,000 | 40,000 | 30,000 | 70,000 | 52,000 |
| • Bypasses, over bridges, safety and drainage measures | Lump sum | 10,000 | Lump sum | 10,000 | Lump sum | 20,000 |
| • Expansion of SH system | 1,000 | 5,000 | 20,000 | 10,000 | 30,000 | 15,000 |
| Total SHs | | 75,000 | | 12,5000 | | 200,000 |

Note: *adjusted on the basis of existing NH length of 65,500km
*Source:* Road Development Plan Vision 2021

The recent trends in vehicle technology emphasize the need for legislation aimed at promoting the road friendliness of heavy vehicles, thereby creating an environment which enhances overall transport capacity and productivity. This includes the provision of road-friendly suspension systems, multi-axles, power steering and improved tyres, etc.

## Conclusion

These proposed reforms will certainly improve the efficiency and quality of trucking services in the country, removing the hurdles in the way of healthy growth within the industry. As a result, the various stakeholders/interest groups will stand to benefit in their area of operation.

## References

Planning Commission Report, 2005.

G. Raghuram and Narayan Rangaraj, 'Synthesis Paper on Strengthening Policy Reforms for Transport Infrastructure Development in India', April 2005, http://www.iimahd.ernet.in/publications/data/2006-04-02raghuram.pdf.

Bibek Debroy and P.D. Kaushik, 'Barriers to Inter-State Trade and Commerce – The Case of Road Transport', RGICS working paper series, No. 35, 2002.

K.L. Thukral, 'Enhancing the Quality of Trucking Services in India', Asian Institute of Transport Develoment, Delhi.

# 2.6

# Partner Selection

*Purvi Sheth, Shilputsi Consultants*

Joint ventures (JVs) in India have so far been formed as a response to the rapid changes in the environment and markets. Companies identify partners to gain competitive advantage in a dynamic and vibrant market.

For an alliance to succeed in India, a method of determining analytical and financial fitness as well as organizational fitness is crucial. Once a venture is formed, effectively managing the interaction and organizational processes will ensure alliance longevity.

Over time, multinational companies have created significant competitive advantage by leading and owning alliance capabilities in India, which are used as templates and directives for ventures in other emerging markets.

## Approach to JVs in India – an evolving perspective

1. *Potential for future growth and new global competitors*: India is viewed as both an emerging market and a strategically competitive base for offshore outsourcing of services and manufacturing. Alliances and partnerships in India offer business advantages along with prospective opportunities for expansion in the subcontinent and Asian region. Businesses contending with established competitor positions can draw on Indian collaborations to counter strong opposition presence.
2. *Liberalization of regulatory regime:* Indian companies are rapidly growing through global acquisitions and mergers. They are open to setting up ventures that are mutually beneficial, allowing the partner to leverage its local strengths and fulfilling their own global aspirations. With the liberalization of several industries and potential non-interventionist government policies in some other sectors, JVs in India can help multinational companies to flourish from a cost and sales perspective.
3. *Important means of foreign investment*: Partnerships are an advantageous route to ultimately making direct investments in India. JVs can become a platform for long-term investment. Acquisition of assets and

establishment of brands through alliances are a good route of entry to the market. The process helps in understanding the landscape and selecting niche areas of operation for long-term returns on investment.

4. *Varying compulsions and challenges for local and foreign companies:* With the rapid rate of market change, Indian companies are increasingly entering international territories and building large visible businesses abroad. Alliances make it easier for Indian companies to influence their partners' global capacities and capabilities, simultaneously enhancing their position in India with foreign technology and brands. International companies gain through Indian partnerships, especially if entering regulated industries, and save costs of investing in large-scale capital at the outset. Alliances allow foreign corporations to establish brands and become familiar with distribution systems, consumption patterns, management practices, etc.
5. *Dilution of comparative advantage and onslaught of information age:* With reduction in global comparative advantages, a JV or collaboration in emerging markets helps to attain global competitive advantage. India has achieved significant visibility and progress in technical know-how, making Indian companies appropriate candidates for international collaborations. As technology and knowledge becomes widely accessible and corporate dominance does not solely rely on IP (intellectual property), businesses with international ambitions need to freely exchange information and ideas. Indian companies today are able to facilitate this exchange as a matter of course.

## Creating successful partnering capability for India

There are some essentials to prepare for before entering any partnership. All organizations, whether foreign or Indian, have peculiar partnering behaviour patterns, their own customs and alliance models.

Prior experience of alliances and processes to build an alliance capability is an important factor for a winning performance. It has been observed that equity levels in an Indian alliance are not correlated with success.

Below are some basic elements to fortify alliance competence in India:

1. *Build trust and share knowledge*: Since liberalization of the economy in the early 1990s, Indian corporations have seen a wide range of alliances and JVs with foreign companies – both Western and Asian. Some have worked and become benchmarks of success, whilst others have failed. Trust is of utmost importance for the success of an alliance. Indian companies may generally not be suspicious of motives but might be

unsure of their partners' longer term objectives. It is necessary to create a feeling of complete faith and absolute trust with your Indian partner to enable learning, increase speed of response and lower transaction costs.

It is vital for foreign companies to believe and have faith in their Indian associates' motives, management and abilities. Make a checklist of questions and request detailed information and evidence, if required, to obtain absolute conviction in your partners' word.

2. *Avoid culture clashes:* Myths and stereotypes are attached to every culture. There is no one culture or trait that binds the Indian workforce. Every Indian organization has its identifiable culture, a combination of traditional Indian practices, as well as contemporary Western processes. In forming a JV in India, extensive due diligence of nuances in interaction, organizational linkages as well as softer aspects of organizational processes will go a long way in making a successful working relationship. Study your own cultural imperatives and map it with those of your collaborators to minimize divergence in working philosophies. Develop conflict resolution mechanisms to drive the success of the venture.
3. *Mutually agree investment plans and performance milestones:* Business objectives of both partners in a venture must be clearly defined at the outset. Not only should aspirations be discussed, but well-framed performance matrices are necessary. To increase chances of a win–win situation, it is useful for both partners to assess and agree if the venture is truly central to the parent company's portfolio, the apparent benefits of the alliance and if the combined force has real power in the market. Any intended investments are best discussed honestly and dormant business goals must be mentioned. Expectations of reciprocal candour should be communicated to the Indian partner company.
4. *Clarify lines of reporting and control*: JV partners are sometimes prone to making assumptions on reporting relationships, control mechanisms and organization design. Management of Indian companies, especially entrepreneurs, may reluctantly agree to be accountable to another person in the partner company's global system. Clearly defined role profiles and accountabilities of management representatives of both sides are very important to maintain smooth working of the entity.

# Selection criteria

There could be several reasons for forming an alliance in India, ranging from external factors like geographical advantages to improvements to the bottom line through better product positioning. The selection criteria would naturally vary accordingly. Some common measures and standards would be:

## For business

1. *Increased competitive positioning / product differentiation:* Multinational companies with modifiable services and products should seek a local partner that has the ability and knowledge to facilitate adaptation to suit Indian preferences, tastes and consumption patterns. It helps to have a collaborator that can strengthen brand position, increase distribution power and distinguish service offerings.

   Some large multinational companies have already been able to launch highly successful and leading global brands with distinctive Indian variances, with the aid of appropriate partners.
2. *Learn critical skills and capabilities:* In JVs, Indian companies look forward to experiencing enhanced business processes, geographical spread and new technologies, whilst foreign companies may seek more understanding of market segments, sales channels and people management. Depending on the most vital learning curve to be honed, as well as the learning intent and capacity, international companies should choose a partner tested in that area. Several Indian organizations offer learning benefits across a range of well-developed capabilities in areas like finance and treasury, regulatory issues, sales and distribution, branding and pricing, vendor development, customer service, human resources (HR) and performance management, etc.
3. *High-value input to influence your costs:* Indian partners can positively impact costs, like providing suppliers to develop better bargaining strength in terms of purchasing power and/or developing favourable long-term contracts. If the JV relies on the Indian partner for significant input in the value chain, organizations known for their power and weight on vendors and suppliers can be chosen as partners. Scale/scope economies in a JV partner's business can also be leveraged. For regulated sectors, a partner with well-established contacts and perceivable bearing with authorities should be a major criterion.
4. *Offer customers fuller range and maintaining a stronger sales force:* For categories that are better valued with supplementary and support products/services, Indian companies with synergies in such areas make excellent JV partners. Several Indian companies have existing well-established product and service ranges with a strong sales team on an India-wide basis. This can be fully leveraged to provide the market with a complete range and assortment of offerings. This combined with distribution strength would make a flourishing business in India.

## Organizational

1. *Cultural compatibility:* Apart from financial due diligence, it is extremely important to do an HR due diligence of a partner. Look for cultural proximities and similarities in order to identify management linkage.

Several traditional family-owned Indian groups have progressed to completely professionally managed, decentralized businesses where decision-making powers are not concentrated with family members. Publicly listed companies are required to have independent directors, and corporate governance is practised as per international norms. Many Indian companies not only recruit qualified talent at all levels and functions but are increasingly selecting expatriates of non-Indian origin for leadership and other managerial jobs. They are becoming multicultural and even offer international level salaries.

However, there are companies that continue to practise certain conventional management procedures. Some even have orthodox management styles that may not be well matched to certain foreign cultures. The closer the value systems, management policies and work ethics of the two companies, the better the chances of a fruitful relationship.

2. *Internal support*: Group support of both partners should be an uncompromised condition for alliance success. If there is little internal managerial and leadership backing and cooperation, the likelihood of success diminishes greatly. It is therefore advisable to speak with the Indian company's managers and teams at various levels, in order to gauge the amount of encouragement and empathy the alliance has gained. Managerial flexibility is another yardstick to measure how fitting a partner would be.
3. *Learning symmetries:* An Indian company and its foreign partner may have divergent learning patterns. Many international companies have found that Indian companies interested in technology gain manage to acquire generic competencies faster, whilst the partner struggles with country-specific issues related to distribution processes, vendor development, financial compliance, etc.

   On the other hand, Indian companies have seen foreign partners use collaborators as short-term options to explore potential growth options, quickly internalizing operational capabilities and leaving the Indian partner with little or no advantage of the alliance. The alliance should facilitate organizational learning and evenness in knowledge for both partners.
4. *Changing priorities:* Both partners may be inclined to change objectives with time. In opting for a partner, the possibility of alterations in direction should be considered. An attractive partner at the time of due diligence whilst entering India may become less appealing by the time an alliance is formed. In selecting an associate, evolving business needs should determine the kind of partner with which a company ultimately makes an alliance. Indian companies may also change their goals with time. Internal governance units can be set up in an alliance to keep a check on shifting priorities.

# Common perceptions of partnerships in India

## Foreign companies

- Indian companies are unable to match investments, yet insist on retaining shareholding and management control.
- Indian family-managed companies run companies for family members.
- Indian companies are looking for easy and immediate returns on their capital investment.

## Indian companies

- Ventures tend to be unstable with a tilt in favour of foreign companies and the expediency of their issues.
- Faith in Indian managerial capabilities and commercial honesty is low.
- Investment capability differential is constantly held and used against the Indian partner.

The views on alliances and JVs in India have evolved over a period of time. JVs are no longer seen as win–lose situations because both partners seek and provide clarity of goals at the time of partnering. There is more transparency of operations and objectives of the alliance, for example, personal wealth versus business growth are verified and confirmed before entering a partnership.

Today, Indian companies have deeper pockets and access to cheaper capital and hence do not simply look for 'rent on assets'. Instead they are keen on attaining global market accessibility, contemporary technology and better profitability for long-term growth. Indian companies, irrespective of size, have been setting their sights on scale and growth. With more professional management and corporate governance norms, powers and resources are not appropriated by family members but shared with stakeholders.

Indian corporations and conglomerates are opening their doors to global talent and paying international level remuneration and perquisites to attract managers. The emphasis is on a long-term view to bringing the most appropriate people into jobs that especially impact the bottom line, customer service and innovation.

International companies in most sectors do not require a 'stepping stone' with increasing possibilities of direct investment. The experience and success of many transnational JVs make international companies less suspicious of the local partners' motives and agenda. Foreign firms look for longer term gain and stability as opposed to 'quick entry' to India. Not only has the position of these companies changed, but the general perception is a great deal more positive than before.

Table 1. The progression of joint ventures in India

| | |
|---|---|
| Early 1990s | JV boom/era of alliances/rush of MNCs* to form collaborations. |
| 1997–2000 | JV boom continues while simultaneous alliance unsteadiness/JV turbulence, disillusionment, distrust is constantly seen among many entities. |
| 2001–2005 | Several dissolved JVs end in FDI*/MNCs integrate local business with global operations/local companies buying out foreign partners/new alliances for partner compatibility and visible competitive advantage. |
| 2006 onwards | Indian companies have access to more capital and look outside India for JVs for access to international markets and technologies/JVs in India are strategic alliances for global 'companies-in-waiting' for FDI* policy changes. |

Note: *FDI = foreign direct investment; MNC = multinational corporation.

# Factors threatening partnership stability in India

1. *Unequal partner contributions:* For every alliance that has failed, there is a partner that felt the imbalance of involvement and contribution. The inequality could be in financial strength, ownership of critical resources, ability to attract management talent or even process to build alliance capability. Most often, the local Indian partner is viewed to be low on these characteristics.
2. *Disparity in decision-making and control:* Several unsuccessful JVs and alliances seem to differ in partner control. In many alliance set-ups, the Indian partner provides operating staff, whilst the foreign partner controls senior management. In some, the foreign partner also manages operations and controls strategy, linking it to the parent company. The domestic partner then provides local expertise and some senior managerial support. Misalignment and lack of management style compatibility may lead to discord and frustration in due course.
3. *Insufficient market growth:* With higher expectations, failure to attain anticipated market potential is another cause of venture collapse. Changes in the environment due to regulatory and market adjustments have created a breakdown in alliances.

# 2.7

# Analysing the Indian Market

*Karthik Ramamurthy, Synovate Business Consulting*

## Introduction

India is like a cellar of wine – only the connoisseur who takes the time to taste, appreciates the differences, and identifies the mature ones, enjoys the wine for a long period of time. Those looking for a quick shot at the available wines seldom get the right one and go back with a bad impression of what is available. The Indian market is diverse in every sense and it takes perseverance and readiness to be flexible to succeed in this market.

This chapter looks at what market analysis means in India and what characterizes the Indian consumer. It also helps understanding of what the supply environment looks like in this market, and provides sources of information, important industry associations and prominent firms that can be contacted for market analysis.

## Defining the Indian market

The aptly named Indian sub-continent is more of a continent than a country, with its numerous religions, languages, dialects, customs and traditions. Spread across 29 states and six union territories, this market of a billion people is something that needs to be well researched and understood before making the entry strategy.

To gauge the vastness of the country, one could simply take a look at the environmental diversity of the country and the seasons that exist within it. Whilst the northern reaches of Kashmir see snowfall, the southern reaches of Kerala see rain for six months every year. These varied environmental conditions have a direct impact on every aspect of the market, be it the type of products that would sell or the kind of supply chain a firm would have to plan to serve the market.

The vastness also means the population is diverse in its language, culture and educational levels. With over 850 languages, each with its own subset of dialects and with a literacy rate of 61 per cent in 2004, whilst it could be a segmentation expert's dream, it could also turn out be a challenge for product and marketing managers.

Additionally, urbanization is a trend that is catching on rapidly, with 28.7 per cent of the population belonging to this category in 2005. This combined with sustained, rapid economic growth clocking around 8–9 per cent year-on-year and increased exposure to foreign media, has led to a renewed thrust on market segmentation, based on 'urban versus rural'.

Customizing products and communication according to the population demographics and consequently diverse usage patterns is the challenge for a firm looking at this market. The good news is that this whole segmentation exercise happens on a pretty large population base and each segment, albeit small in terms of percentages, is large in terms of absolute numbers.

Thus, it is not a coincidence that India today is on every multinational company's radar and there is an increased thrust towards an India-specific strategy. The trillion dollar plus Indian GDP in purchasing power parity (PPP) terms is now ranked fourth place and with 40 per cent of the population under the age of 15 years, the future is increasingly looking more promising and is not a mere speculation.

## Market research in the Indian context

Doing a thorough market analysis in India can be confusing. The challenge in this vast country is not so much how and where to position a brand or product but knowing whom to target and where. Targeting the right audience among consumer segments can be difficult, meaning it is essential for marketers striving to woo the consumer classes to get the 'benefit-image-price' and 'consumer equation' right.

One uniform strategy cannot be adopted for the Indian market. Additionally, the Indian consumer is evolving into an aspirational class, splashing out on luxury items like plasma TVs, cars and watches. This propensity to spend has been enabled by higher disposable income and easy availability of credit. This is a sea change over the market that existed a decade ago.

The most important challenge faced by a market researcher in India is the myriad of languages to deal with. Although English is the most prevalent business language, consumer insights may not be well covered in English alone. There are 10 major languages that are spoken and have to be considered whilst covering the market. There are also challenges in the translation of questionnaires, as well as their responses – there is a lot of difference in the spoken and theoretical language. Adequate lead time needs to be given to complete this, as a result of which the project launch takes time.

Culturally, too, there is a challenge in the interviewing process. For example, when there's a group discussion scheduled, there are bound to be drop-outs or delays at the last minute. Therefore, the sample size of respondents to be taken should be almost double that of the successful numbers intended. In case of high-net worth individuals or senior personnel, additional gestures like personally escorting them have to be provided to ensure that there is participation and cooperation.

Similarly, there is a difference between attracting respondents in large cities versus smaller ones. The respondents in smaller cities tend to be more cooperative and willing compared to larger ones, where incentives are almost a must for participation.

Another aspect to be considered is the use of technology enablers to streamline the research process. Computer-Aided Telephonic Interviewing (CATI), which is pretty popular internationally for fast turnaround and cost minimization, has its limitations in an Indian context. This could be attributed to lack of penetration of phone lines across the strata of society and also to the cultural lack of interest in answering the phone. So, CATI is seen to be effective only in the more affluent areas, which constitutes around 10 per cent of the country.

Whilst on the subject of respondents, it is also important to look at business respondents. These typically would need to be covered to gain an understanding of the business environment including competition, channels, raw material suppliers, business partners and government agencies. These respondents, unlike the developed markets, have an inherent tendency to be suspicious of giving interviews and sharing information. They tend to respond either vaguely or provide responses that do not necessarily reflect reality in the market. Therefore it is imperative that cross-checks are done continually on the veracity of information collected from the respondents before using that information for modelling the market.

# Macro level characteristics of the Indian market

The key areas to be looked into at great depth through market research and analysis are:

- consumers;
- competitors;
- distribution channels;
- suppliers; and
- regulatory environment.

## Consumers

The Indian market shows differences in consumer behaviour from one region to another in terms of usage, preferences, brands, tastes, etc. Cases of marketers finding growth in shampoo demand in a particular region driven by usage for washing cattle, or washing machines being used for making

*Lassi* – a traditional drink made out of yoghurt – characterize the Indian market!

Rural India constitutes approximately 70 per cent of the country's population. Although in terms of buying power urban India would rate higher, the rural market has been showing rapid growth in recent years. This is generating demand for some products that were previously unfamiliar. Micro-serving by converting of sample packs into single-serve sachets is one such example.

As a result of the increasing penetration of cable television and electronic media, advertising plays a vital role in moulding the consumer mindset for buying certain products. Given the global exposure, Indian consumers are becoming brand-conscious when it comes to such names as Nike, Adidas, Honda, Toyota, etc. Consumers are differentiating products not only based on quality but also on brand perceptions such as premium, economy, value for money, etc. Consumers are open to global brands and also associate them with an individual's status in the society.

In such a dynamic environment, it is becoming essential for a player to continually gather market feedback and use it effectively for differentiating the consumer segments and addressing the needs accordingly by appropriate product positioning and effective communication.

## Distribution channels

India is a sub-continent, nearly 2,000 miles from north to south and 1,800 miles from east to west with varying terrains. The population is spread widely across the geography. Rural India forms a sizeable market and, more importantly, a rapidly growing market. It poses a challenge for a firm to distribute its product to these up-country markets. To overcome this challenge, marketers are adopting different distribution channels to reach the consumer. Cut-throat competition is forcing the market players to adopt highly dynamic and innovative channel 'push strategies', such as higher margins and non-cash incentives. Market analysis would help understand the appropriate channel mix, channel margins as well as distribution support systems such as logistics and warehousing.

## Competitors

The Indian market poses a unique challenge to a foreign player. For example, the Indian retail market is dominated by the relationship driven *Kirana* shops (small unorganized players) with over 90 per cent of the market share. Similarly, a multinational hardware supplier would find the Indian market crammed with 'grey market products' (illegally imported products). Multinational corporation (MNC) players in certain industries like apparel, footwear and watches eyeing the Indian market would find themselves already present in the form of counterfeits. Thus, a new market entrant faces competition, not only from domestic and MNC players but also from unorganized grey market and counterfeit players.

Financial information such as sales, revenue, profit, etc., available for companies through public sources does not always represent the realities unless it is a publicly listed company. Market research and analysis agencies with local presence and expertise help new entrants understand the competition with a thorough all-round diligence.

### Suppliers

To set up a manufacturing plant it is critical to have a reliable, consistent and affordable source of raw material. Sourcing from a local supplier versus importing raw material is a dilemma faced by a new entrant whilst considering the quality and price implications. Some large MNC fast-food chains have 'developed' local suppliers by imposing global standards, thus ensuring reliable quality at an affordable cost. Market analysis would help with a diligence of claimed capabilities versus the ground realities in terms of quality, capacity, processes, governmental clearances, financials, clients, etc., and this is crucial to ensure a long term, stable sustenance.

### Regulatory environment

Governmental policies play a vital role in determining the course of action for doing business in India. Though the market is opening up for foreign investment, there are still governmental controls on the market. Global retailers' entry into the country is an example of a sector that is being debated and there are restrictions on foreign players. Certain industries require compulsory licensing to operate. A foreign company can invest in India either through automatic approval by the Reserve Bank of India (RBI) or through the Foreign Investment Promotion Board (FIPB). Understanding duty structures on imported raw materials/finished goods is critical. Knowledge of the basic tax structure is also imperative for a new business. Market analysis can give an overview of these aspects, which would help an entrant make a 'go/no-go' decision, but a legal and financial expert would be a wise choice in order to obtain more detailed advice.

## Data – availability, accuracy and timeliness

One of the largest drawbacks in India is the availability of data in the public domain. Even countries like China are better documented. Whatever is available is either outdated or is highly fragmented, with no single authoritative source. For example, the latest government census data available is for 2001, and there have been major changes in the market in the last five years. Using this could lead to a distorted market model.

Another key consideration is that whilst data may be maintained in hard copy, the digitization process is only a recent phenomenon and progress is slow. This can be prominently seen in dealings with the Registrar of Companies (RoC). Individual RoC offices have different levels of digitization, making it extremely difficult to get similar data for companies across India. This is also the case with vehicular databases, which are maintained by individual Road Transport Offices in each city or town.

Of course, there are private firms that have taken up this opportunity and make data available at a cost. However, again this data is limited by the capabilities of private firms to comprehensively cover the widely spread market. Only limited investments are possible so as to not make the report prohibitively expensive. Examples of agencies providing such services are CMIE (www.cmie.com), Indiastat (www.indiastat.com), and Euromonitor (www.euromonitor.com).

Recently, there has been a government initiative to give the public access to information under the control of public authorities through the Right to Information Act. This enables access to information for a fee and within a specific timeframe. Of course, this is limited to the requested data and cannot be used as a definitive source for information on a continual basis and is not centralized in any form.

Other sources of overall information on India are the India Brand Equity Foundation (www.ibef.org), the National Informatics Centre (indiaimage.nic.in), individual central government departments (india.gov.in) and individual state governments.

## Trade and market research associations

Looking specifically at conducting market research, the Market Research Society of India (MRSI; www.mrsi-india.com) is a non-profit autonomous market research body formed by a large fraternity of research suppliers and users spread across India. Established in January 1988, the MRSI was formed to maintain standards of excellence in the market research industry. It is a proactive and neutral society, striving to promote the needs of market research in India. The MRSI has over 40 corporate members and is involved in furthering market research interests through a variety of events.

Apart from this, there are nodal trade bodies that provide assistance in the form of information, access to Indian firms and also provide vertical specific networking opportunities through events conducted both within India and abroad. A few of the prominent trade bodies are the Confederation of Indian Industry (www.ciionline.org), the Associated Chambers of Commerce and Industry of India (www.assocham.org) and the Federation of Indian Chambers of Commerce and Industry (www.ficci.com). Additionally, there are industry-specific associations, like the National Association of

Software and Service Companies (www.nasscom.org), the Society of Indian Automobile Manufacturers (www.siamindia.com), and the Cellular Operator's Association of India (www.coai.com), etc., which can be contacted for industry-specific insights and information. Statistics, reports and news are usually available from these organizations and they also help companies from abroad network with Indian firms in the domain.

## Agencies for market research and analysis

There are a number of agencies that provide market research and analysis services. The prominent players who specialize in market research are:

- Synovate India Pvt. Ltd (www.synovate.com)
- AC Nielsen (www.acnielsen.co.in)
- the Indian Market Research Bureau (www.imrbint.com)
- TNS Global (www.tns-global.com)
- Frost & Sullivan (www.frost.com)

Apart from market research firms there are also other providers of detailed market analysis including management consultants such as:

- McKinsey & Co (www.mckinsey.com)
- The Boston Consulting Group (www.bcgindia.com)
- Ernst & Young (www.ey.com), KPMG (www.in.kpmg.com)
- A.T. Kearney (www.atkearney.com)
- boutique market related strategy consultants such as Synovate Busines Consulting (www.synovate.com/ bc)

The easiest way to approach these firms is to access the website and the contact details of their India office would be available. The recommended approach for quick response would be to call up the agency. While evaluating the firms it is critical to look into details of past engagements in the industry of interest as well as the Indian market. Most critical in market analysis is the methodology of collecting market information and whether the agency outsources the field coverage to a third party. Outsourcing could jeopardize the quality and validity of the data which in turn would affect the models used for analysis and subsequent business recommendations.

In conclusion, there are a few golden rules to succeed in India:

- enter the market with a long-term vision;
- research the market well;
- use multiple sources to corroborate information; and
- hire locally experienced personnel or choose a local partner for entry.

# 2.8

# Marketing

*Darrell Kofkin, Global Marketing Network*

## Overview

India is undergoing unprecedented change. It is one of the fastest growing large economies in the world, with a population of around 1 billion people, with huge human and natural resources, and with costs that are at the very low end of the global average.

India's large English-speaking population certainly enhances it as an attractive business destination. India represents an economic opportunity on a massive scale, both as a global base and as a domestic market. It is an opportunity that India is anxious to grasp. Emerging from decades of economic isolationism, India's reform process is now bringing this billion-person economy into the global arena.

India has grown at over 5 per cent over the last five years. It is estimated that the economy will expand by 9 per cent in 2007, and it is expected to grow by around 8 per cent in 2008, with growth being driven primarily by improvements in infrastructure and increased private consumption. Compared to the European growth of less than 2 per cent on a 10-year average and the US growth of around 3 per cent, India will be one of the world's biggest two economies by mid-century. Yet despite this rapid growth, consumer markets in India remain largely untapped and relatively undeveloped, although that is changing fast. This is in part the legacy of 40 years of relative isolation from the global economy, as postcolonial India attempted to build a self-reliant economy behind high-tariff walls that discouraged foreign investment.

The Indian economy is on the cusp of something big. India's constraints, infrastructure, saving, foreign direct investment and politics are well known. Yet the consumption potential – the organic basis of sustainable growth and development – is real.

## The Indian consumer

The Indian consumer is hardly a powerful force on today's global stage. But it is incremental change that always drives powerful macro and market trends. And Indian consumption is accelerating off a low base.

Private consumption currently accounts for 64 per cent of GDP – higher than in Europe (58 per cent), Japan (55 per cent), and especially China (42 per cent). India's transition to a 7 per cent growth path in recent years is very much an outgrowth of the emerging consumerism of one of the world's youngest populations. This should provide powerful leverage to the Indian economy that is rarely found in the externally dependent developing world.

According to the recent data from '*The Marketing Whitebook*' by *Businesworld*, India has around 208 million households. Of these only a little over 6 million are 'affluent' that is, with household income in excess of 215,000 Indian rupees (INR). Another 75 million households are in the category of 'well off', immediately below the affluent, earning between INR 45,000 and INR 215,000. In the recent past, the organized consumer goods sector has concentrated almost exclusively on the 'affluent' category.

Consumers are getting richer, leading to competition in the marketplace for consumer products. The result is that consumer companies are increasingly concerned with marketing issues, as they seek to differentiate their products and communicate their values to potential customers.

Indian consumers are becoming increasingly sophisticated and knowledgeable about products; media channels that allow companies to communicate with consumers are growing in diversity and reach.

An important challenge for large global companies is to gain an understanding of Indian consumers. Multinational companies tend to have preconceived ideas about Indian consumers. You have to accept that Indian consumers would not buy exactly the same products as the rest of the world.

The challenge for organized retailers, distributors and consumer goods manufacturers is to capture more consumers in the large category of 'well off', as well as increasing consumer goods penetration and returns in the small category of 'affluent'. One visit to a shopping mall in Mumbai on a Sunday afternoon and it is bustling with activity. The locals are buying in India.

Disposable income is concentrated in urban areas and in well off and affluent classes; income distribution is unequal compared to other Asian economies. Personal cars, for example, are restricted to the 'affluent'. The 'well off' can afford several consumer durables: in order of preference according to current levels of penetration, these include colour televisions, refrigerators, washing machines and air conditioners.

## The importance of marketing

India's major consumer companies all have sophisticated marketing and product development plans. Moreover, the multinationals that are operating in India have business models that are tailor-made to local markets and customs. And all of the banks are focused on consumer-oriented growth strategies, especially in the mortgage finance and credit and debit card businesses.

Smart companies are making brands more relevant to the Indian consumer by regionalizing their brands. There is also the need to identify future growth segments and start building a knowledge base from this perspective. ITC (Indian Tobacco Company) has managed the transition in recent years from a company that mostly had an understanding of male preferences (cigarettes) to understanding the housewife as well.

Companies should ride both on well-entrenched trends and on those which are yet to be established. The focus on health and well-being is an emerging trend which companies like Pepsi (through Tropicana) are riding on. On the other hand, Hindustan Lever has identified 'return to nature' and 'increased social consciousness' as factors to tailor its communication for Surf.

Consumer companies say the most attractive factor is the sheer size of the Indian market. They also consider that advertising is developed – most global advertising companies have established operations in India.

Innovative marketing can be the solution to tackling the fragmentation and relative poverty of much of the Indian market. For example, the sachet phenomenon is an example of reaching to the bottom of the pyramid. It is a recognition that a lot of people in India are just not willing to buy a whole bottle of shampoo. This does not mean that they would not buy shampoos. Customer retention is also still a challenge, with loyalty schemes becoming increasingly popular.

Foreign brands remain very powerful in India. Foreign brand power is most visible in clothing and personal care products, but increasingly brands have to be associated with value. Foreign brands used to command a premium but increasingly the consumer wants to know that they are getting a good deal.

## Communicating to the Indian consumer

The growth in media channels brought about by economic liberalization has made people increasingly aware of brand values.

Advertising is of increasing concern to companies, as channels multiply and product offerings become more sophisticated. Advertising is becoming a bigger and bigger part of the marketing mix. Advertising is a must because markets are growing and, as a result, competition is increasing. The biggest challenge is to identify consumer insights to make relevant advertisements.

They are also concerned about the profusion of media channels – 'media clutter' – and the increasing number of brands competing for the same space. Consumer product companies also feel that a big challenge is measurement of the impact of advertising and promotional activities.

The biggest issue in marketing is media fragmentation. Years ago you could run an ad on television and know 80 per cent of the television owners would see it. Now India has so many channels and it is difficult to identify the appropriate fora.

There is increasing concern that advertising messages can only travel limited distances in the Indian market. A lot of companies are not able to reach further down, towards the bottom of the 'consumer pyramid'. How do you talk to someone who is illiterate, who does not have access to a television or a radio? Increasingly companies will have to seek multiple advertising channels.

## The growth of rural marketing

In the early 2000s, around 700 million people (70 per cent of the Indian population) lived in 627,000 villages in rural areas. Of these 90 per cent were concentrated in villages with populations of less than 2,000. Today, the real growth is taking place in the rural–urban markets, or in the 13,113 villages with a population of more than 5,000.

According to a study conducted in 2001 by the National Council for Applied Economic Research (NCAER), there were as many 'middle income and above' households in rural areas as there were in urban areas. There were almost twice as many 'lower income households' in rural areas as in urban areas. There were 2.3 million 'highest income' households in urban areas as against 1.6 million in rural areas.

NCAER projections indicated that the number of 'middle income and above' households was expected to grow to 111 million in rural India by 2007, compared to 59 million in urban India. Gone are the days when a rural consumer had to go to a nearby town or city to buy a branded product. The growing power of the rural consumer is forcing big companies to flock to rural markets.

Thanks to the growing penetration of television in rural areas, consumer awareness in rural areas had increased. Rural expenditures on FMCG (fast moving consumer goods) are growing at an impressive rate of 20–25 per cent. Several companies are taking rural marketing seriously.

This is throwing up major challenges for marketers. Servicing rural markets involves ensuring availability of products through a sound distribution network, overcoming prevalent attitudes and habits of rural customers and creating brand awareness.

Price sensitivity is another key issue. Rural income levels are largely dependent on the vagaries of monsoon, and the demand is not easy to predict. Most of the companies targeting rural India have started tinkering with pack sizes and creating new price points in order to reach out to rural consumers since a significant portion of the rural population are daily wage workers.

Thus, sachets and miniature packs, as in the case of shampoo sachets priced at 1 paisa (Re) and 2 paisas (Rs) or toothpaste at Rs 10, have become the order of the day in hinterland India and help improve market penetration.

Yet driving consumption of goods in rural areas is not just about lowering prices and increasing volumes but also about product innovation and developing indigenous products to cater to their demands. For example, soap makers use advanced technology to coat one side of the soap bar with plastic to prevent it from wearing out quickly.

In order to efficiently and cost-effectively target the rural markets, companies have to cover many independent retailers since in these areas, the retailer influences purchase decisions and stocks a single brand in a product category.

In such an environment, being first on the shelf and developing a privileged relationship with the retailer is a source of competitive advantage to consumer goods companies.

A further challenge is to gain acceptability for the product or service. One company which has reaped rich dividends by doing so is LG Electronics. In 1998, it developed a customized television for the rural market and christened it Sampoorna. It was a runaway hit, selling 100,000 sets in the very first year. Because of the lack of electricity and refrigerators in the rural areas, Coca-Cola provides low-cost ice boxes, a tin box for new outlets, and thermocol box for seasonal outlets.

With large parts of rural India inaccessible to conventional advertising media – only 41 per cent of rural households have access to television – building awareness is another challenge.

Companies need to turn to innovative methods of advertising like fairs or *haats* to reach their potential customer base. Several years ago, for example, many companies congregated at the Ganges River for the Kumbh Mela festival, where about 30 million people, mostly from rural areas, were expected to come over a span of one month. The companies provided 'touch and feel' demonstrations and distributed free samples. This is proving to be extremely effective in advertising to the rural market.

Hindustan Lever relies heavily on its own company-organized media. These are promotional events organized by stockists. Godrej Consumer Products, which is trying to push its soap brands into the interior areas, uses radio to reach the local people in their language. Coca-Cola uses a combination of television, cinema and radio to reach 53.6 per cent of rural households. It doubled its spend on advertising on Doordarshan, the Indian public television broadcast channel, which alone reached 41 per cent of rural households. It has also used banners and posters and tapped all the local forms of entertainment and local language advertising. Philips India uses wall writing and radio advertising to drive its growth in rural areas.

# Future outlook

According to MGI (McKinsey Global Institute), if India continues on its current high-growth path, incomes will almost triple over the next two decades, and the country will climb from its current position as the 12th largest consumer market to become the world's fifth largest consumer market by 2025.

The combination of more income per person, more people and moderating savings will fuel a quadrupling of India's consumer market over the next two decades.

MGI forecasts urban consumption both to accelerate and to continue to grow faster than the overall economy. With almost half of the middle class being 'new consumers' at any point in time loyalties are up for grabs.

An analysis of rural consumption shows that while its growth will continue to lag behind growth in wealthier urban areas, it will nonetheless accelerate from a compound annual rate of 3.9 per cent during the past two decades to 5.1 per cent during the next two decades.

Many companies agree that Indian consumer markets are changing fast, with rapid growth in disposable incomes, the development of modern urban lifestyles and the emergence of the kind of trend-conscious consumers that India has not seen in the past. Indians are travelling abroad a lot more. They get exposed to what is happening in other markets, and they bring back new attitudes and preferences.

But with those changes, companies are adamant that while there are growth opportunities for consumer companies, there are few easy pickings. You cannot sell junk in India. In India you have to give value. It is simply not enough to be a foreign brand anymore.

Companies expect that the next cycle of change in Indian consumer markets will be the arrival of foreign players in consumer retailing. If retailing is liberalized, say companies, growth will be boosted, so will be competition. Indian companies know Indian markets better, but foreign players will come in and challenge the locals by sheer cash power, the power to drive down prices. That will be the coming struggle. The key challenges for multinationals will be to meet middle class aspirations at Indian prices and adapt products and services to meet Indian needs and task points as well as building brands and overcoming infrastructure, regulatory and distribution hurdles.

# Part 3

# Finance, Tax and Accounting

# 3.1

# Direct Taxation Issues

*KPMG India*

In India, taxes are levied by the central and state governments and also by local government bodies. Principal taxes, including income tax, central sales tax, custom duties, central excise duty and service tax are levied by the central government. On the other hand, states levy taxes such as state excise duty, VAT (value-added tax), entry tax and stamp duty. Local government bodies levy octroi duties and other taxes of a local nature like water tax and property tax.

Income is taxed in India in accordance with the provisions of the Income Tax Act, 1961. The ministry of finance (Department of Revenue) through the CBDT (Central Board of Direct Taxes) – an apex tax authority – implements and administers direct tax laws.

India has embarked on a series of tax reforms since the early 1990s. The focus has been on rationalization of tax rates and simplification of procedures.

## Direct taxes

India follows a residence-based taxation system. Broadly, taxpayers may be classified as 'residents' or 'non-residents'. Individual taxpayers may also be classified as 'residents but not ordinary residents'. The tax year in India runs from 1 April to 31 March of the following calendar year for all taxpayers. Taxable income has to be ascertained separately for different classes of income (called 'heads of income') and is then aggregated to determine total taxable income. The 'previous year' basis of assessment is used, ie. any income pertaining to the tax year is offered to tax in the following year (known as the assessment year).

Income tax is levied on taxable income, comprising income under the following heads:

- salaries;
- income from house property;
- profits and gains of business or profession;

- capital gains; and
- income from other sources.

Generally, the global income of domestic companies, partnerships and local authorities are subject to tax at flat rates, whereas individuals and other specified taxpayers are subject to progressive tax rates. Foreign companies and non-resident individuals are also subject to tax at varying rates on specified incomes which are received/accrued or deemed received/accrued in India. Agricultural income is exempt from income tax at the central level but is taken into account for rate purposes. Income earned by specified organizations, eg. trusts, hospitals, universities, mutual funds, etc., is exempt from income tax, subject to the fulfilment of certain conditions.

India adopts the self-assessment tax system. Taxpayers are required to file their tax returns by the specified dates and pay the tax. The tax officer may choose to make a scrutiny assessment to assess the correct amount of tax by calling for further details.

Generally, taxpayers are liable to make income tax payments as advance tax, in three or four instalments, depending on the category they belong to, during the year in which the income is earned. Balance tax payable, if any, can be paid by way of self-assessment tax at the time of filing the return of income. Employed individuals are subject to tax withholding by the employer on a 'pay-as-you-earn' basis. Certain other specified incomes are also subject to tax withholding at specified rates.

# Residential status

## Individual

Depending upon the period of stay in India during a given financial year, an individual may be classified as a resident or a non-resident in India or 'not ordinarily resident' in India.

## Company

A resident company is a company formed and registered under the Companies Act, 1956, or one whose control and management is situated wholly in India. An Indian company is always an Indian resident. Consequently, an Indian company that is wholly owned by a foreign entity and managed from India by foreign individuals/companies is also considered a resident Indian company. A non-resident company is one whose control and management are situated wholly outside India.

# Types of taxes

## Annual income tax

Annual income tax is levied on income earned for a financial year as per the rates declared by the annual Finance Act.

## Minimum alternate tax

With a view to bring zero taxpaying companies having book profits under the tax net, the domestic tax law requires companies to pay MAT (minimum alternate tax) in lieu of the regular corporate tax, in a case where the regular corporate tax is lower than the MAT.

However, MAT is not applicable to:

- income exempt from tax (excluding exempt long-term capital gains from tax year ending 31 March 2007);
- income from units in specified zones including SEZs (special economic zones) or specified 'backward' districts; and
- income of certain ailing industrial companies.

MAT is levied at 10 per cent (plus applicable surcharge and education cess[1]) of the adjusted book profits of companies where the regular corporate tax payable is less than 10 per cent of their book profits. Surcharge is applicable at 10 per cent in the case of companies, other than a foreign company, if the adjusted book profits are in excess of $235,000. Education cess is applicable at 3 per cent on income tax (inclusive of surcharge, if any).

A tax credit, being the difference of the tax liability under MAT provisions and regular provisions, can be carried forward for set off in the year in which tax is payable under the regular provisions. Such set off shall be allowed on the difference of tax as per regular provisions and as per MAT provisions. However, no carry forward shall be allowed beyond the seventh assessment year succeeding the assessment year in which the tax credit becomes allowable.

## Dividend distribution tax

DDT (dividend distribution tax) is a tax payable on the dividend declared, distributed or paid. Dividends paid by an Indian company are currently exempt from income tax in the hands of the recipient shareholders in India. However, the company paying the dividends is required to pay DDT on the

[1] Education cess is a widely used term in India that refers to any hypothecated tax.

amount of dividends declared, at the rate of 16.99 per cent (inclusive of surcharge and education cess). An exemption from this tax has been granted in the case of dividends distributed out of profits of SEZ developers.

The Finance Act 2008 has granted the following exemption. A domestic company will not have to pay DDT on dividends distributed to its shareholders to the extent of dividends received from its subsidiary if:

- the subsidiary has paid DDT on such dividend received; and
- such domestic company is not a subsidiary of any other company.

A company would be a subsidiary of another company if such company holds more than half in nominal value of equity share capital of the company.

## Tonnage tax on shipping companies

Indian shipping companies are taxed on a presumptive basis. Tax is levied on the notional income of the shipping company arising from the operation of ships at normal corporate tax rates. The notional income is determined in a prescribed manner on the basis of the tonnage of the ship. Tax is payable even in the case of loss. The scheme is applicable to shipping companies that are incorporated under the Indian Companies Act (with its effective place of management in India), with at least one ship with minimum tonnage of 15 tonnes and holding a valid certificate under the Merchant Shipping Act, 1959. Shipping companies can opt for this scheme or for taxation under normal income tax provisions. Once the scheme has been opted into, it applies for a mandatory period of 10 years and other income tax provisions do not apply.

## Fringe benefit tax

FBT (fringe benefit tax) is a tax payable by the employer on benefits (provided/deemed) that employees (past or present) receive as a consideration of their employment. FBT is leviable on every employer, excluding individuals, HUFs (Hindu Undivided Family – a special community-based entity in India) and certain institutions enjoying certain exemptions.

Certain expenses are directly covered within the ambit of FBT. In respect of expenditure such as entertainment expenditure, conferences etc., a certain percentage of these expenses are deemed fringe benefits, upon which FBT is leviable. FBT is leviable at the rate of 30 per cent plus applicable surcharge and education cess.

The due date for filing the return of fringe benefits in the case of a company or a person whose accounts are required to be audited under the Act is 30 September following the end of the financial year. In any other case, the due date is the 31 July following the end of the financial year.

The manner of payment of FBT is similar to that of advance tax. FBT should be paid in each quarter, on or before the 15th day of the month following such quarter, except for the quarter ending on 31 March, when the FBT will be payable on or before 15 March of the relevant financial year.

## Securities transaction tax

STT (securities transaction tax) is levied on the value of taxable securities transactions at specified rates.

The taxable securities transactions are:

- the purchase/sale of equity shares in a company or a derivative or a unit of equity-oriented funds entered into a recognized stock exchange; and
- the sale of unit of an equity-oriented fund to the mutual fund.

The rates of STT are shown in Table 1.

Table 1. Rates of STT for seller

| From 1 June 2006 | |
|---|---|
| Purchase/sale of equity shares, units of equity-oriented mutual fund (delivery based) | 0.125% |
| Sale of equity shares, units of equity-oriented mutual fund (non-delivery based) | 0.025% |
| Sale of derivatives | 0.017% |
| Sale of unit of an equity-oriented fund to the mutual fund | 0.25% |

## Commodities transaction tax

The CTT (commodities transaction tax) is levied on the value of taxable commodities transactions at specified rates as shown in Table 2.

Table 2. Rates of CTT

| | |
|---|---|
| Sale of an option in goods or an option in commodity derivative | 0.017% (by seller) |
| Sale of an option in goods or an option in commodity derivative, where option is exercised | 0.125% (by purchaser) |
| Sale of any other commodity derivative | 0.017% (by seller) |

## Banking cash transaction tax

The BCTT (banking cash transaction tax) is levied on the following 'taxable banking transactions' entered with any scheduled bank on any single day:

- the withdrawal of cash from any bank account other than a savings bank account; and
- the receipt of cash on encashment of term deposit(s).

The value of the above transactions chargeable to BCTT is 50,000 Indian rupees (INR; approximately $1,175) or more, in the case of individuals and HUFs and INR 1 million (approximately $2,350) or more, in the case of persons other than individuals and HUFs. The BCTT will be payable by the person from whose account the cash is withdrawn.

The BCTT is levied at the rate of 0.1 per cent of the value of each taxable banking transaction. No BCTT shall be charged on or after 1 April 2009.

## Wealth tax

Wealth tax is leviable on specified assets at 1 per cent on the value of the assets held by the assessee in excess of the basic exemption of assets amounting to INR 1.5 million (approximately $35,200).

# Tax rates

## Individuals

Individuals (excluding women and senior citizens) are liable to tax in India at different rates of tax. See Tables 3–5 below.

Table 3. Individual slab rates of income

| Income slab | Effective tax rate (including surcharge of 10% and education cess of 3%) |
|---|---|
| Up to $3,500 | NIL |
| $3,500 to $7,000 | 10.3% |
| $7,000 to $11,700 | 20.6% |
| $11,700 to $23,500 | 30.9% |
| Above $23,500 | 33.99%* |

*Where the income exceeds $23,500, surcharge at 10 per cent would be leviable on the total tax payable.

Table 4. Women's slab rates of income

| Income slab | Effective tax rate (including surcharge of 10% and education cess of 3%) |
|---|---|
| Up to $4,200 | NIL |
| $4,200 to $7,000 | 10.3% |
| $7,000 to $11,700 | 20.6% |

| | |
|---|---|
| $11,700 to $23,500 | 30.9% |
| Above $23,500 | 33.99%* |

*Where the income exceeds $23,500, surcharge at 10 per cent would be leviable on the total tax payable.

Table 5. Senior citizens'(individuals of the age of 65 years or more) slab rates of income

| Income slab | Effective tax rate (including surcharge of 10% and education cess of 3%) |
|---|---|
| Up to $5,200 | NIL |
| $5,200 to $7,000 | 10.3% |
| $ 7,000 to $11,700 | 20.6% |
| $11,700 to $23,500 | 30.9% |
| Above $23,500 | 33.99%* |

*Where the income exceeds $23,500, surcharge at 10 per cent would be leviable on the total tax payable
Note: Income slabs rounded off to nearest $100; $1 = INR 42.55.

## Capital gains tax

Gains arising from the transfer of long-term capital assets are taxed at special rates/eligible for certain exemptions (including exemption from tax where the sale transaction is chargeable to STT). Short-term capital gains arising on transfer of assets other than certain specified assets are taxable at normal rates. The capital gain rates are shown in Table 6.

Table 6. Capital gains tax rates

| | |
|---|---|
| Long-term capital gains* | NIL |
| Short-term capital gains* | 15 % |

*Subject to payment of STT.

## Taxability of non-resident Indians

Non-resident Indians may also be liable to tax in India on a gross basis depending upon the type of income received.

## Foreign nationals

Indian tax law provides for exemption of income earned by foreign nationals for services rendered in India, subject to prescribed conditions. For example:

- remuneration from a foreign enterprise not conducting any business in India, provided the individual's stay in India does not exceed 90 days and the payment made is not deducted in computing the income of the employer; and

- remuneration received by a person employed on a foreign ship, provided his stay in India does not exceed 90 days.

## Companies

A resident company is taxed on its global income. A non-resident company is taxed on income received/accrued or deemed received/accrued/arisen in India. The scope of Indian income is defined under the Act. The tax rates for the tax year 2008–2009 are:

- domestic company – 33.99 per cent (income tax 30 per cent plus surcharge of 10 per cent thereon [if the total income exceeds $235,000] plus education cess of 3 per cent on income tax including surcharge); and
- foreign company – 42.23 per cent (income tax 40 per cent plus surcharge of 2.5 per cent thereon plus education cess of 3 per cent on income tax including surcharge).

Additionally, a company is required to pay the other taxes, eg. FBT, STT, BCTT and MAT.

# Modes of taxation

## Gross basis of taxation

Certain specific income streams earned by non-residents are liable to tax on a gross basis in certain cases, ie. a specified rate of tax is applied on the gross basis and no deduction of expenses is allowed. The details of the nature of income and applicable rate of tax are as shown in Table 7 below.

Table 7. Income stream and rate of tax

| Income stream | Rate of tax |
|---|---|
| Interest | 21.115% |
| Royalties | 31.673/21.115/10.558%* |
| Technical know-how fees | 31.673/21.115/10.558%* |

*The rates are in the case of a foreign company and are inclusive of surcharge of 2½ per cent and education cess of 3 per cent on tax and surcharge in respect of agreements made on or before 31 May 1997; or after 31 May 1997 but before 1 June 2005; and after 1 June 2005, respectively. In the case of other non-residents, the basic tax rate would be increased by a surcharge of 10 per cent where income exceeds INR 1 million (approximately $23,500) and education cess of 3 per cent on tax and surcharge.

## Presumptive basis of taxation

Foreign companies engaged in certain specified business activities are subject to tax on a presumptive basis, ie. income is recognized at a specific percentage of gross revenue and thereafter tax liability is determined by applying the normal tax rates on deemed income. Certain activities taxed on a presumptive basis along with the basis of taxation are set out below in Table 8.

Table 8. Activities and their taxation

| Activity | Basis of taxation | Effective tax rate (including surcharge of 10% and education cess of 3%) |
|---|---|---|
| Oil and gas services | Deemed profit of 10% of revenues | 4.223% |
| Execution of certain turnkey contracts | Deemed profit of 10% of revenues | 4.223% |
| Air transport | Deemed profit of 5% of revenues | 2.112% |
| Shipping operations | Deemed profit of 7.5% of revenues | 3.167% |

## Deductions allowable from business income

Generally, all revenue expenses incurred for business purposes are deductible from the taxable income. The requirement for deductibility of expenses is that the expenses must be wholly and exclusively incurred for business purposes; that they must be incurred or paid during the previous year and supported by relevant papers and records. Expenses of a personal or capital nature are not deductible. Income tax paid is not allowable as a deduction. Depreciation on specified capital assets at prescribed rates is also deductible.

Expenditure incurred on taxes (excluding income tax) and duties, bonus or commission to employees, fees under any law, interest on loans or borrowings from public financial institutions and interest on loans and advances from scheduled banks are deductible only if they are paid during the previous year. Alternatively, they are deductible if they are paid on or before the due date for furnishing the return of income, and the return is accompanied by evidence of such payment. However, interest on capital borrowed for the acquisition of assets acquired for the extension of an existing business is not allowed as a deduction until the time that such assets are actually put to use.

Employee contributions to specified staff welfare funds – that is, provident funds, gratuity funds, etc. – are treated as employer income and are allowed as deduction only if actually paid during the previous year on or before the applicable due date. However, employer's contributions to these funds are deductible even if paid before the due date of the filing of the return of income.

Salaries, interest, royalties, technical service fees, commissions or any other amount payable outside India or in India to a non-resident (other than a foreign company) or a foreign company, on which the applicable withholding tax has not been withheld or after deduction has not been paid are not deductible. Such amounts are deductible in the year in which the withholding tax is paid. Where, in respect of these payments, tax has been deducted in the relevant year but paid in the subsequent year within the prescribed time limit, such payments made are deductible in the relevant year. However, if the tax so paid in the subsequent year is not paid within the prescribed time limit, the deduction is allowed only in the subsequent year.

Similarly, any payment made to residents for interest, commission or brokerage, rent, royalty, fees for professional or technical services, contract/sub-contract payments, where taxes have not been withheld or if taxes have been withheld incorrectly under the prescribed regulations, will be disallowed in the hands of the payer. The deduction for such a sum will be allowed in the year in which the withholding taxes are paid.

## Head office expenditure

Foreign companies operating in India through a branch are allowed to deduct executive and general administrative expenditure incurred by the head office outside India. However, such expenditure is restricted to the lower of 5 per cent of adjusted total income (as defined) or expenditure attributable to the Indian business.

In cases where the adjusted total income for a year is a loss, the expenditure is restricted to 5 per cent of the average adjusted total income (as defined).

## Bad debts

Bad debts written off are tax deductible. Provision for doubtful debts is not tax deductible. Banking companies are allowed a deduction for provisions for bad and doubtful debts up to 7.5 per cent of total income or 10 per cent of their assets classified as doubtful assets restricted to the provision for doubtful debts made in the books. Banks incorporated in a country outside India and public financial institutions are allowed a deduction for provisions for doubtful debts up to 5 per cent of income, as specifically defined for this purpose. Bad debts actually written off by banks and public financial institutions, in excess of the accumulated provision for doubtful debts, are deductible.

## Grouping/consolidation

No provisions currently exist for the grouping/consolidation of losses of entities within the same group.

## Withholding of taxes

Generally, income payable to residents or non-residents are liable to withholding tax, a tax 'withheld' by the payer and given directly to the relevant tax authority, especially for overseas and non-resident tax payers by the payer (in most cases individuals are not obliged to withhold tax on payments made by them). The rates in the case of residents would vary, depending on the income and the payee involved, eg. in the case of rent, the rate is 15 per cent if the payee is an individual and 20 per cent in all other cases.

Except where preferential tax rates are provided for under DTAAs (Double Tax Avoidance Agreements), payments to foreign companies/non-residents are subject to the withholding tax rates as shown in Table 9.

Table 9. Withholding tax rates applicable to foreign companies/non-residents

| Type of income | Foreign companies* | Other non-residents# |
|---|---|---|
| Interest on foreign currency loan | 21.115% | 22.66% |
| Winnings from horse races | 31.673% | 33.99% |
| Royalties and technical services fees payable under an agreement approved by the government of India in accordance with the new industrial policy | 10.558%; 21.115% | 11.33%; 22.66% |
| Winnings from lotteries and crossword puzzles | 31.673% | 33.99% |
| Long-term capital gains | 21.115%† | 22.66%† |
| Any other income | 42.23% | 33.99% |

*Rate includes income tax plus 2.5 per cent surcharge and 3 per cent education cess thereon.
#Rate includes surcharge of 10 per cent where income exceeds $23,500 and education cess of 3 per cent.
†Other than exempted long-term gains.

# Carrying forward losses and unabsorbed depreciation

This is subject to the fulfilment of the following prescribed conditions:

1. Business loss can be carried forward for eight consecutive financial years and can be set off against the profits of subsequent years. Losses

from a speculation business can be set off only against gains from speculation business for a maximum of four years.

2. Unabsorbed depreciation may be carried forward for set off indefinitely.
3. Capital losses may also be carried forward for set off for eight subsequent financial years subject to fulfilment of certain conditions. Long-term capital losses can be set off only against long-term capital gains, whereas short-term capital losses can be set off against short-term as well as long-term capital gains. These losses cannot be set off against income under any other head.
4. Carry back of losses or depreciation is not permitted.

## Corporate reorganizations

Corporate reorganizations, such as mergers, de-mergers and slump sales, are either tax neutral or taxed at concessional rates subject to the fulfilment of prescribed conditions.

## Foreign institutional investors

To promote the development of Indian capital markets, qualified FIIs (foreign institutional investors)/subaccounts registered with the SEBI (Securities and Exchange Board of India) and investing in listed Indian shares and units are subject to tax as per beneficial regime.

In addition, there is a surcharge of 2.5 per cent in the case of companies and 10 per cent in the case of non-corporate entities where the income exceeds INR 1 million (approximately $23,500) and education cess of 3 per cent. Additionally, capital gains earned by an FII are not subject to withholding tax in India.

The rate of tax on other short-term capital gains is 30 per cent plus surcharge and education cess; and on long-term capital gains is 10 per cent plus surcharge and education cess.

## Relief from double taxation

For countries that have DTAAs (Double Tax Avoidance Agreements) with India, bilateral relief is available to a resident in respect of foreign taxes paid. Generally, provisions of DTAAs prevail over the domestic tax provisions. However, domestic tax provisions may apply to the extent that they are more beneficial to the taxpayer. The DTAAs would also prescribe rates of tax in the case of dividend income, interest, royalties and fees for technical services that should be applied if the rates prescribed in the Act are higher. Business income of a non-resident may not be taxable in India if the non-resident does not have a permanent establishment in India.

For countries with no DTAA with India, a foreign tax credit is available under Indian domestic tax law to a resident taxpayer in respect of foreign taxes paid. The amount of credit allowable should be the lower of the tax in the foreign country or the Indian tax attributable to the foreign income. Currently, there is no carry forward/carry back of excess tax credits.

# Tax incentives – SEZs

## SEZ developer

An SEZ developer is entitled to claim an income-tax holiday for a period of any 10 consecutive years out of 15 years beginning from the year in which such SEZ is notified by the central government. Such deduction shall be up to 100 per cent of the profits derived from business of developing/developing and operating/developing, operating and maintaining SEZs.

## SEZ unit

A unit which sets up its operations in a SEZ is entitled to claim an income-tax holiday for a period of 15 years commencing from the year in which such unit begins to manufacture or produce articles or things or provide services. The benefits are available against export profits, as under:

1. deduction of 100 per cent for the first five years;
2. deduction of 50 per cent for the next five years (unconditional); and
3. deduction of 50 per cent for next five years (subject to conditions for creation of specified reserves).

## Offshore Banking Units and International Financial Service Centre units set up in SEZs

OBUs (offshore banking units) and IFSCs (international financial service centres) in SEZs are entitled to claim an income-tax holiday of 100 per cent for the first five years and 50 per cent for the next five years.

## Export-oriented units

Undertakings set up in EPZs (export processing zones)/FTZs (free trade zones), EHTP (electronic hardware technology park), STP (software technology park) or 100 per cent EOUs (export-oriented units) are eligible for a deduction of 100 per cent on the profits derived from exports for 10 consecutive years from the year in which such undertaking begins manufacturing or producing articles or things or providing services. Such deductions would not be available after 31 March 2010.

# Transfer pricing

In the case of businesses carried on by multinational companies, detailed provisions relating to transfer pricing were introduced by the Finance Act, 2001 in order to facilitate the computation of reasonable, fair and equitable profits and tax in India. The Indian transfer pricing provisions generally follow OECD (Organization for Economic Co-operation and Development) guidelines, albeit with some significant differences, such as a wider definition of the term 'associated enterprise', and the concept of arithmetical mean as opposed to internationally followed statistical measures of median/arm's length range.

In simple terms, transfer pricing regulations require cross-border transactions between associated enterprises to be undertaken on an arm's length basis. In this regard, Section 92 of the Income Tax Act, 1961 provides that the price of any transaction between associated enterprises, either or both of whom are non-resident for Indian income tax purposes (international transaction), shall be computed having regard to the arm's length price. Two enterprises are considered to be associated if there is direct/indirect participation in the management or control or capital of an enterprise by another enterprise or by the same persons in both the enterprises. Further, the transfer pricing regulations have prescribed certain other conditions that can trigger an associated enterprise relationship. Significant conditions among these include:

- direct/indirect shareholding, giving rise to 26 per cent or more of voting power;
- dependency relating to the source of raw materials/consumables, as well as dependency relating to customer(s) for manufactured/processed goods, price and other conditions being influenced by the other contracting party;
- authority to appoint more than 50 per cent of the board of directors or one or more of the executive directors;
- dependency in relation to IP (intellectual property) rights (know-how, patents, trademarks, copyrights, trademarks, licences, franchises, etc.) owned by either party; and
- dependency relating to borrowings, ie. advancing of loans amounting to no less than 51 per cent of total assets or provision of guarantee amounting to not less than 10 per cent of the total borrowings.

## Determination of arm's length price

The Indian transfer pricing regulations require an arm's length price in relation to an international transaction to be determined in accordance with the most appropriate method from the following:

- CUP (comparable uncontrolled price);
- RPM (resale price method);
- CPLM (cost plus method);
- PSM (profit split method); and
- TNMM (transactional net margin method).

Unlike the OECD guidelines, there is no order of preference prescribed, although in practice transfer pricing authorities do attempt to use traditional methods such as CUP, RPM and CPLM before accepting a profit-based approach. The choice of the most appropriate method is required to be made having regard to factors that inter alia include nature and class of the transaction, the classes of associated enterprises undertaking the transaction and the functions performed by them.

## Burden of proof and assessment

The burden of proving that the international transactions comply with the arm's length principle lies with the taxpayer. Furthermore, the Act requires every person entering into an international transaction to maintain prescribed information and documents relating to international transactions. The documentation requirements laid down by the Indian transfer pricing regulations are detailed and prescriptive, and failure to maintain/furnish prescribed documentation attracts penalties that can extend up to 4 per cent of the value of the international transaction entered into by the taxpayer.

Furthermore, every taxpayer entering into an international transaction is required to file a report (referred to as an accountant's report) along with a tax return, setting out prescribed details in respect of international transactions and associated enterprises. The accountant's report forms the basis on which the transfer pricing authorities undertake an audit. Under prevailing regulations, taxpayers reporting international transactions with associated enterprises exceeding INR 150 million (approximately $3.5 million) are subjected to a transfer pricing audit. To the extent of transfer pricing adjustments made as a result of the audit, taxpayers lose any tax exemption to which they are otherwise entitled. There are also potential penalties amounting to one time to three times of the incremental tax, arising as a result of any adjustment. There is a separate penalty of INR 100,000 (approximately $2,300) for not furnishing the accountant's report.

Indian transfer pricing regulations are in an evolving stage, with only three years of audits having been completed. At present there is limited administrative guidance/judicial precedent available. Furthermore, it is pertinent to note that Indian transfer pricing regulations do not have provisions for either advance pricing arrangements or safe harbours. However, taxpayers are provided a limited safe harbour to the extent that the transaction value of the international transaction can vary to the extent of 5 per cent of the arm's length price.

# 3.2

# Indirect Taxation Issues

*KPMG India*

The ministry of finance (Department of Revenue) through the CBEC (Central Board of Excise and Customs), an apex indirect tax authority, implements and administers Cenvat (Central Excise), Customs and Service Tax laws. Circulars, notifications and clarifications issued by the CBEC supplement these indirect tax laws. Issues involving the interpretation of tax laws are decided by the judiciary, which is independent of the legislature.

## Customs duties

Customs duties are levied on import of goods into India at the rates specified in the Customs Tariff Act, 1975. The effective rates of customs duties may vary pursuant to general and/or specific exemption or concession notifications issued by the government of India in this regard.

Customs duties currently comprise the following:

- BCD (basic customs duty): The current general peak rate is 10 per cent.
- CVD (countervailing duty): This duty is equivalent to central excise duty leviable on a like product manufactured in India. The current rate applicable to the majority of the industrial products is 14 per cent plus 2 per cent education cess and 1 per cent secondary and higher education cess ('SHE cess'), taking the effective rate to 14.42 per cent. This duty is calculated on the value of the product and BCD.
- Education cess: This cess is levied at 2 per cent on the amount of BCD and CVD.
- SHE cess: This is levied at 1 per cent on the amount of BCD and CVD.

ADC (additional duty of customs) is levied in lieu of VAT (value-added tax), local taxes and other charges leviable on like goods on their sale, purchase or transportation in India. Presently, this duty is levied at 4 per cent on most items, with a few exceptions. This duty is levied on the value of the product, BCD and CVD.

In addition, the government also levies anti-dumping and safeguard duties on specified products to protect domestic manufacturers. These duties are levied for specified periods.

Valuation, for the purpose of levy of customs duty, is generally on the basis of value at arm's length price between unrelated parties plus freight and landing charges.

## Import–export policy

The import of goods into and export of goods from India is regulated by the Foreign Trade Policy issued from time to time by the ministry of commerce. The policy remains in force for five years and is amended from time to time. The policy currently in force is for the tax year period 2004–2009. The majority of goods are now freely importable.

## Central excise duty

Cenvat is levied on goods manufactured and produced in India. It is generally levied on an *ad valorem* basis at the rate of 14.42 per cent (a basic rate of 14 per cent, education cess of 2 per cent and SHE cess of 1 per cent). The effective rates may be lower pursuant to general/specific notifications issued by the government granting whole or partial exemption from duty. The duty, in most cases, is levied on the basis of the value of the excisable goods.

Cenvat is levied on the transaction value of excisable goods if such goods are sold for delivery at the time and place of removal. Such transaction value would apply:

- where the buyer is not a related person; and
- where the price is the sole consideration.

In other cases, the value of excisable goods is determined in the manner prescribed under the relevant valuation rules.

Cenvat is payable by the manufacturer but is, ordinarily, recovered from the buyer as part of the consideration for the sale of goods. Under the Cenvat Scheme, a manufacturer can be credited back the Cenvat or additional duties of customs (ie. CVD) paid on specified inputs and capital goods used in the manufacture of excisable goods. The manufacturer can also be credited back the service tax paid on eligible input services. The credit can be utilized to discharge output Cenvat liability on finished excisable goods.

## VAT

Currently, all states in India are governed under the VAT regime. The last state to replace local sales tax with VAT is Uttar Pradesh (which switched from local sales tax to a VAT regime effective from 1 January 2008). VAT is not much different from local sales tax regimes except that it captures value addition at each level of the distribution network. State VAT continues to be a tax on the sale of goods and does not include taxation of services. The standard rate of VAT is 12.5 per cent and there is a reduced rate of 4 per cent (generally available for information technology products, industrial inputs, agricultural equipments, etc.)/1 per cent (generally applicable on gold, silver, precious stones, including jewellery made of such precious metals and stones). Besides that, there are exemptions and increased rates of 20 per cent for specified products (eg. petroleum products).

State VAT is levied on the movement of goods within a state. If the sales transaction involves the movement of goods from one state to another (interstate), the tax is levied under the CSTA (Central Sales Tax Act, 1956). This Act also covers transactions of the import of goods into or the export of goods out of India. Sales tax/VAT is not imposed on the import of goods into the country or the export of goods out of the country. CST is levied by the central government and administered by the state governments and the tax is levied at the origination of transaction (origin-based levy). The revenue collected under the CSTA is retained by the state governments. The rates of tax under the CSTA depend on the VAT rate applicable in the originating state. The standard rate of CST is 2 per cent (on submission of statutory declaration in Form C, by the purchasing dealer) or the lower rate applicable in the state of the dispatch if the purchaser is purchasing the same for resale or for use in manufacturing goods for sale or for other specified purposes and both the seller and buyer are registered dealers. Otherwise, the CST rate is the applicable rate under VAT laws of the state of dispatch.

States also levy tax on transactions which are 'deemed sales', like works contracts and leases. Essentially, a works contract is for carrying out a composite scope of work involving supply of labour and material where the property in the materials passes during the course of execution of the contract. Lease is a transaction involving the transfer of rights to use goods.

In addition to VAT, some states also levy turnover tax or entry tax. VAT is payable by the seller to the state VAT authorities. Ordinarily, VAT is recovered from the buyer as a part of consideration for the sale of goods.

## Service tax

Service tax is levied on the notified services by the central government. The rate of service tax is currently 12 per cent. Education cess at 2 per cent and SHE cess of 1 per cent are levied on the service tax. Thus, the effective rate of service tax works out to 12.36 per cent.

Service tax is charged on the gross value of services and is generally payable on a receipt basis. It is an indirect tax – payable by the service provider but ordinarily recovered from the recipient of services. The law requires separate mention of service tax amount in the invoices.

Ordinarily, every person liable to pay service tax is required to register himself or herself with the service tax authorities and comply with procedural requirements like paying taxes, filing returns, etc. Further, with effect from 18 April 2006, where any taxable service is provided by a person who has his or her place of business outside India and such service is received by a person having a place of business in India, such service is also deemed a taxable service and is liable to be taxed in the hands of the recipient (under 'reverse charge mechanism'). The taxability of such transactions is governed under the Taxation of Services (provided from outside India and received in India) Rules, 2006.

There is a basic exemption limit of INR 1 million ( $23,348), which means that service providers providing taxable services up to the aforementioned amount will be exempt. A mechanism for credit of service tax on input services and Cenvat on inputs and capital goods used in providing output services is also in place.

The government has notified 'Export of Service Rules, 2005', which defines what constitutes the 'export of services'. These rules have been effective from 15 March 2005. When two or more services are bundled together, they are classifiable under the category that gives essential character to the service. Classification rules are in place from 14 May 2003. If, in the case of composite activities, one or more of the activities are liable to service tax and others are not, service tax would ordinarily be payable only on the charges received for the services to which the tax is applicable. This can be relevant where the charge for each activity can be separately identified/ determined (as a separate scope of work) and is not incidental to the main service.

Service tax/Cenvat incurred on input services/goods is available as credit, which can be used as a set off against output service tax liability. However, with respect to common service/inputs (used for providing taxable as well as exempt output/services) allocation principles have not been well articulated in law. The language of the law is broad and generic and uses terms such as 'directly or indirectly', 'in any manner' and separate books of accounts', which raise a number of issues regarding the scope of the specific category of service. Revenue authorities have been issuing explanatory circulars from time to time in relation to specific issues. Yet there remains considerable ambiguity in the applicability of the service tax law to various services.

Service tax is currently levied on more than 100 notified categories of services. Six more taxable services have been brought under the service tax net with effect from 16 May 2008 post the enactment of Finance Bill, 2008.

## Octroi duty

Octroi duty is a local authority levy, which is imposed on the entry of goods into a municipal/local area for use, consumption or sale. This is only applicable in a few states. No credit is available with respect to octroi payments in terms of state VAT laws.

## Entry tax

Some of the states impose entry tax on the entry of goods within state limits for use, consumption or sale. Again, the rates vary from state to state. Generally, entry tax paid in a state is eligible for claiming as input tax credit against the state VAT/CST liability of that state. The constitutional validity of the levy of entry tax is currently a subject matter of dispute at various judicial forums including the Supreme Court on certain specific grounds and is pending final decision.

## Research and development cess

R&D (research and development) cess is a special levy at a rate of 5 per cent on all payments made for the purchase of technology from abroad under a foreign collaboration agreement, including royalty payments, payments for technicians, lump sum payments and payments for design and drawings. The cess is required to be paid by the importer on or before remitting any money towards payment of such imports. Service tax laws provide for an exemption from service tax on account of R&D cess payments under specific taxable service categories.

# Repatriation of foreign exchange

The FEMA (Foreign Exchange Management Act), 1999 forms the statutory basis for exchange control management in India. The RBI (Reserve Bank of India) administers the exchange management regulations for the government.

India does not have full capital account convertibility as yet. However, there have been significant relaxations in the recent past in both current accounts and capital accounts, related to the withdrawal of foreign exchange. Payments made in connection with services procured in the ordinary course of business are regarded as current account transactions, provided such payments do not alter the payer's assets and liabilities outside India. Withdrawal of foreign exchange for current account transactions is regulated as is shown in Table 1.

In the case of some of the transactions listed in Schedules II and III, prior approval is not required if the payment is made out of funds held in the EEFC (exchange earner's foreign currency) account of the remitter. It is clarified by the RBI that remittances for all current account transactions, other than those prescribed in aforesaid schedules, may be made without

Table 1. Withdrawal of foreign exchange for current account transactions

| Prescribed schedule | Drawal of foreign exchange | Approving authority |
|---|---|---|
| I | Completely prohibited | n/a |
| II | Prior approval if it exceeds the prescribed limits | Concerned ministry/ department of government |
| III | Prior approval if it exceeds the prescribed limits | Reserve Bank of India (RBI) |
| All other current account transactions | No limits | No approval required |

any specific approval. Some of the relevant current account payments are discussed below.

## Dividends

Dividends can be remitted without any specific approval from the RBI.

## Royalty payments under technical collaboration

Royalty payments under technical collaboration are covered under Schedule II as shown in Table 2.

Table 2. Royalty payments under technical collaboration

| Prescribed schedule | Nature of remittance | Approving authority |
|---|---|---|
| Schedule II | Remittance under technical collaboration agreements where:<br>• payment of royalty exceeds 5 per cent on local sales and 8 per cent on exports; or<br>• lump-sum payment exceeds $2 million. | Prior approval of ministry of industry and commerce |

However, no approval is necessary if remittance is made out of the EEFC account of the remitter.

Under FDI (foreign direct investment) guidelines, an Indian company can also pay brand royalty (on use of trademarks and the brand name of the foreign collaborator without technology transfer) under the automatic route to the extent of 2 per cent for exports and 1 per cent for domestic sales.

In the case of technology transfers, the payment for the use of the trademark and brand name subsumes into the technical know-how royalty and therefore additional brand royalties cannot be paid.

## Consultancy services

Remittances for any consultancy service procured from outside India and not involving transfer of technology are covered in Schedule III. Remittance up to $1 million per project can be made without any approval of the RBI. In the case of consultancy services in relation to infrastructure projects, the above limit is extended to $10 million. However, no such approval is necessary if remittance is made out of the EEFC account of the remitter.

## Import of goods

Payments in connection with the import of goods and services in the ordinary course of business are generally permissible and can be undertaken freely through the direct filing of required documents with the authorized dealer/banker. The guidelines for imports contain specific provisions relating to the period of settlement, charging of interest, etc.

## Repatriation of capital

Foreign capital invested in India is generally allowed to be repatriated, along with capital appreciation, if any, after the payment of taxes due on them. Generally, the repatriation of capital may take place in the following scenarios:

- the winding up of the company in India; and
- the sale of shares in the company to a third party.

## Netting

Foreign receivables and payables may not be netted off and the Indian company is obliged to realize the entire export proceeds and pay for the import of goods and services separately. Specific relaxation exists in the regulations for some cases. The RBI also gives case-specific approvals based on industry practice and internal norms.

## Other remittances

1. No prior approval is required for remitting profits earned by Indian branches of companies (other than banks) incorporated outside India to their head offices outside India.
2. Remittances of winding up proceeds of a project office of a foreign company in India are permitted under the automatic route subject to the fulfilment of necessary compliances.

3. Winding-up proceeds of a branch/liaison office of a foreign company in India are permitted subject to RBI approval.

# 3.3

# Accounting and Audit Requirements

*KPMG India*

Chartered accountants in India are regulated by the ICAI (Institute of Chartered Accountants of India), constituted under the Chartered Accountants Act, 1949, an act of Parliament. It is thus the statutory body in India to which all chartered accountants must belong in order to conduct statutory audits in India. The MCA (ministry of corporate affairs) exercises supervision over the ICAI.

The accounting standards were earlier issued under the authority of the Council of the ICAI. The ICAI, recognizing the need to harmonize the diverse accounting policies and practices in use in India, first took on the task of laying down standards of accounting in India in 1977, in the guise of the ASB (Accounting Standards Board). However, the accounting standards issued by the ICAI were mandatory only for its members. It was the Companies (Amendment) Act, 1999 that gave legal recognition to the accounting standards, thereby making them mandatory for companies.

The accounting standards are designed to apply to the general purpose financial statements and other financial reporting, to which members of the ICAI are subject. They apply in respect of any enterprise (whether organized in corporate, cooperative or other forms) engaged in commercial, industrial or business activities (however small), irrespective of whether it is profit oriented or established for charitable or religious purposes. The accounting standards will not, however, apply to enterprises only carrying on activities that are not of a commercial, industrial or business nature (eg. collecting donations and giving them to flood-affected people). The 'general purpose financial statements' for a company include a balance sheet, a statement of profit and loss, a cash flow statement (wherever applicable) and statements and explanatory notes, which form part thereof, issued for the use of various stakeholders, governments, their agencies and the public. The enterprises are classified on factors such as listing, nature of activities, turnover, use of public funds, etc. Small and medium-sized enterprises have been granted certain specific exemptions.

As per the Indian Companies Act, 1956, for companies, the accounting standards have to be prescribed by the central government in consultation with the NACAS (National Advisory Committee on Accounting Standards). Pending notification of standards, the government recognized the ICAI standards as mandatory standards for the purpose of compliance with the Act. Subsequently in December 2006, the government in consultation with NACAS issued rules notifying the accounting standards under the Companies Act. With this, the ICAI is a recommendatory body (to NACAS) as far as standard setting for companies is concerned. Companies are thus required to follow the notified standards while other enterprises continue to follow standards issued by the ICAI. The ICAI has also revised its standards to harmonize them with the notified standards.

Whilst formulating the accounting standards, the ASB of the ICAI takes into consideration the applicable laws, customs, usages and business environments prevailing in India. The ICAI, being a fully fledged member of the IFAC (International Federation of Accountants), is expected, *inter alia*, to actively promote the IASB's (International Accounting Standards Board) pronouncements in the country with a view to facilitating the global harmonization of accounting standards. Accordingly, whilst formulating the accounting standards, the ASB gives due consideration to IASs (International Accounting Standards)/IFRSs (International Financial Reporting Standards) issued by the International Accounting Standards Committee/ IASB, as the case may be, and tries to integrate them, wherever possible, according to the conditions and practices prevailing in India.

The Indian Accounting Standards, like IASs/IFRSs, are principle-based standards. They describe the accounting principles and the methods of applying these principles in the preparation and presentation of financial statements in order to give a true and fair view. They are mandatory in nature. Any deviation from the accounting standards is required to be adequately and appropriately disclosed in the audit report.

Additional accounting principles and practices have also been recommended by the ICAI through guidance notes that form an integral part of the financial reporting framework. There are other pronouncements, such as opinions issued by the Expert Advisory Committee of the ICAI and research publications providing useful and practical guidelines. The documents do not legally enjoy the authoritative status of a mandatory or recommendatory document but nevertheless provide valuable support in understanding accounting treatment applicable to specific issues, and the members are expected to comply with these pronouncements.

## Financial reporting

Apart from the accounting standards, the financial statements also need to comply with the relevant statutory requirements, eg. the Companies Act which mandates the format of the financial statements and the information to be included therein. In this context, it should be noted that apart from ICAI, there are other independent regulators in India governing companies which may lay down specific accounting and/or disclosure norms for financial reporting. An example of this would be the SEBI (Securities and Exchange Board of India), which regulates the functioning of stock exchanges and protects the interests of investors, for listed companies. Another example is the RBI (Reserve Bank of India), the apex bank in India, for banks, non-banking financial institutions and financial and foreign exchange markets. There is also the IRDA (Insurance Regulatory and Development Authority) for insurance companies. In specific circumstances such as mergers and amalgamations, the legal system, through the courts, also provides accounting norms.

Whilst issuing accounting standards, the ICAI makes an effort to ensure that these conform with the provisions of applicable laws, customs, usages and the business environment in general in India. However, if a particular accounting standard is found to be not in conformity with law, the provisions of the said law will prevail. Thus, statutes like the Companies Act, etc., supersede the accounting standards and may require some deviation.

Taxable income is calculated in accordance with tax laws. In some circumstances, the requirements of these laws to compute taxable income differ from the accounting policies applied to determine accounting income. Thus, a particular item of revenue or expense may be treated differently in the general purpose financial statements and for the computation of taxable income. The effect of this difference is that the taxable income and accounting income may not be the same.

In addition to the statutory financial statements, SEBI requires the listed companies to submit and publish quarterly financial results. The financial results are also subject to a limited review/audit by auditors. Consolidated quarterly financial results are recommended but it is mandatory for listed companies to publish annual consolidated financial statements. In addition, detailed corporate governance norms have been prescribed by SEBI through the Listing Agreement required to be entered into by a listed company with the stock exchange.

In sync with the global trend, ICAI has proposed full convergence with IFRSs with effect from accounting periods commencing on or after 1 April 2011. India may thus join 100 plus countries (including those of the European Union) which require or permit the use of IFRSs. As part of ICAI's roadmap, IFRSs would be applicable to public interest entities (ie. listed entities, banks, insurance entities and large-sized entities as defined) as has been the case in other countries. As regards SMEs (small and medium-sized enterprises), ICAI has proposed the application of the proposed 'International Financial Reporting Standard for Small and Medium-sized Entities' (with or without modifications). The proposed standard represents a simplified set of standards for SMEs with disclosure requirements reduced, methods for recognition and measurement simplified and topics not relevant to SMEs eliminated.

Convergence with IFRS has its own regulatory challenges as listed below:

- The central government will have to prescribe IFRSs as accounting standards under Section 211. Presentation requirements of Schedule VI would require review.
- Regulators like SEBI, RBI and IRDA would need to accept IFRSs. This implies that the present set of rules of accounting prescribed by these regulators will have to be thoroughly reviewed.
- Corresponding amendments in taxation laws may also be required, eg. the tax treatment of unrealized gains due to fair value measurements.
- A rule would need to be enacted that accounting treatment in any proposal/scheme submitted to the court/tribunal for approval would need to comply with IFRSs.
- IFRSs require greater use of fair value measurements. It is a moot question whether capital, money, debt, foreign exchange and other markets in India possess necessary depth and breadth for providing reliable fair values on measurement of various assets and liabilities.
- Identification and recruitment of IFRS resources will require sufficient time and merits immediate attention. With limited IFRS trained experts, companies will have to, in all probability, supplement their efforts by educating the existing staff.

MCA has also indicated its support for convergence by issuing a press release stating that it would continue to notify the standards to be followed by Indian companies based on the standards recommended by the ICAI and approved by NACAS. While doing so, the process of convergence with IFRSs would be continued so that the financial information disclosed by Indian companies compares well with that disclosed by non-Indian companies in compliance with IFRS.

The last few years have seen many developments relating to financial reporting by corporates, which in turn influence the auditing profession. The issues of transparency, accounting practices and corporate governance have come to the fore as high agenda items in organizations worldwide. The parameters of financial reporting need a constant review, as they have to keep pace with the fast changing milieu and the corresponding expectations of society in general and the specific users of financial statements in particular. In India, financial reporting is, in any case, in a stage of transition – a stage where hectic changes are being introduced to catch up with the developed world. The ICAI has taken a big leap in financial reporting by introducing new accounting standards and other technical pronouncements as well as taking the decision to converge with IFRS. This has been further supported by the initiatives taken by the MCA and SEBI with the objective to tighten the regulatory regime for corporates, ensure better corporate governance practices and protect investors' rights.

# Part 4

# Legal and Regulatory Framework

# 4.1

# Administrative Barriers to Entry

*Diljeet Titus and Pragya Dhamija, Titus & Co. Advocates*

India is a developing country and is suffering from problems typical of a nation trying to quickly and efficiently join the league of developed nations. The government, on its part, has been trying to improve the business climate by further relaxing the foreign direct investment (FDI) policy and streamlining procedures. These efforts will yield results in the medium term and will certainly make India a better place to live, work and invest.

Although the Indian government has greatly improved the investment climate since the launch of the economic liberalization and globalization programme 15 years ago, it has not been able to completely dismantle the barriers hampering free flow of FDI and foreign institutional investment. These blocks and challenges, however, are not insurmountable and can be overcome by foreign entrepreneurs with sound business acumen, adequate drive and some patience.

Anyone who has closely observed India's march to economic freedom since July 1991 would vouch that these obstacles will be removed sooner rather than later. However, the option before an investor today is either to wait until India's road to investment is free of all possible barriers or venture out on that road regardless, after taking reasonable precautions.

Amidst these alternatives, what a company wanting to participate in the Indian resurgence needs to do is to view the obstacles as challenges and work out an effective business plan to overcome them successfully. Many of the Fortune 500 companies and small and medium-sized enterprises (SMEs) that have opted for the latter are now running profitable businesses in India.

Some of the major impediments that an investor is likely to encounter in India are as follows.

## Entry restrictions

The government has slowly and gradually opened various sectors to FDI. There are several sectors where 100 per cent FDI is allowed under the automatic route. At the same time, there are sectors that are only partially open to FDI.

The government has also banned FDI in certain sectors, for reasons such as public order, national security and national interest. The sectors in which foreign investment is prohibited include the following:

- atomic energy;
- lottery business;
- gambling and betting;
- agriculture (excluding floriculture, horticulture, development of seeds, animal husbandry, pisciculture and cultivation of vegetables, mushrooms, etc., under controlled conditions, and services related to agro and allied sectors) and plantations (excluding tea plantations);
- retail trading (except single brand product retailing).

The government has made some concessions with regard to the retail trade of single brand products. It has allowed FDI up to 51 per cent in the retail trade of single brand products with prior government approval. The initiative is aimed at attracting investment in production and marketing of quality goods.

## Sectoral caps

A foreign investor is required to keep his/her investment in the Indian companies below a prescribed threshold. These restrictions are prescribed by the government in its FDI policy. For instance, FDI is only permitted up to 26 per cent in the insurance sector, subject to the licensing requirement of the Insurance and Regulatory Development Authority (IRDA) of India. Similar restrictions are imposed in sectors like FM broadcasting, defence industries and print media. The government has also imposed a 49 per cent cap on investment in asset reconstruction companies.

As far as the telecommunications sector is concerned, the government has allowed FDI up to 49 per cent in basic, cellular, value-added services and global mobile personal communications by satellite. The foreign investment is permitted up to 74 per cent, subject to the approval of the Foreign Investment Promotion Board (FIPB). In certain sectors like airports, atomic minerals and the exploration and mining of diamonds, FDI is also allowed up to 74 per cent.

The government may have valid reasons for imposing sectoral FDI caps, but they do create operational problems for foreign as well as domestic investors. For instance, if an insurance company needs additional capital of 100 crore rupees, the foreign investor will be required to contribute 26 crore rupees, whilst the Indian partner will have to provide 74 crore rupees to maintain the mandatory FDI: Indian investment ratio. The inability or even unwillingness of the Indian partner to come up with larger sums may create problems for the joint venture (JV).

The sectoral caps also create problems relating to ownership and control. It is ironic that a foreign investor, with deep pockets, larger resources and more experience, has to play the role of a junior partner in the JV.

## The Small Scale Industry sector

The Small Scale Industry (SSI) units enjoy certain privileges in India. These relate to taxes and the items reserved for exclusive production by SSI units. The government has permitted FDI up to 24 per cent in SSI units, provided they are not engaged in the production of something prohibited under the FDI policy.

The SSI units are also allowed to issue shares or convertible debentures to foreign investors in excess of 24 per cent, provided they give up the SSI status, do not engage in the manufacture of items reserved for the SSI sector and keep the foreign investment within the prescribed sectoral cap.

The FDI policy, therefore, restricts the entry of FDI in the SSI sector.

## Remittances

There are various restrictions on remittances, especially with regard to fees and royalties, which a foreign investor can charge for passing technology to an Indian business partner. The remittances are governed by the Foreign Exchange Management (Current Account Transactions) Rules, 2000, issued by the Reserve Bank of India (RBI) in exercise of the powers conferred by the Foreign Exchange Management Act (FEMA), 1999. Under the present regulations, the payment of a technical fee and royalty is allowed under the automatic route, subject to the following limitations:

- The lump sum payments shall not exceed $2 million.
- The royalty payable should not be more than 5 per cent for domestic sales and 8 per cent for exports.
- The royalty limits will be net of taxes and will be calculated according to standard conditions.
- The royalty will be calculated on the basis of the net ex-factory sale price of the product, exclusive of excise duties, minus the cost of the standard bought-out components and the landed cost of imported components, irrespective of the source of procurement, including ocean freight, insurance, custom duties, etc.

The approval of the ministry of commerce and industry would be needed for remittances more than $2 million and royalties in excess of 5 per cent of local sales and 8 per cent of exports.

# Tax rates

India has been witnessing frequent changes in tax rates. As per the tradition, the finance minister of the country presents a budget on the last working day of February every year proposing changes in rates of several taxes. The rates are altered primarily with a view to raising additional resources. The government also takes into account various economic, social and political factors whilst revising the tax rates. The changes, however, can adversely affect the business plans of corporates.

For instance, the government reduced the peak customs duty to 12.5 per cent from 15 per cent and increased the service tax rate from 10 per cent to 12 per cent in February 2006. These changes have a bearing on the cost of goods imported and those produced indigenously.

The effective import duty, after taking into account additional customs duty and education cess, works out to be around 37 per cent on most of the items. As the government is committed to lowering the customs duty to Association of South East Asian Nations (ASEAN) levels, there is a strong likelihood of rates going down further in the near term and imports becoming cheaper.

As far as service tax is concerned, the government wants to earn more revenue from this tax, as services account for about 54 per cent of the country's gross domestic product. There is a possibility of the service tax rate going up further in the near future. The increase in service tax will make domestic goods more expensive.

The finance ministry also keeps on experimenting with new taxes. The latest in the list is the fringe benefit tax. These taxes impose additional burdens on the industry.

The government has been talking about the need for a stable fiscal regime and also appears to be working towards it. However, until such a regime is firmly in place, investors will have to live with sudden changes in tax rates.

# Multiplicity of laws

There is no dearth of laws in India. An investor is expected to have a fair knowledge of various important commercial laws and ensuing legal obligations. The important laws that have a bearing on trade and commerce are listed as follows:

- Indian Contract Act, 1872;
- Foreign Trade (Development and Regulation) Act, 1992;
- Foreign Exchange Management Act, 1999;
- Income Tax Act, 1961;
- The Companies Act, 1956;
- Indian Partnership Act, 1932;

- Arbitration and Conciliation Act, 1996;
- The Monopolistic and Restrictive Trade Practices Act, 1969;
- Consumer Protection Act, 1986;
- The Sale of Goods Act, 1930;
- Customs Act, 1962;
- Central Excise Act, 1944;
- Central Sales Tax Act, 1956;
- Sales Tax (value-added tax in certain states) laws and local levies of relevant states;
- Negotiable Instruments Act, 1881;
- Insurance Act, 1972;
- General Insurance Business (Nationalization) Act, 1972;
- Trade Marks Act, 1999;
- The Copyrights Act, 1957;
- The Railways Act, 1890;
- Industrial Disputes Act, 1947;
- Trade Unions Act, 1926.

The above is only an illustrative list. There are several other laws concerning use of land, pollution control, etc., which an investor has to keep in view whilst undertaking any manufacturing or trading activity. Many laws, like the Urban Land (Ceiling and Regulation) Act, 1976, are archaic and have lost their relevance, but as long as they are on the statute book, investors have no choice but to abide by them.

In addition, an investor is also required to deal with the countless agencies which often do not work in tandem, causing delays and cost overrun.

## Judicial delays

Though the idiom 'justice delayed is justice denied' sounds like a cliché, it very aptly describes the Indian judicial scene. Indian courts are flooded with civil and criminal cases and it can take years to settle a dispute. The delay can be frustrating for both the litigating parties, more so when the disputes are of a commercial nature and the need for quick resolution is pressing.

The government has been trying to address the problem of mounting cases by setting up specialized tribunals. The National Tax Tribunal (NTT) is being set up to adjudicate tax-related disputes. It is hoped that the NTT will develop some kind of expertise and ensure expeditious resolution of disputes. The NTT will have branches in all states. The appeal against the ruling of NTT shall lie in the Supreme Court.

The government has also decided to set up a National Company Law Tribunal (NCLT) to deal exclusively with company law-related issues and disputes. The NCLT, as a specialized body, will help in improving corporate culture and facilitate mergers and acquisitions. It is also likely to expedite the process of winding-up of companies. The government, however, has yet to set up the tribunal.

These tribunals will definitely ease some pressure on regular courts. However, that may not be enough. All these tribunals cannot be a substitute for an efficient and credible judicial system, necessary to provide comfort and confidence to foreign investors.

## Labour laws

India needs to thoroughly update its labour laws, which remain predominantly socialist. At present, a manufacturing unit is required to follow up to 45 different labour laws, many of which are either redundant or completely out of touch with the liberalization and globalization paradigm.

These archaic laws often give rise to serious problems. They have skewed the production structure of the Indian manufacturing industry, which despite abundant labour, prefers to invest in labour-saving technology. The Contract Labour Act of 1970 bars companies from hiring temporary workers for their core business activities. In practical terms, such regulations impair the capacity of a company to meet any sudden spurt in demand.

The government needs to abandon redundant regulations, consolidate existing laws, improve dispute resolution and reduce unnecessary interference by the state or its agencies in business activities.

## Poor infrastructure

Physical infrastructure, which includes airports, ports, roads, rail, etc., is fairly weak and worn out in India. This is immediately apparent on arrival at any Indian airport. The road network is also poor and good highways are few. India's ports are yet to be adequately modernized. The turnaround time is high and ships have to wait for days before loading and unloading. The country also suffers from a power shortage. The problem becomes acute in summer months when the demand for power goes up.

The government is not oblivious to these problems and has taken various initiatives to improve the physical infrastructure under the public–private partnership route. It has appointed a private company to modernize Delhi Airport. The ambitious National Highway Development Project is under way and has started yielding results. Similarly, the private sector is becoming involved in the development of ports. Many private companies are participating in the generation and distribution of electricity. The sector is also engaged in the running of the goods train and the operation of container services.

Investors are also taking a keen interest in the development of infrastructure facilities in India. However, much more effort is needed to improve the physical infrastructure of a vast country like India. Although the infrastructure sector *per se* offers many opportunities for long-term investment, for entrepreneurs setting up manufacturing units, poor infrastructure is an important issue and cannot be brushed aside.

Poor infrastructure affects the productivity of the economy as a whole. It also has a telling effect on key economic parameters like GDP and per capita income. It reduces the comparative advantage of those industries that are heavily dependent on efficient infrastructure facilities for performance and growth.

## Corruption

Even though corruption is an offence under the Prevention of Corruption Act, 1988, it has become a major problem in India. Transparency International's Corruption Perceptions Index (2005) has placed India in 88th position. India, however, is generally much less corrupt than countries like Russia, the Philippines, Pakistan, Nepal, Iraq and Bangladesh according to the index.

The increase in corruption can be attributed to several factors, such as cumbersome procedure, poor computerization, excessive discretionary powers, frequent interaction between businesspeople and government officials, low wages of government employees, increasing consumerism, etc.

The government is conscious of the need to reduce corruption and has taken various initiatives in the recent past. Courts and the media have also been playing a constructive and proactive role in exposing and containing corruption. The incidence of corruption is likely to decrease in future, with government departments opting for a system of online filing of applications and granting of approvals.

# 4.2

# Business Structures

*Diljeet Titus and Garima Bhagat, Titus & Co. Advocates*

Taking advantage of the business opportunities that India offers, several Fortune 500 companies have established a presence in the country through subsidiaries, joint ventures and technical collaborations. It is now time for others, especially small and medium-sized enterprises, to join the race, follow the route that suits them the best and fruitfully tap the growing business opportunities in India.

Foreign entrepreneurs can follow one of the several investment routes to set up commercial establishments in India and take advantage of the rapidly growing economy, increasing size and purchasing power of the domestic market and widening business opportunities being offered by the country.

In addition, India's dynamic and competitive private sector accounting for over 75 per cent of the country's GDP presents to overseas entrepreneurs considerable scope for joint ventures and collaborations.

## Legal structures

A foreign company interested in doing business in India can enter the country through one of the following routes:

- open a liaison office;
- set up a branch office;
- incorporate a company under the Companies Act, 1956 through joint ventures and wholly owned subsidiaries.

## Liaison offices

Liaison offices, which act as channels of communication between the principal place of business or head office and entities in India, maintain themselves out of inward remittances received from abroad through normal banking channels.

A foreign company can set up a liaison or representative office in India after obtaining prior approval of the Reserve Bank of India (RBI) under the Foreign Exchange Management (Establishment in India of a Branch or Office or Other Place of Business) Regulations, 2000.

A liaison office can be the preferred choice when the intention of the foreign company is limited to liaising with its customers in India and to promote export and import. However, as no manufacturing, trading or any other commercial activity is allowed to form a liaison office, it can neither generate any revenue/income in India nor repatriate any money out of India except winding up proceeds after closure of the liaison office.

## *Permitted activities*

A liaison office is only permitted to undertake the following activities:

- representation of the parent company/group companies in India;
- promotion of export and import from/to India;
- promotion of technical/financial collaborations between parent/group companies and companies in India;
- acting as a communication channel between the parent company and Indian companies.

In essence, a foreign company may, with the prior approval of the RBI, set up a liaison office in India, which will be allowed to function only as a non-trading and non-revenue earning office. The option to open a liaison office is often viewed as the first step towards exploring the investment climate and business opportunities in India.

## *Tax levied*

For purposes of taxation, a liaison office is treated as a distinct taxable entity, separate from its non-Indian components. Since a liaison office cannot undertake any commercial activity, it makes no profit and therefore no corporate tax is levied on it. However, expenses of a liaison office which fall under transfer pricing regulations (ie. related party transactions) may be subjected to tax at the rate of 42.23 per cent. A liaison office may also be liable to pay tax on 'fringe benefits' provided or deemed to have been provided by the office to its employees in India. Fringe benefits include boarding and lodging expenses, travel expenses, etc., which are provided or deemed to have been provided by an employer to its employee. Fringe benefits tax is levied at the rate of 31.672 per cent (30 per cent fringe benefit tax + 2.5 per cent surcharge + 2 per cent education cess (tax) + 1 per cent secondary and higher education cess) on the value of the fringe benefits provided by a liaison office to its employees in India.

# Branch offices

An Indian branch office of a foreign company can be set up with the prior approval of the RBI under the 2000 Regulations. A branch office, as defined by Section 2(9) of the Companies Act, 1956 (CA56), in relation to a company means:

- any establishment described as a branch by the company;
- any establishment carrying on either the same or substantially the same activity as is carried on by the head office of the company;
- any establishment engaged in any production, processing or manufacture.

A branch is basically an extended arm of a foreign company and can undertake various activities on behalf of the parent company. A branch, however, is not allowed to undertake any manufacturing activity independent of the parent company. The foreign parent company is liable for all activities of its Indian branch. Due to restrictions on day-to-day operations and higher incidence of taxation, opening a branch office is not a popular route to enter India.

## *Permitted activities*

A branch office is only permitted to undertake the following activities:

- export/import of goods;
- rendering professional or consultancy services;
- carrying out research work in which the parent company is engaged;
- promoting technical or financial collaboration between Indian companies and parent or overseas group companies;
- representing the parent company in India and acting as a buying/selling agent in India;
- rendering services in information technology and development of software in India;
- rendering technical support to the products supplied by parent/group companies;
- representing a foreign airline/shipping company.

## *Tax levied*

For purposes of taxation, a branch office is treated as a distinct taxable entity, separate from its non-Indian components. Profits made in India are liable to be taxed at the rate of 42.23 per cent (40 per cent basic tax +2.5 per cent surcharge + 2 per cent education cess + 1 per cent secondary and higher education cess) for the tax year ending 31 March 2008.

# Company

Indian laws allow foreign companies to set up permanent establishments in the country in the form of companies to run business operations. When a foreign company has wider business plans and does not merely intend to establish its presence in India (through liaison or branch offices), then it would normally opt for incorporating a company in India. This allows a foreign company the flexibility to engage in different business activities in India, exercise due control over the day-to-day affairs of the company, own properties in India and repatriate returns in the form of dividends which are tax-free in the hands of shareholders.

Foreign investors can incorporate companies in India either as a wholly owned subsidiary (WOS) of the parent company (ie. 100 per cent owned and controlled by the foreign parent company) or a joint venture (JV) company along with an Indian partner. WOSs and JVs are governed by the provisions of the CA56, which was enacted half a century ago to oversee the functioning of corporations in India. The CA56 draws heavily from the Companies Act of the United Kingdom. WOSs and JVs incorporated in India are treated on a par with domestic Indian companies and are required to abide by all applicable Indian laws.

## *Types of companies*

In India, a company can be incorporated either as private or public. It can then be further classified as a limited or unlimited liability company. A company can be limited by shares or by guarantee. In the former, the personal liability of members is limited to the amount unpaid on their shares, whilst in the latter the personal liability is limited to a pre-determined amount.

The key distinguishing features of a private company and a public company are:

1. A minimum of seven shareholders (subscribers) are required to form a public company, whereas in the case of a private company only two shareholders (subscribers) can incorporate a company.
2. A private company must have a minimum paid-up capital of 100,000 Indian rupees (INR), whereas a public company must have a minimum paid-up capital of INR 500,000.
3. There is no ceiling on the number of shareholders of a public company, whereas in the case of a private company the number of shareholders cannot exceed 50. The joint holders are counted as one shareholder for this purpose.
4. A public company can invite the public to subscribe to its share capital, whereas a private company is prohibited from doing so.

5. The shares of a public company are freely transferable, whereas transfer of shares of a private company is subject to restrictions provided in its Articles of Association.
6. A public company can accept/renew deposits from the public, whereas a private company cannot accept/renew deposits, except from its members, directors or their relatives.
7. A private company can commence business immediately after incorporation but a public company cannot do so till the certificate for commencement of business is granted to it by the Registrar of Companies (RoC).

# Wholly owned subsidiaries and joint ventures

WOSs and JVs are the most sought after routes for foreign companies wanting to establish a base in India. For this, an Indian company with limited liability is incorporated in India. The liabilities of the company may be limited to Indian operations only. Depending upon the business sector, a foreign company can invest in India either under the automatic route (ie. without any regulatory approval) or under the pre-approved Foreign Investment Promotion Board (FIPB) route in terms of the government's foreign direct investment (FDI) policy.

Similarly, JVs can be set up in India subject to the regulatory framework and sectoral investment caps prescribed in the FDI policy. The equity ownership between two partners of a JVC (joint venture company) can be in the ratio of 50:50 where both parties have equal voting rights and powers, 51:49 where one of the parties has a slight voting edge and can generally resolve matters in its favour by simple majority, or 76:24 where the majority party has 'super majority', which is needed to pass special resolutions in terms of the CA56. Further, the JVs can be set up as financial collaborations (ie. equity participation) or technical collaborations wherein one of the partners supplies technology and know-how to run the business or as a combination of both financial and technical collaboration. Indian laws allow enough flexibility to foreign partners to structure their investment in the most preferred form.

The liberalized FDI policy permits foreign investment in almost all the sectors and also allows repatriation of profits in the form of dividends to the parent companies outside India. It is also possible for a parent company outside India to exercise control over the day-to-day affairs of the WOS or the JV as Indian laws allow non-residents to occupy key management positions in companies in India.

## *Procedure for incorporation*

A company can be incorporated in India by making certain prescribed filings with the relevant RoC in the state in which the company is to be incorporated.

The RoC first approves the proposed name of the company and thereafter allows incorporation of a company after approving its bylaws, ie. the Memorandum of Association and Articles of Association of the company.

The incorporation process takes around 30–45 working days. On receiving the Certificate of Incorporation (in the case of a private company) and the Certificate of Commencement of Business (in the case of a public company), the WOS or the JV (as the case may be) can commence business operations in India.

Thus, a foreign company may consider establishment of a private limited company in India as its WOS or JV since it has perpetual succession. Unlike a branch or liaison office it does not require any further approval from any other regulatory authority for its continued existence or expansion of its activities.

## Typical issues

Some of the typical issues to consider when setting up a WOS or a JV are as follows:

1. *Shareholding pattern and board constitution:* A foreign investor can structure the shareholding of a company and the composition of the board of directors within the parameters set out in the CA56. Private companies enjoy greater flexibility in terms of shareholders' rights and constitution of the board of directors in comparison to public companies.
2. *Exit mechanism:* A foreign investor must also draw up a suitable exit strategy with respect to the WOS or the JV. The exit strategy may include winding-up, transfer of shares, put and call options, reduction of share capital, etc.
3. *Governing law / jurisdiction*: Indian courts respect and honour the choice of law and jurisdiction expressly agreed between the parties. Where the parties have actually expressed their intention on a matter, their intention will be effectuated. The only limitation on this rule is that the intention of the parties must be expressed, *bona fide*, and should not be opposed to Indian public policy. However, in instances where the overriding balance of convenience and interest of justice are in favour of adjudication of dispute by an Indian court, the court will hear the suit.
4. *Dispute resolution*: The focus of a foreign investor while drafting clauses pertaining to dispute resolution should be on resolving differences through arbitration as it has a distinctive edge over the ordinary process of litigation. It is also necessary to ensure that the resulting judgement or award can be enforced in India as a decree of an Indian court. For example, a judgement is enforceable in India if it has been delivered by a superior court in a reciprocating territory[1] as recognized by the

[1] All courts in Hong Kong, Singapore, Aden, Fiji, Trinidad & Tobago, New Zealand, Papua New Guinea and Bangladesh have been notified as superior courts. In the United Kingdom, the house of Lords, Courts of Appeals, the High Court of England, the High Court of Northern Ireland, the Court of Session in Scotland, the Court of Chancery of the County Palatine of Lanchester and of Durham are notified as superior courts.

government. Similarly, a foreign arbitral award is enforceable in India if the arbitration award was delivered in a territory which is a party to, and has ratified the New York Convention of 1958 on the Recognition and Enforcement of Foreign Arbitral Awards, or the Geneva Convention of 1927 on the Execution of Foreign Arbitral Awards.

## *Tax on WOSs and JVs*

The profits earned by companies incorporated in India are subject to a lower tax rate of 33.99 per cent (including 30 per cent corporate tax +10 per cent surcharge + 2 per cent education cess + 1 per cent secondary and higher education cess) for the tax year ending 31 March 2008, in comparison to branch offices of foreign companies. In addition, companies are subject to fringe benefit tax, withholding tax, dividend distribution tax, etc., are also required to comply with other tax regulations provided in the Income Tax Act, 1961.

# 4.3

# Investment Facilities for NRIs / PIOs and Other Foreign Investors

*Diljeet Titus and Pragya Dhamija, Titus & Co. Advocates*

To attract investment from Indian people living abroad, the Indian government has over the years significantly relaxed the regulatory norms for foreign direct investment (FDI), portfolio investment and real estate investment by non-resident Indians (NRIs) and persons of Indian origin (PIOs).

India also relaxed the investment procedure for other foreign investors as part of the ongoing economic liberalization and globalization process initiated by the government about 15 years ago.

Presently, apart from the few restricted activities, India welcomes foreign investment in almost all sectors either under the "automatic route" or the "government approval route" subject to certain guidelines and investment caps. Today these sectoral investment caps too are being gradually lifted.

## NRIs/PIOs

An NRI, according to the Reserve Bank of India (RBI) guidelines, is a person who is a citizen of India but resides abroad.

As regards PIO, for the purposes of opening and maintenance of various types of bank accounts and making investment in shares and securities in India, a foreign citizen (not being a citizen of Pakistan or Bangladesh) can be a PIO if:

- he/she at any time held an Indian passport; or
- he/she or either of his/her parents or any of his/her grandparents was a citizen of India by virtue of the Constitution of India or the Citizenship Act, 1955.

- the person is a spouse of an Indian citizen (or persons referred in the earlier two categories).

For the purpose of acquisition and transfer of immovable property a PIO must not be a citizen of Sri Lanka, Afghanistan, China, Iran, Nepal or Bhutan.

## Special facilities

The Indian government offers special investment and banking facilities to NRIs/ PIOs which are as follows:

1. *Investment on repatriation basis*: The government allows NRIs/PIOs to invest in India on a repatriation as well as a non-repatriation basis. The facility to invest on a non-repatriation basis, it should be noted, is not available to other foreign investors. NRIs/PIOs as stipulated by the RBI can invest on a repatriation basis in:
   - government dated securities/treasury bills;
   - units of domestic mutual funds;
   - bonds issued by a public sector undertaking in India;
   - non-convertible debentures of a company incorporated in India;
   - shares in public sector enterprises being disinvested by the Indian government, provided the purchase is in accordance with the terms and conditions stipulated in the notice inviting bids;
   - shares and convertible debentures of Indian companies under the FDI scheme (including automatic route and Foreign Investment Promotion Board (FIPB) schemes);
   - shares and convertible debentures of Indian companies through the stock exchange under the Portfolio Investment Scheme (PIS);
   - perpetual debt instruments and debt capital instruments issued by banks in India.
2. *Investment on a non-repatriation basis:* NRIs/PIOs on a non-repatriation basis can invest into a wide variety of instruments, which include:
   - government dated securities (other than bearer securities)/treasury bills;
   - units of domestic mutual funds;
   - units of money market mutual funds in India;
   - non-convertible debentures of a company incorporated in India;
   - the capital of a partnership firm or proprietary concern in India, not engaged in any agricultural or plantation activity or real estate business;
   - deposits with a company registered under the Companies Act, 1956 including an non-bank financial company (NBFC) registered with the RBI, or a body corporate created under an act of Parliament or State Legislature, a proprietorship concern or a partnership firm;

- shares and convertible debentures of Indian companies other than under the PIS;
- commercial papers issued by an Indian company.

3. *Purchase of immovable property:* NRIs/PIOs are allowed to acquire in India immovable property other than agricultural/plantation property or a farmhouse out of repatriable or non-repatriable funds. There are no restrictions on the number of properties which an NRI/PIO can acquire and hold in India. He/she is also not required to file any document with the RBI in this regard. NRIs/PIOs can also acquire commercial or residential property by way of a gift from persons living in India or another NRI or PIO. A foreign national of non-Indian origin resident outside India cannot purchase any immovable property in India.

   An NRI is permitted to sell commercial/residential property to a person resident in India or another NRI or PIO. A PIO, however, can sell his/her property only to a resident and not to another NRI. As far as agricultural land, plantation property or farm houses are concerned, an NRI/PIO can sell/gift them only to residents.

   NRIs/PIOs are also allowed to repatriate sale proceeds of immovable property subject to certain conditions, the first being that the commercial/residential property must have been acquired by way of inward remittances through normal banking channels or by debit to a Non-Resident (External) Rupee (NRE)/Foreign Currency Non-Resident (Bank) (FCNR(B)) account. Secondly, the amount to be repatriated should not exceed the amount paid for acquisition of the property. And thirdly, the amount remitted should not exceed $1 million in a calendar year.

4. *Banking facilities for NRIs / PIOs:* The RBI allows NRIs/PIOs to open and operate the following bank accounts in India:
   - NRE account: Under the scheme, NRIs/PIOs can open authorized dealers savings account. The interest rate on these accounts is the same as paid on domestic savings deposit by Indian banks. For the NRE term deposit schemes ranging from one year to three years, the interest rates on repatriable deposits may go up to 75 basis points over LIBOR (London Interbank Offered Rate). The method for determination of interest rates will also apply to term deposits with a maturity period of more than three years. Individuals and entities from Bangladesh or Pakistan subject to prior approval of the RBI can also open an NRE account under the scheme with authorized dealers.
   - FCNR(B) account: Deposits under this account can be made with authorized dealers in six specified currencies which include the US dollar, pound sterling, euro, Japanese yen, Australian dollar and Canadian dollar. The maturity for such deposits can vary from one year to five years. The interest rates, which may either be fixed or floating, are required to be within the ceiling rate of LIBOR minus 25 basis points for respective currencies except for the Japanese yen for which the prevailing LIBOR will be the cap.

- Non-Resident Ordinary (NRO) Rupee account: Under this scheme any person resident outside India (including NRIs/PIOs) can open savings, current, recurring or fixed deposit accounts with authorized dealers. These accounts are normally operated for crediting rupee earnings/income such as dividends and interest. The current interest rate for a savings account is 3.5 per cent. The banks are free to determine interest rates for term deposits. The authorized dealers can allow remittances up to $1 million for *bona fide* purposes, per calendar year from balances in NRO accounts subject to payment of taxes.

5. *Facilities for returning NRIs / PIOs:* The RBI regulations allow returning NRIs/PIOs to continue to own and invest in foreign currency, foreign security or any immovable property situated outside India, if such investments are made from funds acquired during the stay abroad. They are also permitted to maintain with an authorized dealer in India a Resident Foreign Currency (RFC) account to transfer balances held in NRE/FCNR(B) accounts. Proceeds of assets held outside India at the time of return can also be credited to the RFC account.

## Investment routes

The government has significantly liberalized FDI policy over the years, resulting in a large increase in inflow of foreign investment into the country. High economic growth and rapidly increasing demand for quality goods and services are expected to make India an even more attractive destination for foreign investment.

Under the liberalized investment regime a foreign investor (other than a citizen/corporate entity of Pakistan or Bangladesh) has the general permission to invest in India through purchase of shares, convertible debentures or preference shares of an Indian company. These investments, however, are subject to the guidelines issued by the ministry of commerce and industry.

An investor can choose one of the following two FDI routes, depending upon the sector and size of the investment.

## The automatic route

Under the automatic route, an Indian company can issue shares/convertible debentures to a foreign company and receive inward remittances without prior approval of any agency provided the investment is within the sectoral cap prescribed by the ministry of commerce and industry.

Foreign investment in all items/activities is allowed under the automatic route except the following:

- all proposals that require an industrial licence – these include the items that can only be produced after obtaining the requisite licence under the Industries (Development & Regulation) Act, 1951;
- foreign investment of more than 24 per cent in the equity capital of units manufacturing items reserved for small-scale industries;
- all items that require an industrial licence in terms of the locational policy notified by the government under the New Industrial Policy of 1991;
- all proposals in which the foreign collaborator had a previous venture/tie-up in India;
- all proposals falling outside the notified sectoral policy/caps or under a sector in which FDI is not permitted and/or whenever any investor chooses to make an application to the Secretariat for Industrial Assistance (SIA) in the Department of Industrial Policy & Promotion within the ministry of commerce and industry for not availing the automatic route.

### *Illustrative list*

The ministry of commerce and industry provides an illustrative list of sectors which can attract FDI up to 100 per cent under the automatic route. The list is as follows:

- most manufacturing activities;
- non-banking financial services;
- drugs and pharmaceuticals;
- food processing;
- electronic hardware;
- software development;
- film industry;
- advertising;
- hospitals;
- private oil refineries;
- pollution control and management;
- exploration and mining of minerals other than diamonds and precious stones;
- management consultancy;
- venture capital funds/companies;
- setting up/development of industrial parks/model towns/special economic zones;
- petroleum products pipeline.

In the infrastructure sector, the following activities are allowed under the automatic route:

- electricity generation (except atomic energy);
- electricity transmission;

- mass rapid transport system;
- roads and highways;
- toll roads;
- vehicular bridges;
- ports and harbours;
- hotel and tourism;
- township, housing, built-up infrastructure and construction development projects.

In the services sector, the following activities are allowed under the automatic route:

- computer-related services;
- research and development services;
- construction-related engineering services;
- urban planning and landscape services;
- architectural services;
- health-related and social services;
- travel-related services;
- road transport services;
- maritime transport services;
- internal waterways services.

Furthermore, the ministry of commerce and industry reviewed the FDI policy in February 2006 and came out with Press Note 4 (2006 series), allowing 100 per cent FDI through the automatic route for the following activities:

- the distillation and brewing of potable alcohol;
- the manufacture of hazardous chemicals;
- the manufacture of industrial explosives;
- the manufacturing activities located within 25 kilometres of the standard urban area limits that require industrial licence under the Industries (Development & Regulation) Act, 1951;
- the setting up greenfield airport projects;
- the laying of natural gas/Liquefied Natural Gas (LNG) pipelines, market study and formulation;
- investment financing in the petroleum and natural gas sector;
- cash-and-carry wholesale trading and export trading;
- coal and lignite mining for captive consumption;
- the setting up of infrastructure relating to marketing in the petroleum and natural gas sector;
- the exploration and mining of diamonds and precious stones;
- power trading subject to compliance with regulations under the Electricity Act, 2003;
- the processing and warehousing of coffee and rubber.

## The government approval route

The following activities are not permitted under the automatic route and thus require government approval for FDI:

- the petroleum sector (except for private sector oil refining, natural gas/ LNG pipelines);
- investing companies in the infrastructure and services sector;
- atomic minerals;
- print media;
- broadcasting;
- postal services;
- courier services;
- the establishment and operation of satellites;
- the development of integrated townships;
- the tea sector;
- asset reconstruction companies;
- single brand retail trading.

For investment in the aforementioned activities, an investor has to approach the SIA for the necessary permission. In doubtful cases where it is not clear whether the sector is within the ambit of the automatic route, it would be advisable to obtain the approval of the SIA.

In certain sectors, FDI proposals are also required to be vetted by the concerned ministries or agencies. For instance, an investor cannot set up an insurance company without obtaining a licence from the Insurance Regulatory and Development Authority, although 26 per cent of FDI is allowed in this sector under the automatic route. Similarly, an investor in the telecommunications sector is required to obtain the approval of the Department of Telecommunications.

The foreign investment proposals which are processed in an objective and transparent manner by the SIA are usually approved within four to six weeks.

## Prohibited sectors

The sectors which are completely banned for foreign investment in India are as follows:

- chit fund companies; [1]
- Nidhi companies;[2]

[1] A chit fund company invites subscribers to contribute a fixed sum of money by way of periodical subscriptions and allows each subscriber in turn to take out the prize money through auctions or any other method .chit fund companies are governed by the provisions of the Chit Funds Act, 1982.

[2] Nidhi companies, also described as Mutual Benefit Societies by the Companies Act, 1956, enable members to save money, invest their savings in such companies and secure loans at favourable rates of interest from them

- lottery business;
- atomic energy;
- gambling and betting;
- retail trading (except single brand retailing);
- agriculture or plantation activities;
- real estate business or construction of farm houses;
- trading in transferable development rights (TDRs)

## Residual category

The government's FDI policy further provides that foreign investment in the residual category (ie. such business activities that do not fall under the automatic route, the government approval route or the prohibited sector) will be allowed without any restrictions (ie. up to 100 per cent) and approvals.

# 4.4

# Mergers and Acquisitions

*Diljeet Titus and Monica Arora, Titus & Co. Advocates*

Mergers and acquisitions (M&A) have been on an upswing in the Indian marketplace, with the country witnessing a significant increase in the number of deals in the recent past. Indeed, the unleashing of the economy makes India one of the most sought after markets for global M&A. There have been major M&A deals in a wide range of sectors including telecommunications, fast moving consumer goods (FMCGs), cement and building materials, oil and gas, automotive, pharmaceuticals and healthcare, etc.

M&A are considered to be well accepted growth strategies adopted by companies seeking to achieve economies of scale, increase the market share, diversify the product range and explore new markets. Other considerations for M&A include backward/forward integration of operations, access to tax advantages, managerial talent, additional financing, research and development capabilities, and the ability to compete favourably.

A merger (also referred to as an amalgamation in this chapter), in the Indian context, comes under the wide ambit of an 'arrangement' in terms of which the share capital of a company is reorganized by an amalgamation of two or more companies. There may be an amalgamation either by the transfer of two or more companies to a new company or by the transfer of one or more undertakings to an existing company. Pursuant to the amalgamation, the transferor company ceases to have an identity and the rights and liabilities are amalgamated in the transferee company. Acquisition, on the other hand, is the purchase of assets or controlling interest in the share capital of an existing company by another existing company.

This chapter primarily focuses only on legal and regulatory considerations for M&A in India.

## Mergers and amalgamations

An amalgamation is regulated by the Companies Act, 1956, and the Company (Court) Rules, 1959 (Rules). A company may merge with another corporate body, whether an Indian company or not, provided the surviving entity of the merger is a company within the meaning of the CA56. A scheme of amalgamation requires the sanction of the High Court (Court). The process to obtain the approval of the Court under the CA56 and the Rules is as follows.

## Application to the Court for convening meetings of members/creditors

After preparing the scheme of amalgamation, an application is made to the Court seeking directions for convening meetings of the members (or any class of them) and/or creditors (or any class of them) of the company to consider and approve the proposal. The application may be made by the company or any creditor or member of the company. Separate applications by way of judge's summons are required to be made by the amalgamating companies to the Court. If the registered offices of the amalgamating companies are situated in the same state/territory over which the same Court has territorial jurisdiction, then one company may file an application and join the other company as a party since there is an identity of interest between the transferor company and the transferee company. A joint application may also be filed. Notice of the application is required to be given to the regional director. The Court is also expected to take into consideration the representations, if any, made by the regional director, before passing an order.

## Members and creditors' meeting

On hearing the application, the Court may:

1. pass an order directing the amalgamating companies to convene separate meetings of their respective members (or class thereof) and/or creditors (or class thereof), on the date, time, venue and quorum fixed for the meetings by the Court; and
2. appoint chairpersons to preside over the meetings.

Notices of the meetings of members and creditors are required to be advertised in such newspapers and in such manner as the Court may direct, but not less than 21 days before the date fixed for the meetings.

At these meetings, the scheme of amalgamation should be approved by the requisite majority.[1] Pursuant to the meetings, the chairperson of each meeting is required to file his/her report within the time stipulated by the High Court or if no time is stipulated, within a period of seven days from the

[1] The requisite majority is three-quarters in value of the creditors, or class of creditors, or members, or class of members (as the case may be), present and voting either in person or, where proxies are allowed, by proxy, at the meeting.

date of the meeting. Within seven days of the filing of the report by the chairperson, each company is required to file with the concerned Registrar of Companies (RoC) resolutions passed at the meeting of its members approving the scheme of amalgamation.

## Final petition for confirmation of scheme of amalgamation

Within seven days of the submission of the chairperson's report, a final petition should be filed with the Court to confirm the scheme of amalgamation, and to request the appropriate orders and directions under Section 394 of the CA56. The Court will fix a date for hearing the petition, and notice of the hearing will be required to be advertised in the same newspaper(s) in which the notice for the calling of the meeting of members and creditors was published. This should be done not less than 10 days before the date fixed for the hearing.

Whilst considering the scheme of amalgamation, the Court must be satisfied that the applicant has disclosed to the Court by affidavit all material facts relating to the company, such as the latest financial position of the company, the pendency of any investigation proceedings by the Company Law Board (CLB) in relation to the company under certain provisions of the CA56. In addition, the Court must be satisfied, among other things, that:

- the scheme submitted for approval by the Court is backed by the requisite majority vote;
- the amalgamation scheme does not violate any provisions of law or is contrary to public policy and the scheme is fair, just and reasonable as a commercial proposition;
- the share exchange ratio is just, proper, and beneficial to the interests of the shareholders.

Once the aforesaid parameters are met and if the Court receives no adverse representation from the regional director, the Court may sanction the scheme and pass such orders and directions for the proper implementation of the scheme. This includes the transfer of property or liabilities of one company to another (not including the power to enforce the transfer of contracts of service or of the rights, duties or powers of an executor), the dissolution of the transferor company without the procedure of winding-up, and the allotment of shares, debentures or other like interests, etc.

Thereafter, the amalgamating companies would be required to file the order(s) of the Court sanctioning the scheme of amalgamation with the RoC having jurisdictions over their respective registered offices within 30 days. Upon filing with the RoC, the order of the Court becomes effective and legally binding.

An order of the Court sanctioning a scheme of amalgamation, being in effect a conveyance, is an instrument liable to stamp duty, the amount of which varies from state to state.

# Acquisitions

Acquisitions may either be in the form of acquisition of shares or acquisition of assets. As acquisition of assets involves complexities and payment of stamp duty, companies usually prefer to acquire a company by acquiring its shares.

## Foreign Investment Promotion Board and Reserve Bank approvals

As per the government's recent policy on foreign direct investment (FDI), a proposal for the acquisition of shares of an existing Indian company by a foreign company will neither require the prior approval of the Foreign Investment Promotion Board (FIPB) nor the Reserve Bank of India (RBI) in sectors other than financial services (ie. banks, non-banking financial services and insurance), provided the following conditions are satisfied:

1. The activities of the investee company are under the automatic route of the FDI policy and do not attract the provisions of the Securities and Exchange Board of India (SEBI) (Substantial Acquisition of Shares and Takeovers) Regulations, 1997 (Takeover Regulations).
2. The non-resident shareholding, after the transfer, complies with sectoral limits under FDI policy.
3. The price at which the transfer takes place is in accordance with the pricing guidelines prescribed by SEBI/RBI.

The onus of complying with the foregoing conditions lies both with the resident seller and the non-resident buyer.

The RBI further provides that the price at which shares can be acquired by a foreign company from a resident shareholder must not be less than:

- the ruling market price in the case the shares are listed on stock exchange;
- the fair valuation of shares done by a chartered accountant as per the guidelines issued by the controller of capital issues in the case of unlisted shares.

If the price of the acquisition of shares is less than the pricing guidelines described above, the parties will have to obtain the prior approval of the RBI, justifying the deviation from the pricing guidelines.

However, in terms of the Foreign Exchange Management (Transfer or Issue of a Security by a Person Resident outside India) Regulations, 2000 (Regulations), FIPB approval is not required for sale and transfer of shares of an Indian company by a person resident outside India to another person resident outside India. This facility is subject to the condition that the transferee does not have a previous venture or investment in India in shares or debentures or a technical collaboration or trademark agreement in the same field in which the Indian company whose shares are being acquired is engaged. Two companies are said to be engaged in the 'same field' if their activities fall under the same four-digit National Industrial Classification Code (NIC) of 1987.

## Compliance with the SEBI Act, 1992

Acquisition of the shares of a listed company (target company) will attract the provisions of the SEBI's Takeover Regulations, which have been recently amended to facilitate M&A transactions in India. The highlights of applicable Takeover Regulations are discussed below:

1. Acquisition of more than 5 per cent, 10 per cent, 14 per cent, 54 per cent or 74 per cent shareholding or voting rights: when an acquirer acquires shares or voting rights which (taken together with shares or voting rights if any already held by him/her) would entitle him/her to exercise more than 5 per cent, 10 per cent, 14 per cent, 54 per cent or 74 per cent shares or voting rights in a company, the acquirer is required to disclose at every stage of the acquisition the aggregate of its shareholding or voting rights in the target company to the target company and the stock exchanges where the shares of the target company are listed.
2. Acquisition of 15 per cent or more shareholding or voting rights: when an acquirer acquires shares or voting rights which (taken together with shares or voting rights if any already held by him/her or by persons acting in concert with him/her) would entitle him/her to exercise 15 per cent or more of voting rights in a company, the acquirer is required to make a public offer (ie. to purchase shares of a minimum 20 per cent of the voting share capital of the target company from members of the public) to acquire shares.
3. Consolidation of holding: under this stipulation, no acquirer who (together with persons acting in concert with him/her) has acquired 15 per cent or more but less than 55 per cent of shares or voting rights in a company will acquire additional shares/voting rights entitling him/her to exercise more than 5 per cent of the voting rights in any financial year ending on 31 March, unless he/she makes a public announcement to acquire shares. It has been further stipulated that an acquirer who (together with persons acting in concert) has acquired 55 per cent or more but less than 75 per cent of shares or voting rights in a target

company may acquire additional shares or voting rights without making a public announcement to acquire shares.

The public announcement of the offer by an acquirer broadly involves the following steps:

1. appoint a Category I merchant banker[1] registered with the SEBI;
2. make a public announcement of an offer (containing, *inter alia*, details of the minimum offer price) through the merchant banker (in one English language national daily newspaper and one Hindi national daily newspaper and one regional language daily newspaper with wide circulation, at the place where the registered office of the target company is situated and at the place of the stock exchange where the shares of the target company are most frequently traded) within four working days of the acquirer entering into the agreement for the purchase of shares of the target company;
3. send a copy of the public announcement to the SEBI through the merchant banker and to all the stock exchanges where the target company is listed;
4. submit a draft letter of the offer to acquire shares of the target company to the SEBI through the merchant banker within 14 days of the date of the public announcement;
5. send the offer letter to all shareholders of the target company not earlier than 21 days from submission of the draft letter to the SEBI.

The offer will be opened not later than 55 days from the date of the public announcement and will remain open for a period of 20 days. The acquirer can acquire the shares of the target company if no other offers are received during the period the offer remains open. If other offers are received from the public, then in addition to the shares proposed to be acquired, the acquirer would be required to purchase shares from the public (which may be up to the minimum offer of 20 per cent of the voting shares of the target company depending on the percentage of offers received from the public).

## Stamp duty

Acquisition of shares attracts payment of stamp duty under the Indian Stamp Act, 1899, or the applicable state stamp Acts. However, if the shares to be transferred are dematerialized before the transfer, the stamp duty can be avoided, since the stamp duty is not payable on transfer of shares in a dematerialized form.

[1] There are four categories of Merchant Bankers depending upon net worth. Category I is the highest category. A Category I Merchant Banker, with a minimum net worth of 50 million rupees, is permitted to perform all functions relating to the management of an issue.

## Role of the Competition Commission

The Competition Act, 2002[1] provides a regulatory framework with respect to competition and prescribes creation of the Competition Commission for implementation of the CA2002. The CA2002 lays down detailed conditions with respect to regulation of combinations and the circumstances in which a merger or acquisition would constitute a combination of enterprises. These conditions include value of assets, turnover of enterprises, etc.

Once the Competition Commission fully comes into operation, parties involved in a merger or acquisition would be required to give notice to the Commission about the existence of a combination and disclose the details of the proposed combination. After all the provisions of the Competition Commission are met, it would investigate the effect of the combination on competition in terms of the provisions of the CA2002 and require the parties to show cause if the combination is likely to cause or has caused an appreciable adverse effect on competition within the relevant market in India. The Competition Commission may also, upon its own knowledge or information relating to a merger or acquisition, inquire into whether such a combination will cause an appreciable adverse effect on competition in India.

[1] As the government has not notified all provisions of the Competition Act, 2002, the legislation at present is only partly operational.

# 4.5

# Employment Issues

*Diljeet Titus and Nishant Malhotra, Titus & Co. Advocates*

The Indian labour laws and practice over the years have evolved to adjust to the forces of liberalization and globalization. The Indian workforce has also matured with time and is not oblivious to the ongoing economic reforms programme. In any case, most of the labour laws do not apply to multinational corporations because they usually offer better salaries and working conditions than those prescribed by the statutes. They can also regulate the terms of employment through a carefully drafted employment contract which should include salary, code of conduct, terms of services, etc. Foreign investors, in practice, can enjoy greater flexibility in terms of the hiring of employees.

Although the labour reforms in India have failed to keep pace with the reforms in other sectors of the economy, industrial strikes have come down significantly after the initiation of the economic reforms programme in 1991, reflecting a marked improvement in the industrial climate over the years.Trade unions in India are not as militant as they used to be in the past, mainly because the post-liberalization workforce, by and large, wants to profit from reforms and not confront them.

## Labour legislation

As far as the Indian labour laws are concerned, they were designed primarily to protect the interest of the working class without discouraging industrialization. These laws were aimed at bringing about harmony between employees and employers, with a view to accelerating the growth of the economy in general and industry in particular.

The Indian labour laws encompass a whole gamut of social welfare legislation involving issues relating to employment – the rights of an employee, industrial and labour disputes, social security and social insurance, trade unions, general welfare of employees, working conditions, working hours and leave, minimum wages, provident fund, insurance, gratuity, bonuses and maternity benefits. These labour laws not only describe the rights and entitlements of an employee but also lay down various obligations for employers. These obligations include registration of a factory or establishment, making prescribed filings with the concerned labour authorities and maintaining different types of registers, records and returns concerning the employees. Any failure to comply with such obligations exposes the responsible director or officer of the factory or establishment to certain liabilities, which may be in the form of monetary fines or imprisonment, depending upon the nature and extent of non-compliance.

These laws seek to achieve industrial amity by providing for conciliation of disputes between employees and employers. As per the provisions of the statutes, the state can refer the unresolved disputes between employees and employer to tribunals for adjudication. To encourage resolution of disputes in an amicable fashion, it has also been provided that stoppage of work, after a reference has been made by the state to the tribunal, would be illegal. These provisions have helped in arresting the growth of industrial unrest and enhancing a sense of security among entrepreneurs (see Table 1).

Table 1. Industrial action (1999–2006)

| *Year* | *Number* | *Strikes*<br>*Man days lost (in million)* |
|---|---|---|
| 1999 | 540 | 10.62 |
| 2000 | 426 | 11.95 |
| 2001 | 372 | 5.56 |
| 2002 | 295 | 9.66 |
| 2003 | 255 | 3.21 |
| 2004 | | |
| 2005 | | |
| 2006 (Jan–Sep) (P) | | |

P- Provisional
Source: *Economy Survey 2006-07*, government of India publication

These laws are also aimed at preventing exploitation and oppression of labour by employers. The applicability of these labour laws primarily depends on the number of employees working in a factory or establishment. However, there are certain labour laws, like the Employees' State Insurance Act, 1948, and Employees' Provident Funds and Miscellaneous Provision Act, 1952, which, once triggered, continue to apply to a factory even though the number of employees falls below the specified limit or until such time as the factory is closed down by the employer. The salient features and relevant issues involved in various Indian labour legislation is discussed below.

# Industrial Disputes Act, 1947

The Industrial Disputes Act (IDA), 1947, was enacted to secure industrial peace and harmony by providing a mechanism for investigation and settlement of industrial disputes through collective bargaining agreements, conciliation and arbitration. An employer is required to comply with the provisions of IDA, irrespective of the number of workers employed, ie. even in the case of a single employee the IDA will apply.

The IDA provides a mechanism for investigation and settlement of industrial disputes without resorting to strikes and lock-outs. It also contains provisions for safeguarding the interest of the workforce as well as employers, with the overall objective of maintaining industrial satisfaction.

It defines 'industrial dispute' as any dispute or difference between employers and employers, or between employers and employees, or between employees and employees that is connected with the employment or non-employment or the terms of employment or the condition of labour of any person. An industrial dispute is said to have arisen when some demand is made by a considerable section of employees and is rejected by the management, or *vice versa*. Certain individual disputes relating to dismissal, discharge, retrenchment or termination of services of an employee are also covered under the IDA.

An employee will be said to be a 'workman' under the IDA if he/she is employed to do any manual, unskilled, skilled, technical, operational, clerical or supervisory work for hire or reward. However, this does not include a person who is employed mainly in a managerial or administrative capacity, or who, being employed in a supervisory capacity, draws wages exceeding 1,600 Indian rupees per month (approximately $40) or exercises functions mainly of a managerial nature.

Pursuant to the IDA, where the employer and the workmen fail to arrive at a settlement through negotiations, the Conciliation Officer intervenes as a mediator to reconcile the difference of opinion and help the workmen and employer reach a successful settlement. Accordingly, where a settlement is arrived at between the employer and its workmen as a result of conciliation proceedings, the memorandum of settlement becomes binding on both the employer and the workmen.

IDA also provides for a referral of the industrial dispute to arbitration by a written agreement between the employer and the workmen at any time before the dispute has been referred to a Labour Court or Tribunal.

However, where an industrial dispute is not settled by negotiations or conciliation, and the workmen and the employer do not agree to refer the industrial dispute to arbitration, the state government can refer the dispute to the Labour Court or the Industrial Tribunal for adjudication. The award of the Labour Court or the Industrial Tribunal is binding on both the employer and the workmen and the award is not subject to any further appeals. However, a writ petition before the High Court and thereafter an appeal before the Supreme Court of India can be filed to challenge the award of the Labour Court.

### *Retrenchment*

Retrenchment refers to termination of services of a workman by an employer, for any reason apart from punishment/disciplinary action. Retrenchment does not cover the following:

- voluntary retirement;
- retirement on reaching the age of superannuation;
- termination as a result of non-renewal of contract of employment;
- termination due to continued ill health.

A workman who has been in continuous service for at least one year can be retrenched when certain specified conditions are fulfilled, such as:

- one month's written notice of retrenchment with reasons has been given, or the employee is paid wages in lieu of the period of notice;
- he/she is paid compensation equivalent to 15 days' average pay for every completed year of service or any part of it exceeding six months;
- notice has been served on the appropriate government.

In case of retrenchment, it would be obligatory for the employer to follow the rule of 'last in first out', which means that the employer would retrench the person last employed in that category, unless there is an agreement to the contrary or on grounds of inefficiency, unreliability or habitual irregularity. The employer, however, will have to prove the existence of such valid reasons in the tribunal or court if the retrenchment is challenged by the retrenched workman. However, with respect to the non-workmen category of employees, an employer can follow the 'hire and fire' rule in accordance with the provisions of the employment agreement entered into with the employee.

## Factories Act, 1948

The Factories Act (FA), 1948, is applicable to all 'factories'. A 'factory' has been defined to mean any premises including the precincts thereof:

1. wherein 10 or more workers are employed on any day of the preceding 12 months and a manufacturing process is carried on with the aid of power; or
2. wherein 20 or more workers are employed on any day of the preceding 12 months and the manufacturing process is carried on without the aid of power.

The FA will thus become applicable to every employer if 20 or more persons are employed. Every employee of the factory will be entitled to the benefits under the FA, once the FA becomes applicable to the factory. The FA places an obligation on the occupier of a factory to ensure the safety and welfare of workers whilst they are working in the factory.

# Trade Unions Act, 1926

The Trade Unions Act (TUA), 1926, provides for the registration of trade unions (including the association of employers) with a view to rendering the lawful organization of labour to enable collective bargaining. It also enshrines the main objects behind establishment of trade unions in India, ie. to regulate the relation between workmen and employer, or between employer and employer, or between workmen and workmen, and imposing restrictive conditions on the conduct of any trade or business. It also provides for various checks on rampant trade unionism. There is also a provision for registration of trade unions. It is effectively controlled by the state governments, which are required to deal with everyday problems and industrial unrest.

# Payment of Bonus Act, 1965

The Payment of Bonus Act (PBA), 1965, applies to all factories and establishments in which 20 or more persons are employed on any day during an accounting year. It entitles all eligible employees to receive a minimum bonus of 8.33 per cent (linked with profits or productivity) from his/her employer in an accounting year.

The bonus has to be paid annually within eight months of the close of the accounting year by an establishment. The establishment is also required to prepare a balance sheet and profit and loss account of the year and calculate the 'gross profit', 'available surplus' and 'allocable surplus' as per the method and formula given in the PBA.

# Shops and Establishments Act

The Shops and Establishments Acts (SEAs) are state laws and every state or union territory has enacted its own SEA and has framed the rules for its enforcement. A typical SEA covers all establishments irrespective of the size, turnover and persons employed and applies to all persons employed, whether directly or through an agency or contractor, and whether for wages or not, in or about the business of an establishment, including the apprentices. It prescribes guidelines with respect to working hours, working conditions, overtime, leave, maintenance of records, etc.

## Equal Remuneration Act, 1976

Under the Equal Remuneration Act (ERA), 1976, remuneration is defined as the basic wage or salary and also includes payments in kind. To provide an equal field for all workers, including those in the informal sector, the ERA requires employers to pay all workers remuneration (whether in cash or kind) which is not less than the amount paid to workers of the opposite sex employed to perform the same or similar work. The ERA also seeks to do away with discrimination against employees working in similar conditions. Being supported by penal provisions and checks in the form of inspectors with powers of entry, examination of workers and inspection of registers, the ERA is a potent weapon against discrimination among employees.

## Employees' State Insurance Act, 1948

The main objective of the Employees' State Insurance Act (ESIA), 1948, is to provide workers medical relief, sickness cash benefits, maternity benefits to women workers, pensions to the dependants of the deceased workmen and compensation for fatal and other employment injuries including occupational diseases through a contributory fund. However, if the ESIA is applicable to an establishment, the provisions of the Workmen Compensation Act, 1923, and Maternity Benefit Act, 1961, will not apply.

## Minimum Wages Act, 1948

The Minimum Wages Act (MWA), 1948, was enacted with a view to providing minimum statutory wages for scheduled employment and obviating the chances of exploitation of labour through payment of low wages. The term 'wage' under the MWA includes all remunerations capable of being expressed in terms of money, house rent allowance, etc., but it does not include the payment made towards provident funds or insurance funds. The state government is empowered to fix minimum rates of wages for different classes of employees – skilled, unskilled, clerical, supervisory, etc. – employed in any scheduled employment which is to be reviewed and revised from time to time.

## Payment of Gratuity Act, 1972

Gratuity is a sort of award that an employer pays out of his/her gratitude to an employee for his/her long and meritorious services, at the time of his/her retirement or termination of his/her services. The gratuity is also payable on resignation or death. Normally a gratuity is paid after five years of continuous service. The five-year condition does not apply in case of death and disability. For every year of completed service, an employee becomes entitled to 15 days of wages as gratuity. The wage last drawn is taken into consideration whilst computing the amount of gratuity.

## Workmen's Compensation Act, 1923

The Workmen's Compensation Act (WCA), 1923, entitles every workman (including those employed through a contractor, but excluding casual employees) and/or their dependants, engaged for the purpose of the business of a company, compensation for suffering an injury in any accident arising out of and in the course of his/her employment. The WCA applies to railways and other transport establishments, factories, establishments engaged in making, altering, repairing, adapting, transport or sale of any article, mines, docks, establishments engaged in construction, the fire brigade, plantations, oilfields, etc.

## Maternity Benefit Act, 1961

The Maternity Benefit Act (MBA), 1961, is applicable where 10 or more persons are employed or were employed on any day of the preceding 12 months. There is neither a wage ceiling for coverage under the MBA nor is there any restriction as regards the type of work a woman is engaged in. Every woman employee, whether employed directly or through a contractor, will be entitled to the benefits of the MBA if she has actually worked for a period of at least 80 days during the 12 months immediately preceding the date of her expected delivery.

## Industrial Employment (Standing Orders) Act, 1946

The objective of the Industrial Employment (Standing Orders) Act (IESOA), 1946, is to define 'service rules' or 'service conditions' for workmen. It requires employers of certain industrial establishments to clearly define, with sufficient precision, the conditions of employment, ie. standing orders or service rules, and to make them known to the workmen employed by them. It also provides for punishment of workmen in a disciplinary action if the act committed by him/her is defined as misconduct, under the standing orders.

# Employees' Provident Fund and Miscellaneous Provisions Act, 1952

The Employees' Provident Fund and Miscellaneous Provisions Act (EPFMPA), 1952, is a central piece of legislation instituting a compulsory contributory fund under various schemes *vis-à-vis* the Employees' Provident Funds Scheme, 1952, Employees' Pension Scheme, 1995, and Employees' Deposit-Linked Insurance Scheme, 1976, and is applicable to every establishment that is a factory employing 20 or more persons.

# 4.6

# Export and Import Issues

*Diljeet Titus and Achint Singh Gyani, Titus & Co. Advocates*

Foreign investors can take advantage of various trade facilitation measures and initiatives undertaken by the ministry of commerce and industry to set up manufacturing units in software technology parks (STPs) and special economic zones (SEZs) to service the growing domestic market and feed the global market. Moreover, an increasing number of free trade agreements and preferential trade pacts that the country has signed or is in the process of signing will open greater business and trade opportunities for foreign entrepreneurs to have manufacturing bases in India.

As the world's second most populous country, India offers vast trading opportunities to global entrepreneurs who can come here to set up manufacturing units and feed the growing domestic market. This, however, is only one part of the unfolding Indian story. More significant is that the country is making sincere and serious efforts to become a manufacturing hub for global exports. The government is seeking to achieve this objective by implementing the SEZ policy on a large scale.

The government, after much debate and discussion, operationalized the policy by introducing the SEZ Rules on 10 February 2006. The policy evoked good response from public and private sector companies, and foreign companies and investors. One of the reasons for this unprecedented response is that the units in the SEZs will also be allowed to sell their products in the Domestic Tariff Area (DTA) after payment of the requisite custom duty. Thus, an entrepreneur in an SEZ can look forward to better infrastructure, less red tape and the global market (including the growing Indian market).

India has already signed free trade agreements with several countries, including Thailand, Sri Lanka and Singapore, and is proposing to have more such pacts with other nations and groupings like the Association of South East Asian Nations (ASEAN) and the European Union (EU). These agreements will open doors wider for entrepreneurs setting up units in India, either in SEZs or on the mainland.

More importantly for India, the SEZ policy, in addition to providing positive business opportunities for domestic and global entrepreneurs, will help the country in generating additional employment, creating more wealth and reducing poverty at a faster pace.

## Indian exports

Indian exports have grown steadily since the onset of the economic liberalization programme in 1991. The opening of the economy has helped India in overcoming impediments that used to hamper export efforts in the past. Indian exporters now have more freedom to import raw material, procure capital at competitive rates from domestic and international markets and concentrate on core business activities. India's exports have risen to a record level across all major commodity groups and destinations during 2005–2006 and the trend is still continuing during this current financial year. Exports crossed the landmark figure of $100 billion to reach $103 billion in the year 2005–2006. During the financial year 2006–2007 exports are estimated to have reached $125 billion. A number of commodities have witnessed very high growth rates across diverse sectors and destinations during 2006–2007. The export of petroleum products went up by 93.4 per cent, coffee 33.86 per cent, carpets 13.93 per cent, engineering goods 44.34 per cent, basic chemicals, pharmaceuticals and cosmetics 22.22 per cent, processed food 25.24 per cent, textiles 10.2 per cent, spices 36.82 per cent and agricultural and allied products 25.29 per cent.

## Foreign trade policy

The Export-Import (EXIM) Policy, as it used to be known, is prepared by the ministry of commerce and industry and lays down the ground rules for the development of foreign trade. It was later re-named the Foreign Trade Policy (FTP) by current Minister of Commerce and Industry, Kamal Nath. The policy is important because it spells out various export promotion schemes and provides a direction to the country's trade. Although the FTP has a life span of five years, it is modified by the ministry of commerce and industry every year through annual supplements. This annual exercise helps the ministry of commerce and industry to take stock of the country's trade and respond to unforeseen developments.

The country's first FTP (2004–2009) was announced by the minister of commerce and industry in 2004. It was formulated with the objective of:

- doubling India's percentage share in global merchandise trade within a period of five years;
- using trade as an effective instrument of economic growth by giving a boost to employment generation.

The ministry of commerce and industry has been trying to achieve these objectives through policy initiatives announced from time to time. The important initiatives and the various export promotion schemes are discussed in the following paragraphs.

# Special economic zones

The SEZ Policy, which came into effect with the introduction of the SEZ Rules in February 2006, seeks to provide significant and sizeable tax benefits, a duty-free environment and a single window clearance mechanism to domestic and foreign entrepreneurs interested in participating in the scheme. The fundamental objective of the SEZ Policy is to create an internationally competitive and stress-free environment for the production of goods and services for exports. The SEZs are also expected to attract foreign direct investment (FDI), facilitate transfer and infusion of technology and generate employment.

The concept of SEZs is not a new one and can be traced back to the EXIM Policy 2000. It took almost six years for the government to formulate a comprehensive SEZ policy, frame laws, get them approved by parliament and finally operationalize the scheme.

The SEZs are primarily enclaves of units operating in well defined areas within the geographical boundary of a country where certain economic activities are promoted by a set of policy measures that are not generally applicable to the rest of the country. In addition, SEZs offer high quality infrastructure and other facilities for duty-free import of capital goods and raw material.

The government has made the SEZ Policy attractive for domestic as well as foreign investors by offering liberal and long-term tax incentives to the developers of the SEZs and the units to be located in those zones. Under the Income Tax Act, 1961 (ITA), a SEZ unit can avail several tax exemptions right from the stage of development of the SEZ up to the point when it begins to earn profits.

Multinational companies have begun to pour in sizeable investments in SEZs. The government has recently cleared the proposal of Reliance Industries to set up three zones covering an area of 345 hectares for biotechnology, light engineering and pharmaceuticals. The government has so far cleared 400 SEZ proposals from different companies and many more are in the pipeline.

# Export oriented units

An exporter undertaking to export the entire production of goods and services (except the sale allowed in the DTA) may set up a unit under the Export Oriented Unit (EOU) Scheme, the Electronic Hardware Technology

Park (EHTP) Scheme, the Software Technology Park (STP) Scheme or the Bio-Technology Park (BTP) Scheme. Units set up under these schemes are allowed to import or procure from DTA all types of essential goods without payment of duty. These units are also allowed duty free import of capital goods without any regard to the age of plants and machinery.

The units set up under the schemes have been extended various fiscal incentives which include exemption from payment of income tax as per the provisions of Sections 10A and 10B of the ITA and freedom to manufacture items reserved for small-scale industries. The units can also benefit from other facilities like permission to retain entire export earnings in the Exchange Earner's Foreign Currency (EEFC) Account and 100 per cent FDI through the automatic route. A unit set up under any of the schemes is not required to furnish bank guarantees at the time of import or go for job work in the DTA provided it has a turnover of 50 million Indian rupees (INR) or more, has been in existence for at least three years and has an unblemished track record.

## Advance Authorization Scheme

The ministry of commerce and industry operates an Advance Authorization Scheme (previously known as the Advance Licence Scheme) under which exporters can procure inputs from abroad without payment of duty. These inputs are required to be physically incorporated into products to be exported. The exporters procuring goods under the scheme are exempted from payment of basic customs duty, additional customs duty, education cess, anti-dumping duty and safeguard duty.

The Advance Authorization for duty-free import is issued on the basis of the standard input/output norms, which are announced by the Director General of Foreign Trade (DGFT). The authorization can also be issued on the basis of ad hoc norms or self-declared norms. It can also be issued either to a manufacturer-exporter or merchandise-exporter tied to supporting manufacturers:

- for physical exports (including exports to SEZs);
- for intermediate supplies;
- to the main contractor for supply of goods;
- to the supply stores on board to outgoing vessels/aircraft, subject to certain conditions.

The advance authorization and the materials imported under the scheme are not transferable, even after the completion of export obligation. The authorization holder, however, has been given the option to dispose of the product manufactured out of the duty-free inputs once the export obligation is completed.

The exporters importing goods under the Advance Authorization Scheme are required to fulfil export obligations prescribed in the Handbook of Procedures.

## Importing in small quantities

Export production requires the use of many inputs in small quantities. Even though such inputs are allowed for import without payment of customs duty under the Advance Authorization Scheme, exporters generally do not import them due to lack of economies of scale and often source them locally at a higher price. The existing Duty Exemption Schemes have been of little help in such cases because of design limitations. The government therefore modified the procedure for such imports by clubbing together the salient features of the Advance Authorization Scheme (which allows imports of inputs before exports) and Duty Free Replenishment Certificate (which allows transfer of import entitlements) into a new scheme called the Duty Free Import Authorization Scheme.

The current scheme offers the facility for import of the required inputs before exports and allows the transfer of scrips once the export obligation is complete. The new scheme came into effect from 1 May 2006.

## Export Promotion Capital Goods Scheme

The Export Promotion Capital Goods (EPCG) Scheme allows exporters to import capital goods for pre-production, production and post-production at 5 per cent customs duty, subject to some export obligation, which varies for different units. For instance, for agro units, import of capital goods at 5 per cent customs duty is allowed, subject to fulfilment of an export obligation equivalent to six times the duty saved over a period of 12 years from the date of issue of authorization. For small-scale industrial units, import of capital goods at 5 per cent customs duty is allowed, subject to fulfilment of export obligation equivalent to six times the duty saved over a period of eight years from the date of the issue of the authorization.

## Duty Entitlement Passbook Scheme

The Duty Entitlement Passbook (DEPB) Scheme provides for neutralization of the incidence of customs duty on the import content of the export product, which is extended through grant of duty credit against the export.

Under the scheme, an exporter is allowed to apply for credit, as a specified percentage of the free on board (FOB) value of exports, made in convertible currency or the payment made from the foreign currency account of the SEZ unit in the case of supply by the DTA to SEZ unit. The credit is availed against such export products and at such rates as may be specified by the DGFT for the import of raw material, intermediates, components, parts, packaging material, etc. The credit can also be utilized by exporters for payment of customs duty on any item which is freely importable.

The ministry of commerce and industry is proposing to replace the DEPB with another scheme, as the former is not considered as World Trade Organization (WTO) compatible. However, the existing scheme will continue until the government finalizes an alternative scheme.

# Starred Export Houses

In a bid to encourage exports, the ministry of commerce and industry accords special treatment to exporters who achieve a certain threshold. The exporters are given the status of One Star Export House to Five Star Export House, depending upon the total FOB export performance during the current, plus the previous three years. The threshold limit for qualifying as the One Star Export House is INR 150 million, Two Star Export House INR 1 billion, Three Star Export House INR 5 billion rupees, Four Star Export House INR 15 billion and Five Star Export House INR 50 billion.

Merchants, manufacturer exporters, service providers, EOUs, units located in SEZs, Agri Export Zones (AEZs), EHTPs, STPs and BTPs are eligible to apply for status as Starred Export Houses.

The Starred Export Houses are eligible for the following privileges:

- authorization/licence/certificate/permission and customs clearances for both imports and exports on a self-declaration basis;
- fixation of input-output norms on a priority basis;
- exemption from compulsory negotiation of documents through banks; the remittance, however, would continue to be received through banking channels;
- 100 per cent retention of foreign exchange in the Exchange Earner's Foreign Currency Account;
- exemption from furnishing of a bank guarantee in schemes under the policy;
- Two Star Export Houses and above are permitted to establish export warehouses, as per the Department of Revenue guidelines.

# Focus Market Scheme

The Focus Market Scheme is aimed at increasing penetration of India's exports in new markets, which had remained neglected because of high freight cost and an undeveloped network. The aim of this scheme is to neutralize the disabilities that prevent exporters from approaching certain important markets.

The Focus Market Scheme is primarily aimed at tapping and enlarging India's share in markets in Latin America and Africa. Under the scheme, an exporter is allowed a duty credit facility at 2.5 per cent of the FOB value of exports on all products to listed countries.

## Focus Product Scheme

The Focus Product Scheme is aimed at giving a boost to the manufacture and export of certain industrial products which could generate larger number of jobs per unit of investment compared to other products.

As far as benefits are concerned, under the Focus Product Scheme an exporter is allowed a duty-credit facility at 2.5 per cent of the FOB value of exports on 50 per cent of the export turnover of specified products, such as leather goods, stationery items, fireworks, sports goods and toys, and handloom and handicraft items.

# 4.7

# Intellectual Property Law

*Diljeet Titus and Manish Gupta, Titus & Co. Advocates*

Following global trends India updated its laws to safeguard investment in intangible property involving intellectual endeavour. India's Trade Related Aspects of Intellectual Property Rights (TRIPS) compliant Trade Marks Act, Copyright Act, Patents Act, Designs Act and other statutes provide adequate protection to intellectual property (IP) rights holders, whether Indians or foreigners.

As a signatory to several international pacts like the agreement on TRIPS, the 1886 Convention for Protection of Literary and Artistic Works (the Berne Convention) and the Convention on Bio-diversity, India is fully committed to providing adequate protection to IP rights. The domestic laws that protect various facets of IP include the Patents Act, 1970, the Trade Marks Act, 1999, the Designs Act, 2000, the Copyrights Act, 1957, and the Biological Diversity Act, 2002.

Foreign investors coming to India to set up a company, enter into a joint venture (JV) or open a branch office, etc. would benefit from an awareness of various IP laws. The important legislations dealing with IP are as described below.

## Trade Marks Act, 1999

Under the Trade Marks Act, 1999 (TMA), a trademark is a name, phrase, sound or symbol used in association with services or products in trade that often connects a brand with a level of quality on which companies build their reputation. Trademarks do not necessarily have to be registered in India. If a company creates a symbol or name it wishes to use exclusively, it can simply attach the TM symbol, signifying an unregistered trademark. Trademarks in India can be registered following the norms and procedure laid down in the TMA. Registered trademarks have a ® symbol over them. As per the law, a trademark is a visual symbol in the form of a word, a device or a label applied to articles of commerce, with a view to indicating that they are manufactured or otherwise dealt in by a particular person or a particular organization as distinguished from similar goods manufactured or dealt in by others.

The TMA, which was approved by Parliament in 1999, came into effect on 15 September 2003. As per the preamble it was "an act to amend and consolidate the law relating to trade marks, to provide for registration and better protection of trade marks for goods and services and for the prevention of the use of fraudulent trade marks". Some significant changes are:

- the recognition of three-dimensional trademarks, which allows shape of goods, packaging and combination of colours to be registered as a mark; the concept of a well known trademark was also introduced;
- the registration of 'collective marks' owned by an association of persons (eg. trade associations, professional bodies, unincorporated associations, etc.) allowed;
- the extension of grounds to seek protection from infringement.

These changes have widened the scope of trademark laws and provide better protection of trademarks and related IP rights. The duration of protection of trademarks is 10 years. However, trademark registration is renewable indefinitely on payment of the requisite fee, for a period of 10 years at a time. It takes 12 months to register a trademark in India.

## Procedure to obtain trade mark registration

An investor has to undergo the following procedure to obtain a registered trademark or a service mark:

1. A trademark application is drafted and filed with the Trade Marks Registry.
2. The application can either be accepted absolutely, conditionally or rejected completely by stating the grounds for doing so.
3. The application, if accepted, is advertised in the Trade Marks journal.
4. Once advertised, the application is open to opposition.
5. If the application is opposed, the applicants are given a hearing, to prove their stand.
6. If the application remains unopposed, it proceeds towards registration and the registration certificate is issued.

## Essential details

In order to prepare and file a trademark application in India, the following details are needed:

- full name of the applicant with complete address;
- trade description of the applicant, ie. manufacturer or distributor;

- copy of the mark to be registered (not necessary for a word mark);
- precise specification of goods or services to be registered under the mark;
- date signifying the beginning of the use of the mark in India; alternatively, a confirmation with regard to the usage of the proposed mark in India is required;
- authorization of an agent (power of attorney) signed by the applicant; however, authorization is not required at the time of filing of the application and can be filed with the office of the Trade Marks Registry subsequently.

## Licensing in trademark

A trademark can be licenced to another party by entering into an agreement called the Trade Mark Licensing Agreement (TM Agreement), wherein the licensor assigns the licensee the exclusive right to use the trademark for a prescribed time period. The licensee can use the mark as per the TM Agreement between the licensor and him/herself. The licensing of the mark should not cause confusion or deception among the general public, ie. should not destroy the distinctiveness of the mark. The trademark should continue to distinguish the goods connected with the proprietor of the mark from those connected with others and also the connection between the goods and the proprietor should continue. A licensee has no right to use the trademark after the expiry of the term of the TM Agreement or after the licence has been revoked or cancelled.

The TMA has made provisions for the 'permitted use' of a trademark by a person other than the registered proprietor and registered user of the mark. At the same time, it has also tried to ensure that proper control over the quality of the goods is exercised and the use of the mark by the licensee is not deceptive in any respect.

# Patents Act, 1970

An invention is a creation of intellect to produce something new, useful and industrially applicable. To encourage more people to use their labour and capital for inventions, it is essential that they be given some form of protection, and commercial gains. Such protection is provided to the inventors in the form of a patent. A patent is the legal right granted to the inventor to exclude anyone else from manufacturing or marketing a product invented by them. A patent can also be registered in a foreign country through the Patent Cooperation Treaty (PCT). TRIPS has made it obligatory for its signatory members to provide the same protection to foreign nationals as they provide to their citizens. A patent confers and secures certain substantive rights to an inventor, like the right to grant licences, right of assignment, etc.

Patents give protection in the form of non-disclosure of technology or a process by the owner or holder for a specified period. During the protection, this technology can be used through licensing/assignment/compulsory licensing. Transfer of technology is the transfer of a patent with respect to a particular product.

For transferring technology, the licensor has to enter into an agreement with the licensee called the Technology Transfer Licensing Agreement. The agreement should properly indicate the objects of the licensed products, the territory for which the agreement has been entered into, the time period, exclusivity of the agreement, proof of up-front payment, a running and minimum royalty, etc. Under this agreement, the licensee authorizes the licensor the use of patented technology, subject to certain terms and conditions whilst safeguarding their interest. This gives the licensee the power to exercise regular checks on the use of the patented transferred technology by the licensor. Moreover, through this agreement, a licensee derives economic and/or commercial returns.

## Recent changes

- Product patenting has been introduced to bring the Indian Patents Act into conformity with the TRIPS Agreement. The term of patent protection has been increased to 20 years.
- All computer programs are in combination with hardware, and all computer programs with technical application to software industry in particular are now patentable.

These changes were made to bring India's patent laws in line with the TRIPS Agreement. With these amendments, the Indian patent legislation now stands on an equal footing with the global ones.

## Procedure to obtain a patent in India

The registration procedure involves the following:

1. A patent application may be made, either alone or jointly with another, by the inventor, assignee, or the legal representatives of the deceased inventor or assignee.
2. The territory, where the applicant or the first mentioned applicant in the case of joint applicants for a patent, normally resides or has domicile or a place of business, or the place from where the invention actually originated, determines where the patent application can be filed.
3. A first examination report stating the objections, if any, is communicated to the applicant or his/her agents. Normally, all the objections must be met within 15 months from the date of the first examination report. An

extension of three months is available, but the application for extension must be made before the expiry of a normal period of 15 months.

4. Notice of opposition must be filed within four months of notification in the *Gazette of India*.
5. When the application is found to be suitable for acceptance, it is published in the *Gazette of India* (Part III, Section 2). It is deemed to be laid before the public, for opposition, on the date of publication in the *Gazette of India*.

## Necessary documents required

The following documents and information are needed to prepare and file a patent application in India:

- international application, if any, as published;
- international preliminary examination report;
- request;
- search report;
- demand;
- written report;
- response to written opinion;
- complete specification (in duplicate);
- abstract of the invention;
- drawings, if any;
- authorization of the agent, signed by the applicant.

# Designs Act, 2000

An article is distinguishable from others not only because of its utility but also because of its visual appeal by virtue of its particular shape, configuration, pattern or ornamentation. Therefore, the design of an article or its packaging has great commercial importance and needs to be protected. These designs are protected under the Designs Act. A design is a shape, configuration, pattern or ornamentation or composition of lines or colours applied to an article, in any form, by any industrial process or means. However, it does not include any mode or principle of construction or anything which is, in substance, a mere mechanical device; neither does it include any trade or property mark or artistic work.

The salient features of the Design Act, 2000, include:

- The protection of the design has increased to 10 years, extendable by a period of five years.
- The scope of definition of the 'article' and 'design' has been enlarged and the definition of the 'original' introduced.

- The international classification system has replaced the earlier Indian classification.

India is a signatory to the 1883 Convention for the Protection of Industrial Property (the Paris Convention). Therefore, design applications, by any person residing outside India, can be made within six months from the date of the first application made in another convention country. However, the convention followed in India is based on a reciprocal basis, ie. if the said country does not offer similar registration rights to Indian citizens for their designs in their country, then citizens of that country are not eligible to apply for registration of designs in India.

## Procedure for the registration of a design

The procedure for registration of a design in India consists of the following steps:

1. submission of application with the Controller of Patents & Designs, Design Office;
2. acceptance/objection/refusal of the application by the Design Office;
3. removal of objections/appeal to central government;
4. decision of the central government;
5. registration of the design.

## Necessary details/documents

To file a design application in India, the following documents and information are required:

- name, address and nationality of the applicant;
- name of the article to which the design is applied;
- classification of the design;
- photographs or drawings of the article in its entirety from different angles in quadruplicate, depicting the front, rear, sides, top, bottom and perspective view;
- power of authority.

# Judicial precedents

Effective enforcement mechanisms in the form of judicial remedies are available to protect IP rights. Two-fold judicial remedies available for protecting IP rights include:

1. civil actions seeking injunction orders against the infringer coupled with damages; and
2. criminal sanctions in the form of fines and imprisonment in the case of infringements.

There is now a substantial body of case law, developed over recent years, where damages have been awarded as an additional deterrent to infringers.

## Civil law precedents

Indian courts strictly enforce the IP rights of the owner and/or holder. Some important judgments relating to IP infringement, wherein the Civil Courts have always shown their enthusiasm to protect the interest of lawful owner/ holder of IP rights, are listed below:

1. Trademark infringement
    - Global repute in a trademark has been recognized, even if the trademark or copyright is not registered in India, and passing off has been restrained. India recognizes the concept of a 'well known trademark' and thus ensures protection under the TMA. For example, the Delhi High Court restrained the misuse of the marks 'CAT' and 'Caterpillar' for footwear in *Caterpillar Inc. vs. Mehtab Ahmed [2002 (25) PTC 438]*.
    - Indian courts have awarded pecuniary penalties for infringement and passing off of trademarks beyond statutory provisions in cases of undue commercial exploitation by infringers. Distinguishing between compensatory and punitive damages, in *Time Incorporated vs. Lokesh Srivastava [2005 (30) PTC 3]*, the Delhi High Court awarded 500,000 Indian rupees (INR) as punitive damages and also awarded INR 500,000 as compensatory damages for loss of reputation and goodwill to the plaintiff.
2. Software piracy
    - In another landmark decision, delivered in *Microsoft vs. Yogesh Papat [2005 (30) PTC 245]*, the Delhi High Court calculated actual loss of business caused to the plaintiff by the defendant selling pirated software as 'freeware' with assembled computers. The court considered the violation of the plaintiff's trademark and copyrights and awarded damages of INR 1.97 million for the violation of the plaintiff's rights by the defendants. This is the highest award for damages given by an Indian court for trademark and copyright infringement.

## Criminal remedies

Effective remedies are also available under Indian penal statutes to punish infringers and check increasing cases of data theft.

1. *Trademark infringement* – TMA provides for imprisonment for a minimum of six months to three years and a fine of approximately $1,100–4,500 to any person who infringes the trademark rights of any lawful owner/holder of a trademark. The offences under this act are cognizable.
2. *Copyright infringement* – under the Copyright Act, 1957, unauthorized copying, selling, hiring or distributing copyright material is an infringement of copyright. Under Section 63 of the Act, the known infringement or abetment to infringement of copyright is a criminal offence, punishable with imprisonment ranging from six months to three years along with a fine of approximately $1,100–4,500.
3. *Patent infringement* – whenever the rights of the patentee are infringed, his/her rights may be secured back through judicial intervention. The patentee has to file a suit for the infringement of his/her rights. The procedure followed in conducting such suits is governed by the provisions of the Code of Civil Procedure, 1908, and the period of limitation for instituting a suit is three years from the date of infringement. The relief which may be awarded in such suits are:
   - interlocutory/interim injunction;
   - damages or account of profits;
   - permanent injunction.
4. *Design infringement* – under the Designs Act, 2000, the remedy available for infringement of a registered design is damages along with an injunction. The Act lays the remedy in the form of payment of a certain sum of money by the person who pirates a registered design.

# 4.8

# Company Dissolution and Liquidation

*Diljeet Titus and Sushmita Ganguly, Titus & Co. Advocates*

The procedure for winding-up a company is quite cumbersome in India and can take years. The problems connected with the winding-up of a company were discussed in detail by the Expert Committee on Company Law headed by Dr J J Irani.[1] The committee made a strong case for streamlining the winding-up process by adopting international best practices. Among other things, it suggested adoption of the United Nations Commission on International Trade Law (UNCITRAL) Model Law on Cross Border Insolvency and the establishment of a panel of administrators and liquidators to reduce disputes and expedite winding-up.

The government is considering the recommendations of the Irani Committee and is likely to incorporate various suggestions whilst formulating new company law. The government had been working on the new legislation and is likely to come up with a draft shortly to replace the Companies Act, 1956.

Meanwhile, the establishment of the tribunal as a specialized body, dealing exclusively with all company law-related issues, disputes and problems will improve matters significantly. The proposed tribunal will deal with winding-up petitions and the companies will no longer be required to approach the overworked High Courts for orders.

Winding-up is the process to end the existence of a company by passing its management to liquidators in order to realize the value of assets to the maximum extent possible, pay off the debts, discharge other liabilities and distribute any surplus among the shareholders.

Described in detail in the Companies Act, 1956, dissolution is the last stage of a company which technically will continue to exist until its affairs

[1] The Ministry of Company Affairs in December 2004 appointed an Expert Committee headed by Dr J J Irani to advise the government on new Company Law. The report of the committee submitted in May 2005 is under consideration of the government.

have been completely wound up and its name removed from the register of companies by the Registrar of Companies (RoC).

# Types of winding-up

The Companies Act, 1956, prescribes two modes for winding-up a company which are as follows:

- *Voluntary winding-up* – The shareholders or the creditors of a company wanting to dissolve the company can opt for voluntary winding-up. Under this mode, no petition is made to court for the winding-up of a company. The process of winding-up begins with the passing of a resolution by the shareholders in the manner prescribed in Section 484 of the Companies Act, 1956 and ends with dissolution of the company.
- *Compulsory winding-up* – Although the term 'compulsory winding-up' is not defined in the Companies Act, 1956, it has been construed to mean the winding-up of a company by court or tribunal. A company may be compulsorily wound up by a court of competent jurisdiction for its failure to follow certain key provisions of the Companies Act, 1956. This procedure for compulsory winding-up is extremely formal and has been prescribed in the Companies (Court) Rules, 1959. The government is proposing to come out with a new set of rules for the compulsory winding-up of companies. However, until the fresh regulations are put in place, the old rules are sufficient.

In both cases, the proceedings for winding-up must be conducted in the National Company Law Tribunal (NCLT). However, as the tribunal has not become functional, the proceedings are being regulated by the High Court of the state in which the registered office of the company is located.

## Voluntary winding-up

Depending on the solvency status of a company, the voluntary winding-up may be further divided into the following two categories.

### *Members' voluntary winding-up*

The members may opt for the voluntary winding-up of a perfectly solvent company for several reasons, such as completion of the task for which the company was incorporated, the inability of the company to run profitably due to circumstances beyond its control, redundancy on account of changes in government policies or any other justifiable reason.

### *Creditors' voluntary winding-up*

The creditors may seek winding-up of a company if they are unable to recover their money from the company and also if there is no likelihood of the company doing well financially in future. This step is initiated when the net worth of a company turns negative and there is no prospect of recovery. Under these circumstances, irrespective of the reasons, it may be prudent for a company to stop further losses by entering into voluntary winding-up.

## The procedure of voluntary winding-up

As far as the procedure for voluntary winding-up is concerned, the members can initiate the process by passing either an ordinary resolution (by simple majority) or special resolution (by super majority), as per the requirement. In the case of fixed duration companies, the members can pass the winding-up resolution by simple majority after the completion of the term prescribed in the Memorandum of Association, Articles of Association or on the occurrence of a specified event.

Voluntary winding-up is a comparatively simple process and foreign entrepreneurs may invest in fixed duration companies if they want to keep an easy exit route open. They may do so by incorporating relevant clauses in the Memorandum of Association and Articles of Association of the company. This option, however, may not be relevant for those entrepreneurs who want to make long-term investment or set up manufacturing bases in the country.

In other cases, the voluntary winding-up proceedings can only be initiated by a special resolution which has to be passed by super majority. All special resolutions, as per the provisions of Section 189(2) of the Companies Act, 1956, are required to be approved by at least three times the number of votes cast against the resolution, ie. 76 per cent of the votes cast.

## Compulsory winding-up

Sometimes it may not be possible for a company to comply with the formalities required for voluntary winding-up of a company. Under compelling circumstances, a company may file a petition for compulsory winding-up in the court of competent jurisdiction.

The circumstances under which a tribunal may compulsorily wind up a company are mentioned in Section 433 of the Companies Act, 1956. Some of the important ones are listed below:

- if a special resolution has been passed by the company deciding to wind up its operations;
- if the company has defaulted in filing statutory reports or holding statutory meetings. (According to Section 165 of Companies Act, 1956,

every company limited by shares and every company limited by guarantee and having a share capital, shall, within a period of not less than one month nor more than six months from the date on which the company is entitled to commence business, hold a statutory meeting of the company. A statutory report setting out all the matters listed in Section 165(2) (3) of the Companies Act, 1956, is required to be prepared by the board of directors of the company and has to be forwarded to every member of the company at least 21 days before the statutory meeting. After obtaining the statutory report certified by the directors and auditors and dispatching it to the RoC for the purpose of registration);

- if, within a year of incorporation, a company does not commence its business operations or, suspends its business;
- if the number of members in a public company falls below seven, or in a private company, below two persons;
- if the company fails to pay debts. A debt is defined as a determined or definite sum of money payable immediately or at a future date. If the company owes to a creditor a sum exceeding 100,000 Indian rupees (INR) and has not paid it for over three weeks after a demand to pay has been made to the company, if a decree of any court or tribunal finds it so, or if the tribunal opines that the company is unable to pay its debts, then an order for winding-up can be passed against it;
- if it is just and equitable in the view of the tribunal;
- if the company has not filed its annual accounts and balance sheets or annual returns with the RoC for any five consecutive financial years;
- if the company acts against the interest of the sovereignty and integrity of India, security of the state, or friendly relations with foreign states, public order, decency and morality;
- if the tribunal opines that under the provisions of Section 424G of the Companies Act, 1956, it should be wound up.

## Who can bring winding-up petitions

An application for winding-up can be brought before the court or tribunal by the following:

- the company;
- any creditor or creditors, including contingent or prospective creditors;
- any contributory or contributories (under Section 428 of the Companies Act, 1956, a contributory means every person liable to contribute to the assets of the company in the event of its being wound up, and includes the holder of any shares which are fully paid up; and for the purposes of all proceedings for determining, and all proceedings prior to the final determination of the persons who are to be deemed contributories, includes any person alleged to be a contributory);

- by all or any of the parties specified in the aforementioned clauses whether together or separately;
- the registrar;[1]
- in cases falling under Section 243 of the Companies Act, 1956, a person authorized by the central government;
- central or state government if the company is working against the interest of the sovereignty, integrity, security of the nation, or against friendly relations with neighbouring states, public order, decency and morality.[2]

# Winding-up of foreign companies

The procedure for winding-up unregistered companies, given in the provisions of Part X of the Companies Act, 1956, applies to foreign companies, whatever be the number of their members. A foreign company incorporated in a foreign country may be wound-up in India if it has an office and assets there, and if a pending foreign liquidation does not affect the jurisdiction to make a winding-up order. Where a foreign company is already being wound-up in the country of its domicile, the winding-up in India will be ancillary to the foreign liquidation, and the liquidator's powers in this country are restricted to dealing with assets in this country.[3] A subsequent winding-up in the foreign country does not affect prior proceedings taken in India, and the liquidator's discretion is not fettered.[4]

Where a body corporate outside India ceases to conduct business in India, it may be wound-up as an unregistered company, notwithstanding that the body corporate has been dissolved or otherwise ceased to exist as such under or by virtue of the laws of the country under which it was incorporated.

Where a foreign company ceases to carry on business in India, its substratum is gone or it carries on *ultra vires* business, it may be wound-up on 'just and equitable' grounds.[5]

The essential conditions pertaining to the winding-up of a foreign company are as follows:

(*a*) if it is dissolved or has ceased to carry on business or is carrying on business only for the purpose of winding-up its affairs;
(*b*) if it is unable to discharge debts;
(*c*) if the tribunal opines it would be 'just and equitable' for the company to be wound-up:
  - winding-up can only be made through the tribunal, ie. voluntary winding-up is not permitted;

1 Section 2(40) of the Companies Act, 1956 defines 'Registrar' to mean a Registrar, or an Additional, a Joint, a Deputy or an Assistant Registrar having the duty of registering companies under the Companies Act, 1956.
2 Inserted by the Companies (Second) Amendment Act, 2002 w.e.f. a date yet to be notified.
3 Re Russian and English Bank Ltd, 1932 (2) Company Cases 424
4 1958 (28) Company Cases 204
5 1972 (42) Company Cases 197 Bombay

- reasons for winding-up a foreign company include:
    - a petition for winding-up may be presented to the tribunal for an order of winding-up;
    - the tribunal may pass the winding-up order after inviting objections against the winding-up petition;
    - after receiving the order from the tribunal, the foreign company is required to file the order with the concerned RoC for dissolution of the company.

## Remittance of winding-up proceeds

The Foreign Exchange Management (Remittance of Assets) Regulations of 2000 deal with the remittance of winding-up proceeds of foreign companies. Under the regulations, the Reserve Bank of India's (RBI) prior permission is required for the remittance of winding-up proceeds of a branch or office (other than project offices) in India of a person resident outside India. Persons who desire to remit such assets need to make an application with the following documents:

- a copy of the RBI's approval to set up the branch/office in India;
- a copy of the RBI's approval to sell immovable properties, if any, held by the branch/ office;
- the auditor's certificate;
- the no-objection or tax clearance certificate from the Income Tax Authority for remittance;
- confirmation from the applicant that there are no legal proceedings in any court in India pending and that there is no legal impediment to remittance.

## Priority of claims

Under voluntary winding-up, the company appoints a liquidator whose job is to realize the value of the company's assets and disburse the amount so realized among different stakeholders in accordance with the provisions laid down in Sections 529, 529A and 530 of the Companies Act, 1956. The liquidator acts as an agent or administrator of the company.

In the case of compulsory winding-up, the tribunal or court appoints an official liquidator to oversee the winding-up of the affairs of the company. The official liquidator, who functions under the direction of the tribunal or court, is responsible to the central government for all acts done during the course of winding-up the company. The liquidator's main task is to realize the assets of the company to the extent possible.

The order of disbursement of realized assets, as provided in different sections of the Companies Act, 1956, is as follows:

1. *Workmen and secured creditors*: The legitimate dues of workers are *pari passu* with secured creditors. The wages include ad hoc interim relief if awarded by any industrial court, retrenchment compensation, accrued holiday remuneration, compensation under the Workmen's Compensation Act and gratuity. These dues have been accorded overriding preferential treatment by Section 529A of the Companies Act, 1956.
2. *Cost of liquidation*: The next priority is given to cost of liquidation. It includes:
   - legal charges incurred by the liquidator on litigation; remuneration of the solicitor(s);
   - Income Tax on income accruing after the commencement of the winding-up proceedings; liquidator's remuneration; rents; incidental charges concerning the winding-up process; and preservation charges for the company's property.
3. *Unsecured creditors*: The unsecured creditors, which include debenture-holders, rank *pari passu* according to their claims.
4. *Equity shareholders*: The surplus left after discharging the liabilities of outsiders is disbursed among preference shareholders and equity shareholders in proportion to their equity.

After the procedure of winding-up is completed and the order for dissolution is obtained from the tribunal or court, the same has to be filed with the RoC. After receiving the order and if there is no reason for any suit to be brought against the liquidator for acting in a manner prejudicial to the interest of the company, the RoC strikes off the name of the company from its register, completing the process of dissolution.

# 4.9

# Dispute Resolution

*Diljeet Titus and Manish Gupta, Titus & Co. Advocates*

The alternative dispute resolution (ADR) systems may not provide a perfect setting for the resolution of commercial disputes expeditiously and to the satisfaction of the warring groups. There are several loopholes in the ADR mechanism which can be exploited by one party to delay resolution of dispute to the detriment of the other party. Although the Arbitration and Conciliation Act, 1996, tried to address various shortcomings of the earlier act, it is not free from weaknesses. There are problems with the new act also. Often parties pursuing vested interests or acting with ulterior motives can raise frivolous disputes to delay implementation of a perfectly justified arbitration award. The delay becomes frustrating and painful, especially when the stakes are high and the urgency to amicably resolve a dispute is pressing.

However, what cannot be disputed about ADR is that it is a much better and swifter way to resolve commercial disputes. It is far superior to approaching a court of law and going through the due legal process which involves significant time and money. What smart companies should try to do is to have a proper arbitration agreement either as part of the contract or as a separate agreement for satisfactory resolution of disputes. This is probably the best way to protect the commercial interest of a company from protracted litigation in future. A proper and well thought out arbitration agreement is undoubtedly the best insurance against financial losses that may arise on account of delay in the adjudication of commercial disputes.

Resolving commercial disputes through ordinary courts of law can be frustrating because the process takes an unreasonably long time and involves large amounts of money. At a time when critical decisions are required to be taken in real time, protracted litigation can jeopardize corporate reputations, harm commercial interests and adversely affect the concerned company's bottom line. The way out of this imbroglio is to opt for out-of-court settlement of disputes. The ADR mechanism provides an opportunity to companies to resolve their differences through a mechanism that is efficient, speedy and cheap. The other big advantage is that under the ADR mechanism the disputing parties are not required to adhere to the cumbersome judicial procedure prescribed in the Civil Procedure Code, 1908, and the Evidence Act, 1872. The parties can settle their disputes through the persons of their choice whose integrity and independence they trust.

Several ADR methods are prevalent in India. Among the ADR methods and systems in vogue, arbitration and conciliation are the most widely used. The other ADR systems, which include mediation, negotiation, facilitation and mini-trial are also slowly and gradually gaining currency in India.

## Arbitration

Arbitration provides a potent alternative to litigation in a court of law. Important reasons for preferring arbitration in the transnational context include hassle-free commencement of proceedings, neutrality of arbitrators and freedom from the hair-splitting rules of evidence. The advantages also include expeditious issuance of an award and simplified enforcement of the award. Further, the process of arbitration ensures privacy and is generally protected by the laws of privilege and confidentiality. This is of great significance in commercially sensitive disputes involving, for instance, know-how, lists of clients, the development of business strategy and other commercially confidential matters. Parties may also request a non-speaking award from the arbitrators to maintain confidentiality.

The law relating to arbitration in India is contained in the Arbitration and Conciliation Act, 1996 (Arbitration Act). The new legislation is an improvement over the Arbitration Act, 1940. The 1996 Act, with a few significant interpolations, is based entirely on the Model Law on International Commercial Arbitration adopted by the United Nations Commission on International Trade Law (UNCITRAL) in 1985. This ensures a certain degree of uniformity with the arbitration laws of other countries.

The Arbitration Act is divided into four parts:

- Part I deals with laws relating to domestic arbitration and international commercial arbitration held in India.
- Part II deals with the enforcement of foreign awards under the 1958 Convention on the Recognition and Enforcement of Foreign Arbitral Awards (New York Convention) and the 1927 Convention on the Execution of Foreign Arbitral Awards (Geneva Convention).
- Part III deals with conciliation.
- Part IV contains supplementary provisions.

The Model Law is not a comprehensive piece of legislation and the Indian Act inherited various weaknesses of the former. Moreover, several problems have arisen during the course of the interpretation and application of the Arbitration Act. Hence, it becomes imperative for an investor to have a clear understanding of the various provisions contained in the legislation and act accordingly.

## Arbitration in India

Arbitration as a mode for settlement of disputes has been in vogue in India for many years. Almost all business transactions carry arbitration clauses. Government contracts usually provide for compulsory arbitration in respect of disputes arising thereunder. A sizeable number of public sector undertakings also follow the same procedure.

Several merchant associations provide for in-house arbitration facilities between their members and their customers. Stock exchanges in India also provide for in-house arbitration for resolution of disputes. The board of directors of each stock exchange constitutes the appellate authority for hearing appeals from the award of the arbitral tribunals.

## Arbitration agreements

The foundation of arbitration is the agreement between the parties to submit the dispute to arbitration. An arbitration agreement is defined in the Arbitration Act as an agreement between the parties to submit to arbitration all or certain disputes which have arisen or may arise between them in respect of a defined legal relationship, whether contractual or not. It must be in writing and may be in the form of an arbitration clause in a contract or in the form of a separate agreement. A good arbitration agreement is one that minimizes complications in the event of a dispute cropping up. However, in practice, parties often fail to carefully draft one.

Before finalizing an arbitration agreement, it is imperative that the terms be thoroughly discussed and negotiated to avoid any misunderstanding in future. An arbitration agreement must primarily address key issues such as place or seat of arbitration, laws applicable to arbitration, number of arbitrators, language, interim measures, enforceability of the award, to name a few, in order to safeguard the interest of the parties to the agreement.

## Arbitration mechanism

The arbitrators shall be appointed by the parties as agreed between them. If the parties fail to reach an agreement, the Chief Justice of India, Chief Justice of a High Court or their nominees may appoint the arbitrator. This is a significant addition not contained in the Model Law. An arbitrator can be challenged only if circumstances give rise to justifiable doubts concerning his/her independence and impartiality or in the case where the arbitrator is not qualified to the satisfaction of the parties.

The rule concerning the substance of dispute is an important provision as far as international commercial arbitration is concerned. The arbitral tribunal is obliged to apply the rules of law designated by the parties as applicable to the substance of the dispute. However, in the absence of any agreement as to the applicability of laws between the parties, the tribunal can apply rules of law it considers appropriate.

The act clearly enumerates the grounds on which the court can entertain the application for setting aside an award. These include incapacity of a party, invalidity of an arbitration agreement, the violation of principles of natural justice and the exceeding of terms of reference by the arbitrator.

The arbitral award has been given the status of a decree of court and made enforceable under the Code of Civil Procedure, 1908. Therefore, an award is not required to be converted into a decree.

## Enforcement of foreign awards

As mentioned previously, the act recognizes awards made under the New York Convention or the Geneva Convention. The provisions regarding enforcement of foreign awards are almost the same as for the awards made under the two conventions. It is obligatory for a party applying for enforcement of a foreign award to produce before the court:

- the original award or duly authenticated copy thereof;
- the original agreement for arbitration or a duly authenticated copy thereof;
- such evidence as may be necessary to prove that the award is a foreign award.

Where the award or agreement is in a foreign language, the party seeking to enforce the award is required to produce a certified translated copy in English. Where the court is satisfied that the foreign award is enforceable, the award shall be deemed to be a decree of that court.

## International arbitration

An international commercial arbitration has been defined as an arbitration relating to disputes arising out of legal relationships, whether contractual or not, considered as commercial under the law in force in India and where at least one of the parties is:

- an individual who is a national of, or habitually resident in, any country other than India;
- a body corporate which is incorporated in any country other than India;
- a company or an association or a body of individuals whose central management and control is exercised in any country other than India;
- the government of a foreign country.

From the above definition it is clear that, unlike domestic arbitration, an international arbitration must essentially be commercial in nature in order to fall under the purview of the act. However, the word “commercial” has been interpreted liberally by the Indian courts taking in its sweep all kinds of businesses and transactions. Where the place of arbitration is outside India, the award is treated as a ‘foreign award’ and its recognition and enforcement is dealt with separately in Part II of the Act. The act recognizes awards made under the New York Convention or the Geneva Convention.

# Conciliation and mediation

Conciliation is a facilitative process in which disputing parties engage a neutral third party to act as a conciliator in their dispute. The conciliator has no authority to make any decision which is binding on the parties, but uses certain procedures, methods and skills to help them arrive at a settlement of their dispute by agreement. The basic objective of a conciliator is to assist the parties, in an independent and impartial manner, in their attempt to amicably settle their disputes.

The Arbitration Act provides that conciliation proceedings can be initiated by a party inviting the other party to conciliate under its provisions. Once the other party accepts, in writing, the invitation to conciliate, the conciliation proceedings start.

The terms ‘conciliation’ and ‘mediation’ are, by and large, used interchangeably. However, in some countries a sort of distinction is made between them according to the initiative taken by the third party. In most cases, a mediator plays a more proactive role than a conciliator in a conciliation process.

Conciliation/mediation offers a much more flexible alternative for a wide variety of disputes, reserving the freedom of parties to withdraw from the proceedings without prejudice to their legal position *inter se* at any stage of the proceedings, maintaining confidentiality of proceedings and ensuring quick resolution of disputes in a cost effective manner.

# Other ADR systems

The following alternative methods of dispute resolution other than arbitration, conciliation, mediation and negotiation are also used:

1. *Mini-trial*: In this non-binding procedure the disputing parties are presented with summaries of their cases to enable them to assess the strengths, weaknesses and prospects of the case and then an opportunity to negotiate a settlement with the assistance of a neutral expert.
2. *Partnering*: This collaborative and non-binding process focuses on the cooperative solving of problems that participants have in common.

Properly applied, it yields reconciliation as opposed to either compromise or concession.

3. *Neutral fact finding*: When the resolution of a dispute requires certain expertise and the issue becomes a stumbling block, either of the parties may agree on a fact-finder, a neutral third party, or the court may select a neutral expert to investigate the issue in question to submit a non-binding report or testify in court. The impartial expert usually investigates the matter presented to him/her and subsequently files a report which establishes the facts in the matter.

## Flaws in the arbitration system

As stated earlier, the Arbitration Act is based almost entirely on the Model Law on International Commercial Arbitration adopted by UNCITRAL and hence suffers from the same demerits as the Model Law. A major flaw plaguing both the Model Law and the Arbitration Act is the provision of a judicial remedy for the removal of an arbitrator in case they are believed or found to be biased. In practice, this provision may amount to questioning the fairness of the arbitration system as a whole.

According to the laws on arbitration, the grounds for objecting to an award under relevant provisions of the Arbitration Act are common to both domestic awards as well as international arbitration awards. The principle of minimal court interference may be good in the case of international arbitration awards. However, as far as Indian awards are concerned, the principle of minimal court interference is not enforced as strictly because often the arbitration awards in India are given by persons who are not well acquainted with law.

The object of reducing the work load of courts at times is defeated as parties feel the necessity of approaching courts for the appointment of arbitrators, for interim measures of protection, for substitution of arbitrators, to challenge interim orders passed by arbitral tribunals or to challenge or enforce arbitral awards.

# 4.10

# Contract Issues, Consumer Protection and Property Issues

*Diljeet Titus and Garima Bhagat, Titus & Co. Advocates*

The Indian Contract Act,1872, provides a legal framework to preserve and protect the sanctity of a commercial agreement formed between two or more parties to undertake a permissible commercial activity.

The legislation dealing with contract, consumer protection and transfer of property are important laws having a bearing on trade and commerce in India. It would be advisable for entrepreneurs to have at least some idea of these laws.

## Contract Act, 1872

A contract which may involve several parties has been described by the Contract Act as 'an agreement enforceable by law'. An agreement is defined as 'every promise and every set of promises forming the consideration for each other'. An agreement will be a contract if it is:

- made by the free consent of the parties competent to contract; consent is said to be free if it is not obtained by coercion, undue influence, fraud, misrepresentation or mistake;
- for a lawful consideration and object (a contract to do something unlawful, eg. murder, extortion, smuggling, etc., is not a valid contract);
- not expressly declared to be void by law.

The Contract Act recognizes the following types of contracts:

1. *Valid contract*: These are the agreements enforceable by law. Such a contract creates an outstanding obligation or legal liability.

2. *Voidable contract*: A voidable contract becomes valid only on fulfilment of certain specified conditions. A voidable contract remains valid until rescinded. The main difference between a valid contract and a voidable contract is that unlike the former, the latter cannot be enforced freely. A voidable contract can only be enforced under specific circumstances.
3. *Void contract*: A void contract is unenforceable under law and cannot give rise to any legal liability.

Every contract has to pass through several stages, beginning with the negotiation, during which the parties discuss and negotiate proposals and counter proposals. They also discuss the consideration, resulting finally in the acceptance of the proposal. In order to convert a proposal into a promise, the acceptance must be absolute and unqualified, and the same should be expressed unequivocally. An agreement is not a contract if there is no intention of the parties to create a legal relationship. The acceptance has to be communicated by the offeree or his/her authorized agent to the offeror. The proposal, when accepted, gives rise to a contract. An agreement enforceable by law becomes a contract as per the provisions of the Contract Act.

## Refusal to perform

The refusal of a party to a contract to perform its part of the contract gives an option to the non-defaulting party to put an end to the contract and regard itself discharged, or to treat the contract as still in existence and affirm its continuance.

A refusal to perform any part of the contract, however small, is a refusal to perform the contract in its entirety if the refusal affects a vital part of the contract and prevents the non-defaulting party to get in substance what it had bargained for. Therefore, if a party commits a material breach or manifests an intention to commit such a breach, it will excuse the other party from the obligation to proceed further.

In the case where the non-defaulting party opts for the rescission of a contract, three legal effects follow:

1. It releases the non-defaulting party from its obligation to perform its part of the contract. The non-defaulting party can bring an action without showing that it could have performed its obligations.
2. The acceptance of the breach by the non-defaulting party also releases the defaulting party from its obligation to perform the contract.
3. The non-defaulting party can sue for damages. Its rights to damages are not defeated by actual or possible supervening events. Subsequent events may affect the amount of damages but not the right to damages. The non-defaulting party can claim damages at once even though its right to future performance of the contract is only contingent.

# Issues under the Contract Act

## Limitation of liability

Parties to a contract may limit their liability to a fixed percentage which can be monetarily assessed, and which is mutually agreed upon and acceptable to all the concerned parties. Parties to a contract may agree and fix the damages payable as liquidated damages, or they may be fixed by statute as in the case of damages against a party to a dishonoured bill of exchange.

## Waiver and promissory estoppel

The Act permits the party to a contract to waive or abandon its right. Under the law, the general principle of waiver allows a party to a contract to voluntarily dispense with or remit wholly or in part the performance of the promise made to him/her, or he/she can accept any promise which he/she thinks fit. Neither a consideration nor an agreement is necessary. Waiver may be oral, in writing or inferred from conduct. Similar to a waiver is the doctrine of promissory estoppel or equitable estoppel, whereby a party who has represented that he/she will not insist upon his/her strict rights under the contract will not be allowed to go back on that position, or will be allowed to do so only upon giving reasonable notice.

## Limitation of time for enforcing rights

In terms of the Limitation Act, 1908, any suit instituted after the prescribed period of limitation will be dismissed, even if limitation has not been set up as a defence. Thus, an agreement which provides that a suit should be brought for the breach of any terms of the agreement within a time shorter than the period of limitation prescribed by law will be void to that extent.

## Restraint of trade clause

In terms of Section 27 of the Contract Act, an agreement which has for its object a restraint on trade, is *prima facie* void unless it falls distinctly within prescribed exceptions. Section 27 is based on public policy and deals with agreements by which a person is precluded altogether for a limited time or over a limited area from exercising his/her profession, trade or business. All covenants in agreements relating to reasonable restraint or partial restraint have to fall squarely within the framework of Section 27 to be saved from being declared void.

## Choice of governing law

Parties to a contract are entitled to agree to the law that shall apply to their contract, including the place and mode of resolving disputes that may arise during the course of the contract. Parties may desire to choose a neutral law, the choice of which may depend not upon the main transaction but an underlying transaction which may have a connection with a different system of law.

In cases where there is no expressed intention of the law applicable, the court may examine the real and common intention of the contracting parties by either implying a term into the contract or by applying the extraneous standard of a reasonable person. Furthermore, under Indian laws, a contract or any clause to that effect cannot negate the jurisdiction of Indian courts. This enables a party to sue in India, irrespective of whether the contract says otherwise.

## Restraint of judicial proceedings

The agreements in total restraint of judicial proceedings are void. However, an agreement by which a party is only partially restrained is not void. Therefore, where parties to an agreement agree that, in the case of any dispute, the suit may be brought at a particular place only, the agreement would not be void, if the court at that place has the jurisdiction to try the suit. A contract by which two or more persons agree that any dispute between them with regard to some specified subject shall be referred to arbitration only is valid. In this case, a suit cannot be brought in a court of law with regard to the dispute concerning the specified subject.

## Reasonableness and equity

A contract can be varied or re-negotiated to the extent provided for in the contract or to the extent provided for in the enabling statute under which the contract was concluded. Any material alteration without obtaining free consent of the other contracting party in the terms of the contract which varies the rights, liabilities or legal position of the parties ascertained by the contract in its original state will not be valid and will be unenforceable.

# Consumer protection

The Consumer Protection Act, 1986, was enacted with the intention of safeguarding the interest of consumers. The Act provides for expeditious settlement of consumer disputes and matters connected therewith.

It is a beneficial statute designed to redress grievances of the categories of consumers mentioned in the Act. As per the Act, the 'consumer' is a person who buys any goods or hires or avails of any services for a consideration. The definition of the consumer does not include those persons who obtain such goods for resale or for any commercial purpose.

To provide fast and simple redressal of consumer disputes, the Act provides for the setting up of quasi-judicial authorities at district, state and central levels. These quasi-judicial bodies are expected to observe the principles of natural justice, provide relief of a specific nature and award, wherever appropriate, compensation to the aggrieved. Penalties for non-compliance of the orders given by the quasi-judicial bodies have also been provided in the Act.

The Act also provides for the establishment of consumer councils such as the Central Consumer Protection Council under the minister in charge of consumer affairs in the central government and the State Consumer Protection Councils under the ministers in charge of consumer affairs in the state governments. Several state governments have introduced rules to implement the Act at state and district levels.

The Act, as per the statement of objects and reasons, primarily seeks to promote and protect the rights of consumers such as:

- the right to be protected against the marketing of goods and services which are hazardous to life and property;
- the right to be informed about the quality, quantity, potency, purity, standard and price of the goods or services, so as to protect the consumer against unfair trade practices;
- the right to be assured – wherever possible – access to a variety of goods and services at competitive prices;
- the right to be heard and to be assured that consumers' interests will receive due consideration at appropriate fora;
- the right to seek redressal against unfair trade practices, restrictive trade practices or unscrupulous exploitation of consumers;
- the right to consumer education.

## Property laws

The Transfer of Property Act, 1882, regulates transfer of immovable property that takes place by the acts of parties, ie. the voluntary transfer of property between two contracting parties. With the exception of certain instances, it does not regulate the transfer by operation of law, such as sale by the order of the court, auction or forfeiture. Also, transfers under the Act are required to be *inter vivos* (where both parties are living). Transfer by wills or inheritance are not governed by the Act.

## Transfer of property

Transfer of property occurs under a contract which is subject to the provisions of the Indian Contract Act, 1872. Thus, the parties entering into a contract for the transfer of property should be competent to enter into a contract. What this means is that the parties should have attained the age of majority, which is 18 years, they should be of sound mind and they should not have been disqualified to enter into contract by some other law applicable to them.

## Transactions not permitted

The Transfer of Property Act prohibits certain kinds of transfers. The transfers disallowed by the Act are *lis pendens,* transfer by person with no interest in property, fraudulent transfers, etc.

The principle of *lis pendens* is laid down in Section 52 of the Act. It is based on the legal maxim that in a pending litigation no new fact should be introduced. Thus, a property which is the subject of an ongoing suit cannot be the subject of a transfer. Also, a person cannot transfer a property without owning the title of that particular property.

Section 53 of the Act bars fraudulent transfers. In the case of fraudulent transfers, the Act empowers creditors of the transferor to sue if a transfer is being made with the intent to defeat or delay their claims. The creditors are permitted to file a suit in a representative capacity or for the benefit of all creditors.

## Sale of property

Sale of property is the absolute transfer of ownership and all rights associated with it in exchange for a price paid or promised or for consideration or part-paid and part-promised. Thus a sale of property entails transfer of complete ownership and presence of two parties between whom the transfer takes place. Furthermore, there has to be a consideration of price. The price may be paid or promised, or part-paid and part-promised. Registration of the instrument of transfer is essential for the sale of any property above the value of 100 Indian rupees (INR). For property below that value, transfer may, or may not be registered. Tangible property above the value of INR 100 may be sold through registered deed.

## Liabilities and rights of seller

The seller has to disclose any material defect in the property or title that the buyer could not find on examination. He/she is bound to: produce documents of the property on request, for examination; answer relevant questions put to him/her by the buyer; execute a proper conveyance upon payment at the proper place and time; take care of the property and related documents as if it were his/her own till the delivery after sale; give possession of the property as required by the buyer; and pay all those encumbrances and public charges that accrue in respect of the property until the date of the sale.

The seller is entitled to rents and profits of the property until the ownership is passed on to the buyer. He/she has the charge upon the property, even if it is in the hands of the buyer, until the entire purchase price is paid.

## The duties and rights of the buyer

The buyer has to reveal any material fact (even those that would increase the value of the property considerably) regarding his/her interest in the property that the seller may not be aware of. It is the duty of the buyer to pay the amount due to the seller in the manner directed by him/her. He/she has to bear any loss to the property in his/her ownership not caused by the seller. He/she is also required to pay all public charges after the ownership has been passed on to him/her.

# 4.11

# Competition Law

*Diljeet Titus and Shamik Narain, Titus & Co. Advocates*

The origin of Competition Law in India can be traced back to Articles 38 and 39 of the Constitution of India. These Articles are a part of the Directive Principles of State Policy. Article 38 of the Constitution of India provides that the government shall secure a social order for the promotion of welfare of the people; and Article 39 states that the government shall, in particular, direct its policy towards securing that:

- the ownership and control of material resources of the community are so distributed as best to serve the common good;
- the operation of the economic system does not result in the concentration of wealth and means of production to the common detriment.

Anti-competitive practices include practices that do or could eliminate the competition a firm faces in a market in which it is engaged, or practices that do or could prevent the emergence of new competitors, or practices that distort competition between firms. The aim of competition law is to prevent anti-competitive practices that have an adverse effect on competition. Competition law is also required to control and regulate unfair, restrictive and monopolistic trade practices, price discrimination and illegal business practices, thereby preventing concentration of economic power and abuse of dominant position.

The Monopolies Inquiry Commission was set up by the government in 1964 to curb concentration of economic power in private hands, which, it was generally believed, led to the then prevailing inequality in the distribution of income and standard of living of the populace of India. On the recommendation of the Monopolies Inquiry Commission, the Monopolies and Restrictive Trade Practices Act ('MRTP Act') was enacted in 1969.

The salient features and relevant issues involved in Indian competition legislations are discussed below.

# MRTP Act

The MRTP Act had been designed as a charter of economic liberty aimed at preserving free and unfettered competition as the rule of trade. The MRTP Act lays down regulatory measures in three distinct areas, *vis-à-vis* concentration of economic power, competition law and consumer protection. The objective of the MRTP Act is to curb monopolistic, restrictive and unfair trade practices, which distort competition in trade and industry and which adversely affect consumer interests. The significant provisions of the MRTP Act are discussed below.

## Monopolistic trade practices

Monopolistic trade practice as defined in Section 2(i) of the MRTP Act means a trade practice which:

- has, or is likely to have, the effect of maintaining either the prices of goods or the charges for the services at an unreasonable level;
- unreasonably prevents or lessens competition in the production, supply or distribution of any goods or in the supply of any services;
- limits the technical development or capital investment to the common detriment or allows the quality of any goods produced, supplied or distributed, or any service rendered, in India to deteriorate;
- increases unreasonably (a) the cost of production of any goods or (b) charges for the provision, or maintenance, of any services;
- increases unreasonably (a) the prices at which goods are, or may be, sold or re-sold, or the charges at which the services are, or may be, provided or (b) the profits which are, or may be, derived by the production, supply or distribution (including the sale or purchase) of any goods or by the provision of any services;
- prevents or lessens competition in the production, supply or distribution of any goods or in the provision or maintenance of any services by the adoption of unfair methods or unfair or deceptive practices.

## Unfair trade practices

As per Section 36A of the MRTP Act, unfair trade practice means a trade practice which, for the purpose of promoting the sale, use or supply of any goods or for the provision of any services, adopts any unfair method or unfair or deceptive practice. The unfair trade practices covered under the MRTP Act are:

- misleading advertisements and false representations;
- bargain sale, bait and switch selling;

- offering gifts or prizes with the intention of not providing them and conducting promotional contests;
- non-compliance of product safety standards;
- hoarding and destruction of goods.

In *Director General of Investigation and Registration vs. Investwell Publishers (P) Limited* (UTP Enquiry No. 146/1987), the MRTP Commission observed that the following are the necessary ingredients of an unfair trade practice as defined in the MRTP Act:

- There must be a 'trade practice' within the meaning of Section 2(u) of the MRTP Act.
- The trade practice must be employed for the purpose of promoting sale, use, supply of any goods or the provision of any services.
- The trade practice should fall within the ambit of one or more of the categories enumerated in clauses (1) to (5) of Section 36A.
- The trade practice should cause loss or injury to the consumers of goods or services.

However, after the amendment of Section 36A by the MRTP (Amendment) Act, 1991, it is no longer necessary to prove loss or injury to the consumer.

## Restrictive trade practices

Under the MRTP Act, restrictive trade practice includes a trade practice which has, or may have, the effect of preventing, distorting or restricting competition in any manner and in particular which tends to:

- obstruct the flow of capital or resources into the stream of production; or
- bring about manipulation of prices, or conditions of delivery or to affect the flow of supplies in the market relating to goods or services in such manner as to impose on the consumers unjustified costs or restrictions.

However, before any trade practice could be regarded as restrictive in nature, some damage must be indicated in the context of the relevant competitive situation.

## MRTP Commission

The MRTP Commission is a quasi-judicial body established under the MRTP Act, 1969. The main function of the MRTP Commission is to enquire into and take appropriate action in respect of unfair trade practices and restrictive trade practices. With regard to monopolistic trade practices, the MRTP Commission is empowered to enquire into such practices either upon:

(*a*) a reference made to it by the Central Government ; or
(*b*) upon its own knowledge or information and to submit its findings to the Central Government for further action.

The MRTP Commission has the powers of a civil court. The MRTP Commission has the power to summon and enforce the attendance of any witness and examine him or her on oath. It can also call for discovery and production of documents, proof by affidavits, issuance of commissions for examining witnesses, summoning records from courts and public offices and obtaining appearance of parties and giving effect to the consequences of non-appearance. The MRTP Commission can also grant temporary injunctions *ex parte* and even award compensation. The MRTP Commission can cause investigations to find out whether its orders have been complied with or not, and even punish for its contempt.

The MRTP Commission also has additional and special powers. Under these special powers, the MRTP Commission can require any person to produce, before an officer of the commission, books, accounts or other documents for examination, which could be retained for the said purpose and require information to be furnished on the trade practice and/or about the trade carried on by any other person, to the extent known to him. But the MRTP Commission cannot order the production of any privileged document or information.

## Need for a new Competition Law

In 1991, the march from a 'command and control' regime to a regime based more on free market principles commenced, and widespread economic reforms were undertaken. The economic reforms undertaken since the early 1990s significantly changed the economic environment in the country. In view of the policy shift from curbing monopolies to promoting competition, there was a need to repeal the MRTP Act. Accordingly, the government, in tune with international trends and to cope with changing realities, enacted the Competition Act, 2002, to replace the existing MRTP Act.

The Act is an omnibus code dealing with matters relating to the existence and regulation of competition and monopolies based on principles well established in the European Commission competition law and the US anti-trust law.

The Act has not completely repealed the MRTP Act. The MRTP Commission is still an active body. The provisions of the MRTP Act are still not repealed; the transition from the MRTP Act to the Act is not complete yet. As of now, only a few provisions of the Act have been brought into force and the process of constituting the regulatory authority, namely, the CCI (Competition Commission of India) under the new Act, is on. The remaining provisions of the new law will be brought into force in a phased manner. For the present, the outgoing law, MRTP Act, and the new law, the Competition

Act, 2002, are concurrently in force, though as mentioned above, only some provisions of the Act have been brought into force.

# The Competition Act, 2002

The Act received the assent of the President of India on 13 January 2003, and was published in the *Gazette* of India dated 14 January 2003. Some of the sections of the Act were brought into force on 31 March 2003 and the majority of the other sections on 19 June 2003. However, the entire Act has still not come into force. The Act provides for a modern framework of competition. It deals with three important aspects.

## Abuse of dominant position

Dominant position means a position of strength, enjoyed by an enterprise, in the relevant market, in India, which enables it to:

(*a*) operate independently of competitive forces prevailing in the relevant market;
(*b*) affect its competitors or consumers or the relevant market in its favour.

Section 4 of the Act prohibits abuse of dominant position by any enterprise. Such abuse of dominant position, *inter alia*, includes imposition, either directly or indirectly, of unfair or discriminatory purchase or selling prices or conditions, including predatory prices of goods or service, limiting production or restricting of goods or provision of service, indulging in practices resulting in denial of market access, making the conclusion of contracts subject to acceptance by other parties of supplementary obligations and using dominant position in one market to enter into or protect another market.

## Anti-competitive agreements

The Act classifies anti-competitive agreements into two categories, namely horizontal agreements and vertical agreements. Horizontal agreements are between two or more enterprises that are at the same stage of production chain and in the same market and vertical agreements are between enterprises that are at different stages or levels of production chain.

The following horizontal agreements are *per se* void:

(*a*) agreements fixing purchase or selling prices;
(*b*) agreements limiting or controlling production, supply, markets, technical development, investment or provision of services;

(*c*) agreements for sharing of market or source of production or services by way of allocation of geographical market or type of goods or services in the market;
(*d*) agreements relating to bid rigging or collective pricing.

The following agreements have been identified as vertical agreements:

(*a*) tie-in arrangement;
(*b*) exclusive supply agreement;
(*c*) exclusive distribution agreement;
(*d*) refused to deal;
(*e*) re-sale price maintenance.

Such agreements are not *per se* void and are not presumed to be anti-competitive. Such agreements shall be regarded as anti-competitive only when its adverse effect on competition is appreciable and the onus lies on the complainant to substantiate this allegation.

## Combinations and regulation of combinations

The Act is designed to regulate the operation and activities of combinations, a term which contemplates acquisitions, mergers or amalgamations. Thus, the operation of the Act is not confined to transactions strictly within the boundaries of India but also such transactions involving entities existing and/or established overseas.

The Act provides that any person or enterprise which proposes to enter into a combination may approach the CCI, by giving notice in the prescribed form with fee, for seeking its approval. The notice should be given within seven days of approval of the proposal for amalgamation by the Board of Directors of the transferor or within seven days of execution of agreement for acquisition. The notice may be given by any party, acquirer, acquired entity or transferor or transferee company. On receipt of notice, the CCI shall inquire whether the disclosure made in the notice is correct and whether the combination has or is likely to have an appreciable adverse effect on competition.

The CCI may also *suo moto* issue a show cause notice to the parties for investigation of combination. After enquiry, the CCI may approve the proposed combination, may propose modification to the combination or may order that the proposed combination be not given effect.

# Competition Commission of India

The CCI was established on 14 October 2003 to prevent practices having an adverse effect on competition, to promote and sustain competition in markets, to protect the interest of consumers and to ensure freedom of trade carried on by other participants in markets in India, and for matters connected therewith or incidental thereto.

In pursuance of achieving and fulfilling such duties, it is empowered to:

(*a*) enquire into anti-competitive agreements;
(*b*) enquire into abuse of dominant position.

In addition to these powers the CCI has *suo moto* power to enquire whether an anti-competitive agreement or abuse of dominant position or any combination within or outside India causes or is likely to cause an appreciable adverse effect on competition.

The provisions concerning the CCI as provided in the Act of 2002 have been amended by the Competition (Amendment) Bill, 2007:

(*a*) the CCI being an expert body which would function as a market regulator for preventing and regulating anti-competitive practices in the country in accordance with the Act, and also have advisory and advocacy functions in its role as a regulator;
(*b*) mandatory notice of merger or combination by a person or enterprise to the CCI within 30 (thirty) days and the imposition by the CCI of a penalty of up to 1 per cent of the total turnover or the assets, whichever is higher, on a person or enterprise which fails to give notice of merger or combination to the CCI;
(*c*) the establishment of the Competition Appellate Tribunal to hear and dispose of appeals against any direction issued or decision made or order passed by the CCI;
(*d*) implementation of the orders of the Competition Appellate Tribunal as a decree of a civil court;
(*e*) filing of appeal against the orders of the Competition Appellate Tribunal to the Supreme Court of India;
(*f*) imposition of a penalty by the CCI for contravention of its orders and in certain cases of continued contravention a penalty which may extend to INR 25 crores or imprisonment which may extend to three years or with both as the Chief Metropolitan Magistrate, Delhi, may deem fit.

# Conclusion

In pursuit of globalization, India has responded by opening up its economy, removing controls and resorting to liberalization. Thus anti-competitive laws play an important role within the country in maintaining the competitiveness in the Indian market.

# 4.12

# Corporate Governance

*Diljeet Titus and Raghav Handa, Titus & Co. Advocates*

Efforts to articulate standards for corporate governance took root in countries like the United States and the United Kingdom and have subsequently spread to other countries. The initiatives taken by the Indian government in 1991, aimed at economic liberalization of the domestic economy, led India to initiate a reform process in order to respond suitably to the developments taking place the world over. Pursuant to the Cadbury Committee Report, the Confederation of Indian Industries, Associated Chambers of Commerce and the Securities and Exchange Board of India constituted committees to recommend initiatives on corporate governance.

The above-mentioned autonomous bodies sought to achieve the following objectives:

(*a*) ensure that there is a properly structured board of directors capable of taking independent and objective decisions;
(*b*) ensure that there is a balanced board of directors as regards the representation of adequate number of non-executive and independent directors to take care of the interests of all the stakeholders;
(*c*) ensure that the board of directors adopts a transparent procedure and practice and its decision making is solely on the basis of adequate information;
(*d*) ensure that the board of directors keeps the shareholders informed of relevant developments impacting the company.

## Evolution and development of corporate governance in India

To ensure that the board of directors effectively monitors the functioning of the management of the company, India has also formulated codes of corporate governance through various committees, the more important ones being:

(*a*) CII Code of Desirable Corporate Governance (1998);
(*b*) UTI Code of Governance (1999);
(*c*) SEBI (Securities and Exchange Board of India) norms based on Kumar Mangalam Birla Committee Report on Corporate Governance (2000);
(*d*) Naresh Chandra Committee on Corporate Audit and Governance (2002);
(*e*) Narayanmurthy Committee on Corporate Governance (2003).

The recommendations of the various committees mentioned above address the following issues:

(*a*) reporting of key information;
(*b*) requiring listed companies to have audit committees;
(*c*) corporate board to give a statement on value addition; and
(*d*) optional consolidation of accounts.

## Principles of good corporate governance

Commonly accepted principles of good corporate governance include:

- *Rights and equitable treatment of shareholders*: Organizations should respect the rights of shareholders and help shareholders to exercise those rights. They can help shareholders exercise their rights by effectively communicating information that is understandable and accessible and encouraging shareholders to participate in general meetings.
- *Risk management*: Organizations should clearly establish the process of identifying, analyzing and treating risks, which could prevent the company from effectively achieving its objectives.
- *Role and responsibilities of the board*: The board as a main functionary is primarily responsible to ensure value creation for its stakeholders. It needs to be of sufficient size and has an appropriate level of commitment to fulfil its responsibilities and duties. The role of the board should be clearly documented in a board charter.
- *Code of conduct*: Organizations should develop a code of conduct for their directors and executives that promotes ethical and responsible decision making. It is important to understand, though, that systemic reliance on integrity and ethics is bound to lead to eventual failure. Systems should be in place to periodically measure, evaluate and if possible recognize the adherence to code of conduct.
- *Disclosure and transparency*: Organizations should clarify and make publicly known the roles and responsibilities of the board and management to provide shareholders with a level of accountability. They should also implement procedures to independently verify and safeguard the integrity of the company's financial reporting.

# Mechanism and control

Corporate governance mechanisms and controls are designed to reduce inefficiencies that arise from moral hazards and adverse selections.

# Internal corporate governance

Internal corporate governance monitors activities and takes corrective action to accomplish organizational goals. Examples include:

- *Monitoring by the board of directors*: The board of directors, with its legal authority to hire, fire and compensate top management, safeguards invested capital. Regular board meetings allow potential problems to be identified, discussed and avoided. Whilst non-executive directors are thought to be more independent, they may not always result in more effective corporate governance and may not increase performance. Different board structures are optimal for different firms. Moreover, the ability of the board to monitor the firm's executives is a function of its access to information. Executive directors possess superior knowledge of the decision-making process and therefore evaluate top management on the basis of the quality of its decisions that lead to financial performance outcomes, *ex ante*. It could be argued, therefore, that executive directors look beyond the financial criteria.
- *Remuneration*: Performance-based remuneration is designed to relate some proportion of salary to individual performance. It may be in the form of cash or non-cash payments such as shares and share options, superannuation or other benefits. Such incentive schemes, however, are reactive in the sense that they provide no mechanism for preventing mistakes or opportunistic behaviour and can elicit myopic behaviour.

# External corporate governance

External corporate governance encompasses the controls external stakeholders exercise over the organization. Examples include:

- debt covenants;
- government regulations;
- media pressure;
- takeovers;
- competition;
- managerial labour market;
- telephone tapping.

# Regulatory regime

In India, the regulatory provisions relating to corporate governance are enunciated in the regulations framed by the SEBI and associated provisions in the CA56 (Companies Act, 1956). Corporate governance principles as per Clause 49 of the Listing Agreement and relevant sections of CA56 are discussed as follows.

## Board of directors

The strength of the non-executive directors should not be less than 50 per cent of the total strength of the board. In the case where the board has a non-executive chairman, independent directors should be at least one-third of the board and in the case where the board has an executive chairman, independent directors should be at least half of the board.

The term 'independent directors' means that besides fees the directors do not have any material pecuniary relationship with the company or its promoters or subsidiaries. All pecuniary relationship or transactions of the non-executive directors *vis-à-vis* the company should be disclosed in the Annual Report.

## Audit committee

(*a*) The audit committee shall have a minimum of three non-executive directors other than managing and whole-time directors.
(*b*) The majority of the non-executive directors shall be independent and at least one of them should have financial and accounting knowledge.
(*c*) The chairman shall be an independent director.
(*d*) The chairman shall be present at Annual General Meeting to answer queries of shareholders.
(*e*) The finance director, head of internal audit and a representative of external auditor, whenever required, shall be present at the meeting as invitees.
(*f*) The company secretary shall act as the secretary to the committee.
(*g*) The audit committee shall meet at least three times a year.
(*h*) The committee shall have such powers and carry out such functions as prescribed.

### *Application of Section 292A in CA56*

Additional provisions that shall be complied with as per Section 292A CA56 are as follows:

(*a*) Two-thirds of total directors of the committee shall be other than managing and whole-time directors.

(*b*) The terms of reference for the committee shall be specified by the board and in addition the committee shall have discussions with external auditors periodically about internal control systems, the scope of audit including the observation of the auditors and review of the half-yearly and annual financial statements before submission to the board.
(*c*) The recommendations of the audit committee on any matter relating to financial management including the audit report shall be binding on the board. If the board does not accept the recommendations of the committee, it shall record the reasons therefore and communicate such reasons to the shareholders.
(*d*) The annual report of the company shall contain the composition of the audit committee.
(*e*) The members of the audit committee shall elect a chairman from amongst themselves.

## Remuneration of directors

The company shall make the following disclosures on the remuneration of directors in the Section on corporate governance in the annual report:

(*a*) full particulars of remuneration like salary, benefits, bonus, stock options, pension, etc.;
(*b*) performance-linked incentives along with the performance criteria and fixed component of incentive;
(*c*) particulars of service contracts, notice period, severance fees;
(*d*) stock option details like whether issue price is at a discount over market price, period of option, etc.;

The remuneration of non-executive directors shall be decided by the board.

### *Application of the provisions of CA56*

Pursuant to Section 309 and Schedule XIII of CA56, the appointment and remuneration payable to all executive directors and payment or commission to non-executive directors must be approved by the company general meeting. The explanatory statement relating to the concerned resolution contains full details of the remuneration payable to the directors. However, the disclosure about service contracts, notice period, severance fees, etc, which are included in the agreement, have not been placed before the general meeting hitherto. Clause 49 of the listing agreement makes it mandatory for the companies to place the above further details before the general meetings.

## Board procedure

(*a*) The new Clause 49 requires companies to ensure that the gap between two board meetings shall not exceed four months.
(*b*) To enable a director not to take up more work than he or she can handle, it has been specified that a director shall not become a member in more than 10 committees nor must a director act as chairman of more than five committees.

Every director isy obligated to inform the company the committee position he/she occupies in other companies and notify changes that take place. Both the above stipulations will in the long run promote a better utilization of the active time of the directors, and these can be easily followed.

## Management

Under this sub-clause, every listed company has been asked to include in its directors' report, or separately, a management discussion and analysis report that shall form part of the annual report to the shareholders. The said management discussion and analysis report should contain a discussion on the following aspects of the operation of the company within the limits of safeguarding its competitive position:

(*a*) industry structure and developments;
(*b*) opportunities and threats;
(*c*) segment-wise or product-wise performance;
(*d*) outlook;
(*e*) risks and concerns;
(*f*) internal control systems and their adequacy;
(*g*) discussion on financial performance with respect to operational performance;
(*h*) material developments in human resources/industrial relations front including number of people employed.

It is also prescribed that the report should contain the disclosures made by the (operating) management to the board relating to all material, financial and commercial transactions in which any person in the management (team) has a personal interest that may be in conflict with the interest of the company, as for instance dealing in shares of the company, commercial dealings with companies in which any person in the management and/or his relatives have personal interest.

## *Application of provisions of CA56: Director's Responsibility Statement*

In this connection, it will be noted that pursuant to Section 217(2) of CA56, the board's report shall, among other things, deal with the changes that have occurred during the financial year:

(*a*) in the nature of the company's business;
(*b*) in the company's subsidiaries or in the nature of business carried on by them;
(*c*) generally in the classes of business in which the company has an interest.

In compliance with the statutory provisions quoted above, the directors' reports of companies contain details of the company's performance during the year under review and the performance of its subsidiaries.

On the other hand, specific details that are required to be reported in the annual reports of companies as per Clause 49 of the listing agreement are of immense value to investors. Such details include opportunities available to and threats facing the company, segment-wise or product-wise reporting of performance, internal control system and their adequacy, etc.

The new provision in sub-section (2AA) to Section 217 of CA56 strengthens the duty of accountability of the directors by making them indicate in the Directors' Responsibility Statement, which will form part of the annual directors' report, the following:

(*a*) that in the preparation of the annual accounts, the applicable accounting standards have been followed along with proper explanation relating to material departures;
(*b*) that directors have selected such accounting policies and applied them consistently and made judgements and estimates that are reasonable and prudent so as to give a true and fair view of the state of affairs of the company at the end of the financial year and of the profit or loss of the company for that period;
(*c*) that directors have taken sufficient and proper care for the maintenance of adequate accounting records in accordance with the provisions of CA56 for safeguarding the assets of the company and for preventing and detecting fraud and other irregularities;
(*d*) that directors have prepared the annual accounts on a going concern basis.

The disclosure of more information about the working of the company, required to be given as per the new Clause 49 and the requirements of the said accountability of the directors as per the new provision in Section 217 of CA56 are welcome steps to ensure a vibrant and transparent capital market and to promote active investor protection.

## Shareholders

(*a*) In the case of appointment of a new director or reappointment of a director, the shareholders must be given:
  (*a*) a brief résumé of the director;
  (*b*) nature of his or her experience in specific functional area;
  (*c*) names of companies in which he or she is director and in which he or she holds membership of committees.
(*b*) The company shall supply quarterly results and presentations made by it to stock exchanges to enable them to put the information on their own website.
(*c*) The company shall constitute a shareholders/investors grievance committee under the chairmanship of a non-executive director specifically to look into complaints in respect of transfer of shares, non-receipt of balance sheet, non-receipt of dividend, etc.
(*d*) The company shall delegate the power of transfer to an officer or to a committee or to the registrar and share transfer agents, and the delegated authority shall attend to share transfer work once a fortnight.
(*e*) There must be a report on corporate governance in the directors' report.

Every listed company is required to include a detailed compliance report on corporate governance. Non-compliance of any item of Clause 49 of the listing agreement discussed above and reasons therefore should be mentioned in the compliance report.

## Certificate of compliance

The company shall obtain a certificate from the auditors of the company regarding compliance of the conditions of corporate governance as per Clause 49 of the listing agreement and annex the same with the directors' report. A copy of the certificate shall also be sent by the company to the stock exchange concerned, along with the annual return.

# Lacunas in existing Clause 49

Clause 49 of Listing Agreement has changed the structure and working of the companies to a great extent. Introduction of corporate governance has infused enhanced transparency and ethics into the structure and working of the companies. Yet there are many lacunas that have to be taken care of in order to ensure better performance and implementation of corporate governance. For example, the present code allows the promoters to gain/

retain control over companies.[1] The main implication of the shareholding pattern is that leaving decision making to companies' shareholders and their boards in effect means giving full freedom to the promoters. In most companies institutional investors, who could have played the monitoring role, have either no presence or are only marginal players. It may seem that India has missed an opportunity to build an ownership structure which while making the promoters genuinely interested also would have kept them on a tight leash.

Private managements probably did not oppose the induction of independent directors initially because first, it was difficult for them to openly oppose the international trend and second, they had the freedom to decide on a director's independence. Promoters being firmly in saddle, the slim possibility of genuine independent directors getting elected to corporate boards have receded further. As a result of this companies have found a way to avoid the probable problems faced by the induction of independent directors. In many companies, the promoters re-designate themselves as non-executive chairmen to enable the company to evade the provision to reserve half of the board seats for independent directors.

However, this is only a part of the problem: the major problem is that some companies are designating the promoter's father-in-law, mother's brother or wife's brother as non-executive chairman as they are not regarded as relatives under the company law. SEBI had to make the Corporate Governance Code somewhat more palatable to them. It is, therefore, debatable to what extent the efforts at improving corporate governance will succeed in the face of high promoter stakes.

The prescribed minimum public shareholding is so low that managements can get through even special resolutions without any hindrance. It is easy

---

[1] The Securities and Exchange Board of India (Substantial Acquisition of Shares and Takeovers) Regulations, 1997, defines a 'Promoter' as – "(a) any person who is in control of the target company; (b) any person named as promoter in any offer document of the target company or any shareholding pattern filed by the target company with the stock exchanges pursuant to the Listing Agreement, whichever is later, and includes any person belonging to the promoter group as mentioned in Explanation I, provided that a director or officer of the target company or any other person shall not be a promoter, if he/she is acting as such merely in his/her professional capacity.

Explanation I: For the purpose of this clause, 'promoter group' shall include: (a) in case the promoter is a body corporate (i) a subsidiary or holding company of that body corporate; (ii) any company in which the promoter holds 10 per cent or more of the equity capital or which holds 10 per cent or more of the equity capital of the promoter; (iii) any company in which a group of individuals or companies or combinations thereof who holds 20 per cent or more of the equity capital in that company also holds 20 per cent or more of the equity capital of the target company; and (b) in case the promoter is an individual (i) the spouse of that person, or any parent, brother, sister or child of that person or of his spouse; (ii) any company in which 10 per cent or more of the share capital is held by the promoter or an immediate relative of the promoter or a firm or HUF in which the promoter or any one or more of his immediate relative is a member; (iii) any company in which a company specified in (i) above, holds 10 per cent or more, of the share capital; and (iv) any HUF or firm in which the aggregate share of the promoter and his immediate relatives is equal to or more than 10 per cent of the total.

Explanation II: Financial Institutions, Scheduled Banks, FIIs (Foreign Institutional Investors) and Mutual Funds shall not be deemed to be a promoter or promoter group merely by virtue of their shareholding. Provided that the Financial Institutions, Scheduled Banks and FIIs shall be treated as promoters or promoter group for the subsidiaries or companies promoted by them or mutual funds sponsored by them."

to let promoters accumulate their holding but difficult to force them to bring it down. Effective steps should be taken at the entry point itself to curb the problem.

If the objective is to have genuine independent directors and constraining the promoters, the recommendations of Asian Development Bank such as placing restrictions on promoter voting and making cumulative voting and representation of minority shareholders mandatory need a fresh look. On certain matters, promoters should be denied the voting rights. Provisions relating to the election of directors should be made more restrictive so that diverse shareholder interests can get representation on corporate boards. For instance, small shareholder representation on company boards could be made mandatory rather than voluntary.

Induction of independent directors is only the first step. For the mechanism to be effective, one needs to continually monitor the characteristics of such directors and a change must be brought about in the definition of 'relatives' so as to enlarge it to include the in-laws of promoters also.

But excessive regulation stifles innovation and growth, which is also a major risk. Shareholder activism needs to be encouraged, or at least not stifled. They are the best check on fraudulent practices of managers and directors. The art of corporate governance lies in establishing convergence between the interests of managers and other stakeholders, and selecting boards that provide this crucial link, ensuring that managers neither abuse their authority nor feel cramped to the extent that they do not feel trusted.

# 4.13

# Financial Services Law and Money Laundering

*Diljeet Titus and Ramandeep Kaur Arora, Titus & Co. Advocates*

Financial services are the services related to money transmission, mortgage, lending, guarantees, life insurance, assurance, pension or investments offered by the banks and financial institutions like non-banking financial companies, insurance companies, etc. Section 2(k) of the SARFAESI Act (Securitization and Reconstruction of Financial Assets and Enforcement of Security Interest Act, 2002) defines financial assistance as any loan or advance granted or any debentures or bonds subscribed or any guarantees given or letters of credit established or any other credit facility extended by any financial institution. Financial institutions are the institutions involved in the management of money.

## Types of financial services

The services that qualify as financial services are set out below.

### Customary services

Customary services, which include lending, mortgage, issue of pay order, demand draft, cheque, letter of credit and bill of exchange, are usually provided by the financial institutions. These services may be provided by public financial institutions, state financial institutions, scheduled commercial banks and the General Insurance Corporation of India.

### Merchant banking services

Many banks have now opened up merchant banking departments which specialize in domestic corporate financing and associated businesses such as underwriting of capital issues, acting as managers to new issues and evaluating customers' existing and proposed new business. These services extend to examination of proposals for mergers and amalgamations of companies and arrangements of loans or short-term finance. The banks also assist in arranging for foreign exchange required by industries for their projects and loans with banks and other institutions outside India.

## Securities and foreign exchange broking

Securities and foreign exchange broking are dealt by the foreign exchange broker. Per Section 65(46) of the FA (Finance Act), 1994, a foreign exchange broker includes any authorized dealer of foreign exchange. As per Section 2(c) of the FEMA (Foreign Exchange Management Act), 1999, the authorized dealer of foreign exchange has been assigned the meaning of 'authorized person'.

## Asset management

Asset management involves taking care of the assets of others on a professional basis and includes managing securities, such as real estate, portfolio management, pension fund management, depository and trust services, all forms of fund management, but it does not include cash management. Asset management companies are the specialized companies incorporated specifically for the aforesaid purposes.

## Advisory and other auxiliary financial services including investment and portfolio research and advice

Financial institutions also act as financial advisors at times and provide the advice to the clients on a demand basis after a detailed research and analysis. These advices are formed in a manner to suit the need of the client. For this purpose, they have either a specialized department or an arrangement with some independent consultants.

## Services by insurance companies and advisers

Insurance companies are gaining recognition with the growing market and more players are entering into the field of insurance to grab their share in the market. Insurance companies provide services not only like life insurance, marine insurance, motor and accident insurance, fire insurance and various other forms of insurance but also are engaged in providing insurance-related advisory services.

# Financial service providers

Financial services can be provided by any of the following entities.

## Banking companies

Per Section 5(c) of the BR Act (Banking Regulation Act), 1949, 'banking company', means any company which transacts the business of banking in India. This means that transacting the business of banking should be the primary aim of the banking company as formed and registered under the CA56 (Companies Act, 1956) and not that banking business has been transacted at any particular point of time. Also, any company which is engaged in the manufacture of goods or carries on any trade and which accepts any deposits of money from the public merely for the purpose of financing its business as a manufacturer or trader cannot be classified as a banking company.

The major portion of financial services in India is provided by the banking companies. The business of a banking company is multifold and ranges from accepting money from the public to carrying on and transacting every kind of guarantee and indemnity business. It further includes: undertaking and executing of trusts; contracting for public and private loans; acting as agents for the government or any other local authority; managing, selling and realizing any property which may come into the possession in satisfaction or part-satisfaction of any suits/claims; acquiring, holding, dealing with any property or right or title or interest in any property which may form the security or part of the security for any loans or advances connected with such security; selling, improving, managing, developing, exchanging, leasing, mortgaging or dealing with all or any part of the property rights. The financial services provided by the banking companies have become more easy and convenient with stiff competition and the advancement of technology.

## Financial institutions

In terms of economics, a financial institution acts as an agent that provides financial services to its clients. Financial institutions generally fall under financial regulation from a government authority. In India, financial institutions are covered by various statutes and are well defined under Section 65(45) of the FA, Section 2(m) of SARFAESI Act, 2002, Section 2(h) of The Recovery of Debt Due To Banks and Financial Institutions Act, 1993 and Section 45-I(c) of RBI Act (Reserve Bank of India Act), 1934. Summarization of these definitions provides that a financial institution means:

- a public financial institution within the meaning of Section 4A of the CA56;
- such other institution as the central government may, having regard to its business activity and the area of its operation in India, by notification, specify, like a chit fund company, a cooperative bank, a housing finance institution and non-banking financial company.

Various types of financial institutions are discussed as below.

### *Public financial institution*

Per Section 4A of the CA56, no institution can be recognized as a public financial institution unless it has been established or constituted by or under the Central Act, or not less than 51 per cent of the paid-up share capital of such institution is held or controlled by the central government. Industrial Credit and Investment Corporation of India Limited, Industrial Finance Corporation of India, Industrial Development Bank of India, Life Insurance Corporation of India, Unit Trust of India and Infrastructure Development Finance Company are the only institutions which are recognized as the public financial institutions.

### *Chit fund company*

A chit fund is a kind of saving scheme practised in India. In a chit scheme, a specific number of individuals come together to pool a specific amount of money at periodic intervals and a chit fund company manages, conducts or supervises as foreman, agent or in any other capacity the chits. Usually, the number of individuals and the number of periods will be same. At the end of each period, there will be an auction of the money. Members of the chit will participate in this auction for the pooled money during that interval. The money will be given to the highest bidder. The bid amount will be divided by number of members, and thus determining per head contribution during that period. Usually the discount will continue to decrease over periods. The person getting money in the last period will receive the full scheme amount. Such chit fund schemes are conducted by organized financial institutions.

### *Cooperative bank*

A cooperative bank means a society which is doing the business of banking and is defined in Section 5(1) of the BR Act, 1949, and includes any society which is functioning or is to function as an agricultural and rural development bank. Section 2(dd) of the Deposit Insurance and Credit Guarantee Corporation Act, 1961, also provides for the cooperative bank as a state cooperative bank, a central cooperative bank and a primary cooperative bank.

## *Non-banking financial companies*

Section 45-I(f) of the RBI Act defines NBFCs (non-banking financial companies) as the companies whose principal business is either receiving of deposits or lending of money. The main emphasis of NBFCs is to provide assistance to the corporate sector and provide finance against the letter of credit or bill of exchange. NBFC also provides financial assistance in the form of lease finance or hire purchase. NBFCs include the following:

- hire purchase finance companies;
- equipment leasing companies;
- loan companies;
- investment companies;
- mutual benefit financial companies.

## *Statutory financial institutions*

Various statutory financial institutions have been established to render financial assistance to industries. Institutions have also been set up for financing agriculture and rural development, export and housing development. Some of the statutory financial institutions include:

- Industrial Finance Corporation of India, a national level development bank set up under the Industrial Finance Corporation Act, 1948;
- Industrial Development Bank of India established under Industries Development Bank of India Act, 1964;
- Industrial Investment Bank of India established in April 1971;
- National Bank for Agriculture and Rural Development set up under the National Bank for Agricultural and Rural Development Act, 1981;
- Rural Infrastructure Development Fund set up in 1995–96 under the aegis of the central government.

In order to meet the term credit needs of medium- and small-scale industries, several states set up State Financial Corporations after being empowered as such by the State Financial Corporation Act, 1951, located in their respective territories. These institutions complement the activities of the Industrial Finance Corporation of India. The assistance of the State Financial Corporations to industrial units is mainly through loans, underwriting of shares, bonds and debentures and guaranteeing of deferred payments in connection with capital goods in India.

## *Qualified institutional buyers*

Qualified institutional buyers include financial institutions, insurance companies, banks, state financial corporations, trustees or any asset management companies making investment on behalf of mutual fund or provident fund or gratuity fund or pension fund or foreign industrial/institutional investors registered under the SEBI (Securities and Exchange Board of India). The term also includes public financial institutions under the Companies Act, scheduled commercial banks, multilateral and bilateral development financial institutions and venture capital funds registered with the SEBI.

## Legal framework

- *Companies Act, 1956*: It is the most comprehensive Act providing for law relating to companies, ranging from incorporation to the winding-up of a company and includes the procedure for the management and administration of a company, share capital and debentures, registration of charges, prevention of oppression and mismanagement.
- *Banking Regulation Act, 1949:* The primary objective of Banking Regulation Act is to protect the interest of the depositor. The scope of this legislation is quite extensive, including:
  - a broad definition of 'banking' so as to include all institutions which receive deposits either for lending or investment;
  - a prohibition on non-banking companies from accepting deposits repayable on demand;
  - the prescription of minimum capital standards;
  - a limit on the payment of dividends;
  - the introduction of a complete system of licensing of banks;
  - the inclusion of banks incorporated outside India;
  - the inspection of books and accounts of a bank by the RBI;
  - the provision for bringing the RBI into closer touch with banking companies; and
  - the introduction of an expedited liquidation procedure.
- *RBI Act, 1934*: the RBI Act provides for the constitution of a central bank in India, ie the RBI. The RBI executes the function of regulating bank notes, keeping reserves with a view to securing monetary stability in the country and operating the currency and credit system to the country's advantage.
- *FEMA, 1999, and its associated Regulations*: FEMA provides provisions regulating foreign exchange with the objective of facilitating external trade, foreign direct and indirect investment in India and promotion of orderly development and maintenance of the foreign exchange market in India.

## Money laundering

In common terminology, money laundering is the practice of engaging in financial transactions in order to conceal the identity, source and destination of the money in question. Broadly stated, it means any process or activity connected with the conversion of proceeds of crime to project proceeds of crime as untainted property.

## Anti-money laundering regime in India

- *The PMLA (Prevention of Money Laundering Act), 2002*: the PMLA declares money laundering a criminal and extraditable offence. It establishes fines and sentences for money laundering offences; imposes reporting and record keeping requirements on financial institutions, banking companies and financial intermediaries; provides for the seizure and confiscation of criminal proceeds and the creation of a Financial Intelligence Unit. This Act also provides for the establishment of Special Courts for offences of money laundering. The provisions of PMLA also seek to promote international cooperation in investigation of money laundering, in line with the Financial Action Task Force recommendations.
- *FEMA, 1999*: FEMA is one of the of the Indian government's primary tools for fighting money laundering in India. The objectives of FEMA include the establishment of controls over foreign exchange, prevention of capital flight and maintenance of external solvency. The Act also imposes fines on unlicensed foreign exchange dealers.
- *The Income Tax Act, 1961*: The Income Tax Act provides a framework for combating money laundering by penalizing acts for tax evasion. The Income Tax Act provides for the prosecution of offences such as concealment, fraudulent removal, transfer or delivery of any property with the intention to evade taxes, wilful failure to furnish the return on income, etc., making false statements in verification or delivery of an account or statement, and wilful failure to produce accounts and documents.
- *Companies Act, 1956*: The Companies Act focuses on promoting good corporate governance practices and stresses investor protection. It deals with issues such as promotion and formation of companies, membership, capital, charge on assets, meetings, conducting audit, etc. Apart from other reasons listed under the Act, companies could also be wound up if the business of the company is being conducted to defraud its creditors or members or if the company is run for a fraudulent or unlawful purpose.
- *Other Acts*: There are several other Acts such as the Arms Act, Ancient Monument Prevention Act, etc. having strict provisions that help in checking money laundering through these means.

# Approach to reforms

The last 10 years have seen major improvements in the working of various financial market participants. The government and the regulatory authorities have followed a step-by-step approach, not a big bang one. The entry of foreign players has assisted in the introduction of international practices and systems. Technology developments have improved customer service. However, some gaps remain, like the lack of an inter-bank interest rate benchmark, an active corporate debt market and a developed derivatives market. On the whole, the cumulative effect of the developments since 1991 has been quite encouraging. An indication of the strength of the reformed Indian financial system can be seen from the way India was not affected by the crisis in its neighbouring countries.

However, financial liberalization alone will not ensure stable economic growth. Some tough decisions still need to be taken. Without fiscal control, financial stability cannot be ensured. In the case of financial institutions, the political and legal structures have to ensure that borrowers repay the loans on time and non-performing assets are minimized. As fraud cannot be totally prevented even with the best of regulation, the aim should be to ensure that fraud is minimized.

# 4.14

# Environmental Law

*Diljeet Titus and Ratnika Sehgal, Titus & Co. Advocates*

In the present scenario, environmental degradation has emerged as a major global threat for human survival. It is for this reason that environmental issues are so often intensely debated. The law relating to the environment is rapidly growing as a complex regulatory mechanism which increasingly reflects public concern over vital issues such as clean water and air, conservation of forests and wildlife, increasing noise and depletion of other natural resources. The recent spate of legislation and policy formulations on environmental issues in India reveal sincere efforts of the government to combat this significant problem. But the environmental situation is not improving satisfactorily even after coming within the purview of various laws and government policy.

## Legal framework

### The Constitution of India

Article 48A of the Constitution specifies that the state shall endeavour to protect and improve the environment and will safeguard the forests and wildlife of the country. Further, under Article 51(1) A (g) of the Constitution, every citizen shall protect the environment.

### Key statutes

The key statutes enacted for the protection of the environment are set out below.

#### *The Environment (Protection) Act, 1986*

The main objective of this Act is to provide for the protection and improvement of the environment (which includes water, air, land, human beings, other living creatures, plants, micro-organisms, etc.) and for matters connected therewith. It is an umbrella legislation for the protection and improvement of the environment along with various other specific laws.

The Act empowers the central government to take all such measures it deems necessary or expedient for the purpose of protecting and improving the quality of the environment and preventing, controlling and abating environmental pollution. In cases of contravention of the provisions of this Act, punishment may extend to five years or a fine which may extend to Rs 1 lakh or both, and in cases where the contravention continues, with an additional fine which may extend to Rs 5,000 for each subsequent day of violation.

## *The Water (Prevention and Control of Pollution) Act, 1974*

This Act establishes an institutional structure for preventing and abating water pollution. The CPCB (Central Pollution Control Board) was constituted under this Act, to keep a check on the activities which are in contravention to the provisions of this Act. It establishes standards for water quality, and effluent discharging industries must seek permission to discharge waste into water bodies.

## *The Air (Prevention and Control of Pollution) Act, 1981*

Air pollution means any solid, liquid or gaseous substances including noise present in the atmosphere in such concentration which may be injurious to human beings or other living creatures or plants or property or environment. This Act aims to prevent and abate air pollution; contravention of the provisions of this Act is punishable with imprisonment for a term of not less than one year and six months but it can extend to six years or a fine or both.

## *The Noise Pollution (Regulation and Control) (Amendment), 2002*

The main factors contributing to noise pollution are vehicular traffic, industrial activities, various electrical appliances, sources of entertainment such as blaring musical systems, TVs, public address systems, running trains and air traffic, splutter of gensets every time power breaks down and so on.

The Environment (Protection) Act (1986) made just a passing reference to noise pollution. Although a notification was further issued in 1989 on ambient air quality standards *vis-à-vis* noise, it hardly made any impact on controlling noise pollution.

Fourteen years later in February 2000, the ministry of environment and forests woke up to the dire need for regulation and formulated the Noise Pollution (Regulation and Control) Rules. The salient features of these rules are that the state governments, being the implementation authorities, should initiate the process of controlling noise pollution by classifying the areas into residential, commercial, industrial and silent zones. The rules further provide that the governments should ensure that the noise levels do not exceed the prescribed limits.

In this regard, the rules further lay down the terms and conditions which are necessary to reduce noise pollution, permit use of loud speakers or public address systems during night hours (normally 10 pm to 6 am); the state governments may permit the use of loud speakers or public address systems during night hours, ie. between 10 pm and 12 midnight on or during any cultural or religious festive occasion of a limited duration not exceeding 15 days in all during a calendar.

## *The Indian Forests Act, 1927*

Although this Act embodies the colonial policies of the pre-independence era, it still remains in force. A state may declare forest lands or waste lands as reserved forests and may sell the produce from these forests. Any unauthorized felling of trees, quarrying, grazing and hunting in reserved forests is punishable with a fine or imprisonment, or both.

## *The Forest (Conservation) Act, 1980*

The Act was promulgated to check deforestation and for matters connected therewith. Any forest land or portion thereof cannot be used for any non-forest purposes or assigned by way of leases or otherwise to any private person or to any authority, corporation, agency or any other organization not owned, managed or controlled by the government, except with the prior approval of the central government. The Act also provides for an advisory committee to advise the central government with regard to the granting of such approval.

## *The Mines and Minerals (Development and Regulation) Act, 1957*

The said Act and rules are intended to regulate the development of mines and minerals under the control of the Union. The intention was that the mineral wealth of the country should be conserved and used in a sustainable manner. Section 4A permits the government to terminate a prospecting licence or mining lease in order to preserve the natural environment or prevent harm to public health, monuments, buildings and other structures. Sections 13 and 15 empower the central government and the states to frame rules to restore vegetation destroyed by mining operations in any area.

## *The Wildlife (Protection) Act, 1972*

The Wildlife Act provides for state wildlife advisory boards, regulations for hunting wild animals and birds, establishment of sanctuaries and national parks, regulations for trade in wild animals, animal products and trophies and judicially imposed penalties for violating the Act.

### *The Biological Diversity Act, 2002*

The said Act provides for the conservation of biological diversity, sustainable use of its components and fair and equitable sharing of the benefits arising out of the use of biological resources associated with it.

### *The PLIA (Public Liability Insurance Act), 1991*

This Act was enacted to provide for public liability insurance for providing immediate relief to the victims of accidents occurring while handling any hazardous substance and matters connected therewith. The Act imposes 'no-fault' liability upon the owner of the hazardous substance and requires the owner to compensate the victims irrespective of any neglect or default on his or her part.

### *The NETA (National Environment Tribunal Act), 1995*

This Act extends the principle of 'no-fault' liability and also received statutory recognition under PLIA. NETA is empowered to impose liability beyond the statutory compensation limits prescribed under the PLIA of 1991. NETA empowers the central government to establish a national tribunal to take up applications for compensation whereby it may determine its own procedure for processing the compensation claims, consistent with the principles of natural justice.

## Concept of sustainable development

The right to a wholesome environment is a fundamental right protected under Article 21 of the Constitution. But the question is – can the environment be protected at the present time when almost all the countries in South-East Asia are still at their developing stages? Development comes through industrialization, which in turn is the main cause behind the degradation of the environment. To resolve the issue, the experts worldwide have come up with a doctrine called 'sustainable development', ie. there must be a balance between development and ecology.

Some of the basic principles of sustainable development as described in the 'Brundtland Report' are as follows:

(*a*) *Inter-generational equity*: The principle talks about the right of every generation to get benefit from natural resources. Principle 3 of the Rio Declaration states that 'The right to development must be fulfilled so as to equitably meet developmental and environmental needs of present and future generations.'

(*b*) *The precautionary principle*: This principle has widely been recognized as the most important principle of sustainable development. Principle 15 of the Rio Declaration states that 'In order to protect the environment, the precautionary approach shall be widely applied by states according to their capabilities.' In other words, it can be explained as follows:

- (*a*) Environmental measures by the state governments and the local authorities must anticipate, prevent and attack the causes of environmental degradation.
- (*b*) Where there are threats of serious and irreversible damage, lack of scientific certainty should not be used as a reason for postponing measures to prevent environmental degradation.
- (*c*) The 'onus of proof' is on the actor or the developer to prove that his or her action is environmentally benign.

(*c*) *Polluter pays principle:* Principle 16 of the Rio Declaration states that 'National authorities should endeavour to promote the internalization of environmental costs and the use of economic instruments, taking into account the approach that the polluter should, in principle, bear the cost of pollution, with due regard to the public interest and without distorting international trade and investment'. It is quite obvious that the object of the principle was to make the polluter liable not only for the compensation to the victims but also for the cost of restoring the damage caused to the environment.

## Role of judiciary

The judiciary in India, more precisely, the Supreme Court and the High Courts, has played an important role in preserving the doctrine of sustainable development. It is worthwhile to mention here that principle 10 of Rio Declaration, 1992 states that 'Environmental issues are best handled with participation of all concerned citizens, at the relevant level. At the national level, each individual shall have appropriate access to information concerning the environment that is held by public authorities, including information on hazardous materials and activities in their communities, and the opportunity to participate in decision-making processes. States shall facilitate and encourage public awareness and participation by making information widely available. Effective access to judicial and administrative proceedings, including redress and remedy, shall be provided.'

The first case on which the apex court had applied the doctrine of sustainable development was *Vellore Citizen Welfare Forum vs. Union of India*. In this case, the dispute arose over some tanneries in the State of Tamil Nadu. These tanneries were discharging effluents in the river Palar, which was the main source of drinking water in the State. The Supreme Court held that 'We have no hesitation in holding that the precautionary principle and polluter pays principle are part of the environmental law of India'. The court also held that 'remediation of the damaged environment is part of the process of "Sustainable Development" and as such polluter is liable to pay the cost to the individual sufferers as well as the cost of reversing the damaged ecology'.

Even before *the Vellore Citizen* case, the Supreme Court had in many cases tried to keep the balance between ecology and development. In *Rural Litigation and Entitlement Kendra, Dehradun vs. State of Uttar Pradesh*, which was also known as *a Doon Valley Case*, a dispute arose over mining in the hilly areas. The Supreme Court, after much investigation, ordered the stoppage of mining work and held that 'This would undoubtedly cause hardship to them, but it is a price that has to be paid for protecting and safeguarding the right of the people to live in a healthy environment with minimal disturbance of ecological balance and without avoidable hazard to them and to their cattle, homes and agricultural land and undue pollution of air, water and environment.'

In another landmark case, *Tarun Bhagat Singh vs. Union of India*, the petitioner through a Public interest litigation (PIL) brought to the notice of the Supreme Court the fact that the State Government of Rajasthan, though empowered to make rules to protect environment, had failed to do so and on the contrary had allowed mining work to continue within the forest area. Consequently, the Supreme Court issued directions that no mining work or operation could be continued within the protected area. But it would be unwise to hold that the courts always favour environment without giving any importance to the development aspect when disputes arise between the environment and development.

In *M.C. Mehta vs. Union of India*, the Supreme Court issued directions towards the closing of mechanical stone crushing activities in and around Delhi, which was declared by the WHO to be the third most polluted city in the world. However, it realized the importance of stone crushing and issued directions for the allotment of sites in the new 'crushing zone' set up at the village of Pali in the State of Haryana. Thus, it is quite obvious that the courts give equal importance to both ecology and development while dealing with the cases of environmental degradation.

## Fly ash notification for thermal power plants

The notification was issued on 3 April 2007. The main objective of the notification is to conserve top soil, protect the environment and prevent the dumping and disposal of fly ash discharged from coal- and lignite-based thermal power plants on land. It also aims to promote the utilization of fly ash in the manufacture of building materials and in construction activity.

The central and the state governments agencies, the State Electricity Boards, the National Thermal Power Corporation and the management of the thermal power plants must facilitate utilization of ash. Public Work

Departments, Housing Boards, etc., are to prescribe the use of ash and ash-based products in their respective schedules of specifications. All local authorities are to specify in their respective building by-laws and regulations the use of ash and ash-based products.

*Responsibilities of the thermal power plants' owners*: Owners of coal- or lignite-based thermal power plants (including captive and/or cogeneration plants based on coal or lignite):

(*a*) may dispose of fly ash through competitive bids to the best advantage of the owners;
(*b*) shall not at any time store more than three months' ash generation in their storage and/or ash ponds. In cases where the quantity of fly ash already in storage and/or ash ponds on and from the date of this notification exceeds three months' generation, the same shall be disposed of within a maximum time of five years from the date of issue of this notification.

# Framing the future effort

The UNFCCC (UN Framework Convention on Climate Change) establishes a foundation and fundamental guiding principles, for such a global approach. To effectively advance the climate effort beyond 2012, the international framework must do the following:

- *Engage major economies*: The immediate imperative is successfully engaging the world's major economies. Twenty-five countries account for 83 per cent of global greenhouse gas emissions, 71 per cent of global population and 86 per cent of global income. There is tremendous diversity within this group. While all should be prepared to commit to stronger action, an equitable approach must be consistent with the principle of 'common but differentiated responsibilities'.
- *Provide flexibility*: To broaden participation, the multilateral framework must be flexible enough to accommodate different types of national strategies by allowing different types of commitments. Each country must be able to choose a pathway that best aligns its national interests with the global interest in climate action.
- *Couple near-term action with long-term focus*: Near-term action is urgently needed on three fronts: achieving immediate, cost-effective emission reductions; fostering the development of breakthrough technologies to achieve deeper reductions in the future and strengthening resilience to the adverse effects of a changing climate.
- *Integrate climate and development*: Countries can contribute to the international effort through actions that serve their development goals while simultaneously delivering climate benefits. In developing countries, efforts will be most successful if complemented by assistance, investment

and access to clean technologies.

- *Address adaptation*: The impacts of climate change are being felt already and are certain to intensify, even if immediate steps are taken to dramatically reduce emissions. These impacts fall disproportionately on the poor, particularly in developing countries. Fairness demands that they be assisted.
- *Be viewed as fair*: A new global bargain on climate change will be possible only if each participating country perceives it to be reasonably fair. Each country will judge fairness in terms it believes it can defend, both before its own citizens and the global community.

# 4.15

# Banking Law and Banking Sector

*Diljeet Titus and Jasman Boparai, Titus & Co. Advocates*

## Banking law and banking sector

In India, the aggregate foreign investment in private banks can be to a maximum of 74 per cent of the paid up capital of the bank, while the resident Indian holding of the capital has to be at least 26 per cent. Foreign banks may operate in India through only one of the following three channels:

- branches;
- a wholly owned subsidiary;
- a subsidiary with maximum foreign investment of 74 per cent in a private bank.

## Regulatory authority governing the banking sector

The RBI (Reserve Bank of India) is the foremost regulatory body for regulating financial institutions and banks in the country. It was established in 1935 under the RBI Act, 1934, and centralized in 1948.

(*a*) The RBI is the sole authority for issuing currency in the country, thus enabling regulation and control of the money supply in the country.

(*b*) The RBI acts as a banker to the central government and on request, for state governments, managing the public debt of the country. It accepts money on account of the government and makes payment on its behalf.

(*c*) It plays a supervisory role to all commercial banks in India. Commercial banks maintain accounts with the RBI and borrow money from it when necessary. The RBI also regulates the activities of these commercial banks by virtue of the powers vested in it under the Banking Regulation Act, 1949, and the RBI Act, 1934. No commercial bank can start its operations without first obtaining a licence from the RBI. The RBI can also revoke such a licence if it is of the opinion that the affairs of the bank are not being maintained in the public interest. The RBI has the power to inspect the working of the commercial banks. It can order audits and ask for accounts as and when it deems fit. The approval of the RBI is necessary for the appointment, reappointment or termination of a manager, chairman or whole-time director. The RBI has been given the power to control the advances given by the commercial banks; in other words it has selective credit control. The RBI can also appoint additional directors in any banking company if it so deems fit.

(*d*) The RBI has the responsibility for maintaining the internal and external value of the Indian rupee.

(*e*) It is also concerned with promoting and developing capital markets adequately over the country.

## Legal framework

### *SARFAESI (Securitization and Reconstruction of Financial Assets and Enforcement of Security Interest) Act, 2002*

The SARFAESI Act, 2002, was passed essentially for the securitization of financial assets so as to generate immediate liquidity, and to *enforce* security, as prior to the act there was no power to do so. It was enacted keeping in mind the changing commercial environment, the asset liability mismatch, the mounting levels of NPA (non-performing assets) and the fact that heavy losses were being incurred on account of unpaid debts. The SARFAESI Act primarily ensures the enforceability of securitization by financial institutions, and banks on account of NPA by creating recourse to Debt Recovery Tribunals. It enacts extremely important provisions relating to three domains: (i) securitization; (ii) resolution of non-performing loans via the asset management route; and, above all, (iii) enforcement of the rights of the secured lender.

#### *Securitization*

SARFAESI defines securitization as the acquisition of financial assets by any securitization company or reconstruction company from any originator, whether by raising of funds by such securitization company or reconstruction company from qualified institutional buyers by issue of security receipts representing undivided interest in such financial assets or otherwise. The central feature of such securitization is therefore the fact that there is a segregation of assets and issuance of securities which are either collateralized by such assets or represented by a beneficial interest in such assets.

#### *Asset reconstruction companies*

The SARFAESI Act allows acquisition of the financial assets of banks and financial institutions by any asset securitization or reconstruction company (including both standard loan assets and NPA) and raising of funds for such acquisition by issue of security receipts formulated for this purpose. ARCs (asset reconstruction companies) have to apply for and obtain a certificate of registration from the RBI. FDI in an ARC is permitted up to 49 per cent of the paid up equity capital of the ARC, subject to the prior approval of the Foreign Investment Promotion Board.

### *Enforcement of security interest*

When any borrower under a liability to a secured creditor under a security agreement makes any default in repayment of a secured debt or any instalment thereof, and his account as a result is classified by the secured creditor as an NPA, the secured creditor can require the borrower by notice in writing to discharge his liabilities in full, failing which the secured creditor will be entitled to exercise any of the rights under Section 13(4). Under the latter section, the secured creditor has a right to take over possession or management of the secured asset of the borrower including the right to transfer by way of lease, assignment or sale and realize the secured asset. The secured creditor also has a right to appoint any person to manage the asset, the possession of which already lies with the secured creditor, or demand payment by any person who has acquired any of the secured assets from the borrower and from whom any money has become due to the borrower, to pay the secured creditor so much of the money as is sufficient to pay the secured debt.

## *FEMA (Foreign Exchange Management Act), 1999*

FEMA, 1999, aims to facilitate external trade and payments for promoting the orderly development and maintenance of the foreign exchange market in India. Per the provisions of FEMA, the acquisition, holding, owning, possession or transferring of any foreign exchange, foreign security or any immovable property situated outside India by a person resident in India is prohibited. However, any person may sell or draw foreign exchange to or from any authorized person, if such sale or withdrawal is a current account transaction. The central government may in the public interest, however, and in consultation with the RBI, impose such reasonable restrictions for current account transactions as may be prescribed. The RBI in consultation with the central government may also specify any class of capital account transactions which are permissible and the limits up to which the Forex shall be admissible for such transactions. The RBI cannot impose any restrictions, however, on the drawal of Forex for payments due on account, amortization of loans or for depreciation of direct investments in the ordinary course of business.

### *NIA (Negotiable Instruments Act), 1881*

Per Section 13 of NIA, 1881, promissory notes, bills of exchange and cheques are negotiable instruments. Negotiable instruments are transferable instruments by their very nature, the property of which can be transferred by mere delivery or endorsement depending on whether the instrument is a bearer or order one. The transferee of the instrument gets a title that is free from the defects and equities of the transferor, depending on the nature of the instrument being bearer or not. Any far-off party liable on the negotiable instrument (holders in due course) can sue or be sued or sue in its own name.

Banks primarily deal with cheques; NIA deals with provisions as to the penalties in case of dishonour of a cheque for insufficiency of funds in an account. If a cheque is wrongfully dishonoured by a bank, the holder of such a cheque can sue any endorser or the drawer of the cheque directly. The Act describes in detail conditions related to payment of cheques and protection to the paying banker under various sections. The concept of 'payment in due course' has been elaborately dealt with in the NIA, and if the conditions of the same have been met with, the drawees are discharged from all liabilities.

## Financial institutions[1]

A distinguishing characteristic of banking financial institutions is that they participate in the economy's payments mechanism by providing transaction services. Banks, subject to legal reserve requirements, can advance credit by creating claims against themselves. Financial institutions, on the other hand, can lend only out of resources put at their disposal by the savers.

Financial institutions have been the primary source of long-term lending for large-scale projects. Conventionally, they raised their resources in the form of bonds subscribed by the RBI, public sector enterprises, banks and others. Financial institutions are increasingly raising resources at the short end of the deposit market.

Financial institutions as categorized by the SARFAESI Act[2] are:

(*a*) public financial institutions within the meaning of Section 4-A of the Companies Act, 1956;
(*b*) any institution specified by the central government under S.2(h)(ii) of the Recovery of Debts Due to Banks and Financial Institutions Act, 1993;
(*c*) the International Finance Corporation established under the International Finance Corporation Act, 1958;
(*d*) any other institution or non-banking financial company as defined in

---

[1] Defined in Section 45-I(c) of the RBI Act.

[2] Securitization and Reconstruction of Financial Assets and Enforcement of Security Interest Act, 2002 under S.2(1)(m).

45-I (f) of the RBI Act, 1934, which the central government may, by notification, specify as a financial institution for the purpose of this act.

This definition includes two parts, one which is listed in the law itself, ie. clauses (i) and (ii) of the above-mentioned Act (and clause (i) of S.2 of the the Recovery of Debts Due to Banks and Other Financial Institutions Act) and the other which needs to be 'notified' by the RBI in terms of the power to notify granted to it, other than the reference to the International Finance Corporation.

The 'to be notified' list empowers the RBI to only notify 'financial companies' as defined in the RBI Act. Under the Act, a company is treated as a financial company based on its business-lending, investment, hire purchase, leasing, etc. Financial companies, unless exempted from the operation of law, require registration with the RBI.

## Non-banking financial companies (NBFCs)

There has been emergence of many companies that are involved in the finance business, providing the corporate sector with funds. The facilities provided by them may match to some extent the facilities provided by commercial banks, but they cannot, yet, be classified as banking companies within the meaning of the enactments pertaining to the RBI.

NBFCs are governed by the Non-Banking Financial Companies Acceptance of Public Deposits (Reserve Bank) Directions, 1998.

NBFCs as per the above directions can be broadly classified into:

(*a*) hire-purchase finance companies;
(*b*) equipment leasing company;
(*c*) loan companies;
(*d*) investment company;
(*e*) mutual benefit financial companies.

Besides the classification as per the RBI guidelines, a few more categories of NBFCs and allied companies operating in the country are as listed below:

- miscellaneous non-banking companies;
- residuary non-banking companies;
- housing finance companies.

These companies have been performing a vital function especially where established financial entities are not accessible to the borrowers.[1] In India, a marked growth in the NBFC sector was noticed in the last two decades.

[1] The monetary and credit policy of the country usually leaves a section of the borrowers outside the purview of the commercial banks and NBFCs thus cater to the needs of such people.

The NBFCs as a group have succeeded in broadening the range of financial services rendered to the public.

One of the main reasons for the popularity of these institutions is customer orientation and higher rate of interest offered by them compared to banks. NBFCs are in a position to pay higher interest to their depositors as many of them can deploy their resources in segments where there are credit gaps at rates higher than those charged by banks. Depositors are taking a risk in placing their deposits with NBFC as they are not sufficiently regulated or supervised. However, the RBI directions of 1998 have taken positive steps toward investors' protection as, for instance, the RBI has been empowered to file a petition for the winding up of an NBFC in certain circumstances.

## Statutory financial institutions

State-level institutions mainly comprise state financial corporations (SFCs) and state industrial investment or development corporations.

### *State financial corporations (SFCs)*

SFCs have been set up by several states under the State Financial Corporations Act, 1951, for meeting the term credit needs of medium- and small-scale industries located in their respective territories. SFCs provide financial assistance to industrial units by way of term loans, underwriting of shares, bonds, debentures and the guaranteeing of deferred payments in connection with the purchase of capital goods in India. They also assist small-scale units with their modernization and technology upgrade programmes by providing soft loans, restructuring sick small-scale units through rehabilitation schemes.

The activities of the corporation are visualized not as a profit earning concern but as an extended arm of the state to harness any potential business of the country to benefit the common person.

### *State industrial development corporation (SIDCs)*

Included in the definition of state financial institutions along with SFCs, SIDCs are categorized as the state-level statutory institutions and are registered under the Companies Act, 1956.

## Monetary systems

Various components of the monetary system with respect to their regulatory authorities, ie. the RBI and the central government (ministry of finance) are as listed below:

- CRR (Cash Reserve Ratio) is the percentage of bank reserves to deposits and notes. The RBI stipulates the CRR – the proportion of deposits that commercial banks must hold in cash to control the availability of money in the market and thereby control inflation and is used as a tool in monetary policy, influencing the country's economy, borrowing and interest rates.
- All scheduled commercial banks are required to maintain minimum CRR balances up to 70 per cent of the total CRR requirement on all days of the fortnight. If any scheduled commercial bank fails to observe the minimum level of CRR, a penalty is imposed.[1] Though central banks rarely alter the reserve requirements, as it would cause immediate liquidity problems for banks with low excess reserves and instead, use open market operations to control monetary supply, lately the RBI ordered commercial banks to hold a larger share of deposits in cash, and raised a key short-term lending rate in a bid to curb high inflation.
- The SLR (statutory liquidity ratio) is the amount which a bank has to maintain in the form of cash, gold or approved securities. The quantum is specified as some percentage of the total demand and time liabilities of a bank. This percentage is fixed by the RBI.[2] At present, all scheduled banks are required to maintain a uniform SLR of 25 per cent of the total of their demand and time liabilities in India as on the last Friday of the second preceding fortnight. The 25 per cent bar is the minimum SLR (the statutory requirements to park their money in government bonds) limit the RBI can fix at present. The objectives of the SLR are to restrict the expansion of bank credit, to augment the investment of the banks in government securities and to ensure the solvency of banks.
- The bank rate is the rate of interest at which the RBI lends to the commercial banks in terms of re-discounting first class bills of exchange or other eligible paper. Whenever the RBI wants to reduce credit, the bank rate is raised and whenever the volume of bank credits is to be expanded the bank rate is reduced. In India, the bank rate has changed frequently from 1951 onwards and today the bank rate stands at 10 per cent.
- RP (rate repurchase) agreements are financial instruments used in the money markets and capital markets. In RP transactions, securities are exchanged for cash with an agreement to repurchase the securities at a future date. The securities serve as collateral for what is effectively a cash loan and, conversely, the cash serves as collateral for a securities loan. RP can be used for leverage, to fund long positions in securities and to

---

[1] On any day(s) during the relevant fortnight, the bank will not be paid interest to the extent of one-fourteenth of the eligible amount of interest, even if there is no shortfall in the CRR on average basis.

[2] As per Section 24(2-A) of the Banking Regulation Act, 1949, banks are required to maintain in (i) cash; (ii) gold valued at a price not exceeding the current market price; or (iii) unencumbered approved securities valued at a price as specified by the RBI from time to time; an amount of which shall not, at the close of business on any day, be less than 25 per cent or other such percentage not exceeding 40 per cent as the RBI may from time to time, by notification, specify, of the total of its demand and time liabilities in India as on the last Friday of the second preceding fortnight.

fund short positions for hedging interest rate risks.

- The prime lending rate is the lowest commercial interest rate charged by banks to their most creditworthy customers (usually the most prominent and stable business customers). The rate is almost always the same amongst major banks. Adjustments to the prime lending rate are made by banks at the same time, although the prime rate does not adjust on any regular basis.

# Conclusion

According to the RBI annual report 2007, there are 29 foreign banks operating in India, with approximately 268 offices across the country, and 34 other foreign banks run Indian operations through representative offices. The current liberal FDI policy and a huge untapped banking market make the Indian banking industry very lucrative for foreign investors.

# 4.16

# Capital Markets

*Diljeet Titus and Ramandeep Kaur Arora, Titus & Co. Advocates*

Capital markets play a significant role in mobilizing funds either to fund start-up costs, sustain operations or to help generate growth. Capital markets serve this requirement by pairing lenders and investors with companies that require funding. The funding may occur in the following three ways:

- borrowing from banks in the form of loans;
- borrowing directly from households and institutional lenders by issuing bonds;
- selling ownership shares in the firm through equity markets. Equity markets are another primary component of capital markets.

## Categories of capital market

Indian capital market primarily comprises two main categories.

### Primary market

The primary market is also called the market for public issues. It refers to the raising of new capital (equity or debt) by companies. Companies may tap the primary or equity market by offering public issues. When a company approaches the public for the first time to subscribe to its shares, it is called the IPO (Initial Public Offering), and when equity shares are exclusively offered to existing shareholders, it is called a 'rights issue'. Investments in new issues or the primary market can be made by NRIs (non-resident Indians) and FIIs (foreign institutional investors) subject to prior approvals of the RBI (Reserve Bank of India) and the SEBI (Securities and Exchange Board of India).

## Secondary market

The secondary market is the financial market for the trading of securities that have already been issued in an IPO. Secondary market operations involve the buying and selling of securities on the stock exchange through its members. It mainly provides liquidity to all the listed securities by enabling a holder to convert the securities into money through the stock exchanges. The secondary market also acts as an important indicator of the investment climate in the economy.

# Regulatory framework

The responsibility of regulating the capital market is shared by the DEA (Department of Economic Affairs), the MCA (ministry of corporate affairs), the RBI and the SEBI. The four main laws that govern the capital market are:

1. the CA56 (the Companies Act, 1956), which sets out the code of conduct for the corporate sector in relation to issue, allotment and transfer of securities and disclosures to be made in public issues;
2. the SCRA (Securities Contracts (Regulation) Act), 1956, which provides for regulation of transactions in securities through control over stock exchanges;
3. the SEBI (Securities and Exchange Board of India) Act, 1992, which establishes the SEBI (the board) to protect investors and to develop and regulate the capital market; and
4. the DA96 (Depositories Act, 1996), which provides for electronic maintenance and transfer of ownership of demat securities.

## CA56

A company may enter into the capital market through an IPO. Part III of the CA56 deals with the procedure to be followed for issuing a prospectus, allotment of shares and prohibitions on allotment in certain cases, eg. where the minimum subscription required has not been received. Further, it prescribes the liabilities of directors in cases of mis-statements made in the prospectus. Part IV of the CA56 broadly deals with the kinds of share capital, debenture share certificate, etc. It also contains, in detail, the procedure to be followed for the transfer of shares and debentures, which is the main activity of the capital market. Other than these, Part IV prohibits the reduction of share capital without permission of the High Court.

## SCRA, 1956

This Act was enacted to prevent the undesirable transactions in securities by regulating the business of dealing therein, by providing for certain other matters connected therewith. The Act provides for:

- the procedure for recognition of stock exchanges in India;
- the procedure for corporatization and demutualization of stock exchanges;
- listing and delisting of securities;
- the constitution of the Securities Appellate Tribunal; and
- the penalties for non-compliance of any of the procedure prescribed thereof in the Act.

The Parliament during its Budget Session 2005–2006 proposed to amend SCRA, 1956, so as to provide a legal framework for the trading of securitized debt including mortgage-backed debt. The bill is still pending before the Parliament.

## The Securities Contracts (Regulation) Rules, 1957

The central government has made Securities Contracts (Regulation) Rules, 1957, as required by sub-section (3) of the Section 30 of the SCRA, 1956, for carrying out the purposes of the Act. The said rules provide for: renewal of recognized stock exchanges in India (Rule 7); qualification standards for membership of a recognized stock exchange (Rule 8); requirements with respect to the listing of securities on a recognized stock exchange (Rule 19). Further, the said rules prescribe that all contracts between the members of a recognized stock exchange shall be confirmed in writing and shall be enforced in accordance with the rules and bye-laws of the stock exchange of which they are members (Rule 9).

## SEBI Act, 1992

This Act was enacted for the establishment of a board to protect the interests of investors in securities and to promote the development of, and to regulate, the securities market and matters connected therewith or incidental thereto. Apart from this, the Act provides for:

- registration of stock brokers, sub-brokers, share transfer agents, etc.;
- prohibition of insider trading;
- procedure for maintaining the accounts;
- penalties for failure to furnish information, returns, etc.;
- establishment of the Securities Appellate Tribunal for the purpose of adjudicating over the disputes arising with respect to the securities and so on.

SEBI has promulgated various regulations which are discussed below.

## SEBI (Prohibition of Insider Trading) Regulations, 1992

Per the said regulation, an insider is prohibited from dealing, communicating or counselling on matters relating to any such information which relates directly or indirectly to a company which if published is likely to affect the securities of the company. Further, it provides for a policy on disclosures and internal procedure for prevention of insider trading.

## SEBI (Merchant Bankers) Regulations, 1992

Per the said rules, no person shall act as a merchant banker or carry on any activity as a merchant banker, unless he or she holds a certificate granted by the SEBI. In this context, the said rules provide for registration and regulation of the activities of 'merchant bankers'; general obligations and responsibilities of merchant bankers, procedure for inspection and action in case of default.

## SEBI (Stock Brokers and Sub-Brokers) Regulations, 1992

Per the said regulation, no stock broker or sub-broker shall buy, sell or deal in securities, unless he or she holds a certificate granted by the board. In this context, the said regulation provides for registration and regulation of the activities of stock brokers and sub-brokers.

## SEBI (Debenture Trustees) Regulations, 1993

Per the said regulation, no person shall act as debenture trustee unless he or she holds a certificate granted by the board. In this context, the said regulation provides for:

(*a*) registration and regulation of the activities of debenture trustees;
(*b*) responsibilities and obligations of the debenture trustees;
(*c*) inspection and disciplinary proceedings, etc.

## SEBI (Portfolio Managers) Regulations, 1993

The said regulation provides for the registration and regulation of the activities of portfolio managers. A portfolio manager is one who, pursuant to a contract or arrangement with the client, advises or directs or undertakes on behalf of the client the management or administration of a portfolio of securities or the funds of the client, as the case may be. A portfolio manager who undertakes on behalf of the client the management or administration of a portfolio of securities is permitted to invest in derivatives, including transactions for the purpose of hedging and portfolio rebalancing, through a recognized stock exchange.

## SEBI (Registrars to an Issue and Share Transfer Agents) Regulations, 1993

The said regulation provides for:

(*a*) the registration of registrar to an issue and share transfer agent;
(*b*) renewal of certificate;
(*c*) conditions of registration;
(*d*) general obligations and responsibilities;
(*e*) procedure for inspection and action in case of default.

## SEBI (Underwriters) Regulations, 1993

Per the said regulation, no person shall act as an underwriter unless he or she holds a certificate granted by the board. In this context, the said regulation provides for the procedure to be followed for the registration and grant of the certificate to carry out the activities of an underwriter. Further, every underwriter shall abide by the general code of conduct as specified in Schedule III of the said regulation.

## SEBI (Bankers to an Issue) Regulations, 1994

A banker to an issue is defined as a bank carrying on all or any of the scheduled activities, such as acceptances of application and application monies, acceptances of allotment or call monies, refund of application monies, payment of dividend or interest warrant. This banker to an issue need to be registered as per the said regulation. Further, it also provides for the renewal and cancellation of the certificate, etc.

## SEBI (Foreign Institutional Investors) Regulations, 1995

Per the said regulation, an FII and its key personnel shall observe high standards of integrity, fairness and professionalism in all dealings in the

Indian securities market with the intermediaries, regulatory and other government authorities. The said regulation makes it compulsory for a person dealing in securities as an FII to obtain a certificate granted by the board.

An FII, under the said regulation, is restricted to invest in the following sectors, namely:

(*a*) securities in the primary and secondary markets including shares, debentures and warrants of companies whether listed on a recognized stock exchange or not;
(*b*) units of scheme floated by domestic mutual funds including Unit Trust of India, whether listed on a recognized stock exchange or not;
(*c*) dated government securities;
(*d*) derivatives traded on a recognized stock exchange;
(*e*) commercial paper;
(*f*) security receipts.

## SEBI (Prohibition of Fraudulent and Unfair Trade Practices Relating To Securities Markets) Regulations, 2003

Per the said regulation, no person shall buy, sell or otherwise deal in securities in a fraudulent manner. It specifically prohibits manipulation of the price of a security, misleading news which may induce sale or purchase of securities, unfair trade practices relating to securities and other offences relating to securities. In cases where any such activity takes place, this regulation gives *suo moto* power to the regulating authority to take action on any information received by the investigating officers. The authority in such a case may cancel or suspend registration of such person involved in any kind of fraudulent activity.

## SEBI (Mutual Funds) Regulations, 1996

Per the said regulation, mutual funds are allowed to invest only in transferable securities either in the money market or in the capital market, including any privately placed debentures or securitized debts. The said regulation provides for (i) the procedure with respect to the registration of mutual funds in India; (ii) the constitution and management of mutual fund and operation of trustees, etc. (iii) the constitution and management of asset management company and custodian; (iv) schemes of mutual fund; (v) valuation policies, procedure for inspection, investigation and action in case of default, appointment of auditor, etc.

## SEBI (Venture Capital Funds) Reglations, 1996

Venture capital is an important source of equity for start-up companies. Any company or trust or a body corporate which proposes to or is desiring to carry on any activity as a 'venture capital fund' shall make an application under this regulation to the SEBI for the grant of a certificate to enable them to conduct such activities. In this context, the said regulation prescribes for:

(*a*) the procedure for the grant of the certificate;
(*b*) investment conditions and restrictions, etc.

Under the said regulations, no venture capital fund shall be entitled to get its units listed on any recognized stock exchange until the expiry of three years from the date of the issuance of units by the venture capital fund.

## SEBI (Custodian of Securities) Regulations, 1996

Custodian of securities are the people who carry on the business of providing custodial services in relation to securities of clients or gold, or gold-related instruments held by mutual funds. Any person who seeks to provide such services must obtain registration under this regulation.

## SEBI (Substantial Acquisition of Shares and Takeovers) Regulations, 1997

The underlying principles behind this regulation are as follows:

(*a*) equality of treatment and opportunity to all shareholders;
(*b*) protection of the interests of shareholders;
(*c*) fair and truthful disclosure of all material information by the acquirer in all public announcements and offer documents;
(*d*) no information to be furnished by the acquirer and other parties to an offer exclusively to any one group of shareholders;
(*e*) availability of sufficient time to shareholders for making informed decisions;
(*f*) an offer to be announced only after careful and responsible consideration;
(*g*) the acquirer and all other intermediaries professionally involved in the offer to exercise highest standards of care and accuracy in preparing offer documents;
(*h*) recognition by all persons connected with the process of substantial acquisition of shares that there are bound to be limitations on their freedom of action and on the manner in which the pursuit of their interests can be carried out during the offer period;

(*i*) all parties to an offer to refrain from creating a false market in the securities of the target company;

(*j*) no action to be taken by the target company to frustrate an offer without the approval of the shareholders.

## DA96

One of the most important changes that affected the capital market in India a decade back was the introduction of the depository system. Prior to this, all the transactions on the stock exchanges involving purchase and sale of shares and other securities used to take place in the physical form with all the attendant shortcomings. The DA96 encourages the free transfer of securities in the market in electronic form instead of transferring it physically. The Act dematerializes the security in the depository mode and provides for the regulation of depositors in securities and for matters connected therewith or incidental thereto.

## The Income-Tax (Eighth Amendment) Rules, 2002

Under, the Income-Tax (Eighth Amendment) Rules, 2002, it is mandatory for a person to quote a PAN (Permanent Account Number), issued by the Income Tax Department, for securities transactions of over Rs 1 lakh.

# Emerging trends

Some of the recent developments in the capital market are as discussed below.

## Negotiated Dealing System

The negotiated dealing system also known as electronic ordering system for trading in securities, mutual funds, provident funds and insurance companies has been launched.

## Anti-Money Laundering Guidelines

The guidelines set out the steps that a registered intermediary and any of its representatives should implement to discourage and identify any money laundering or terrorist financing activities. The guidelines have taken into account the requirements of the Prevention of the Money Laundering Act, 2002, as applicable to the SEBI registered entities.

## Capital market and banks

In a bid to tighten capital market exposure on banks and noting that the banks have extended large loans to various mutual funds, RBI is streamlining norms for banks' capital market exposure with a view that lenders should not guarantee payments to stock on behalf of FIIs.

# Conclusion

Recent years have witnessed significant reforms in the capital market. It is well known that the trading platform has become automatic, electronic, anonymous, order-driven, nationwide and screen based. An investor today need not wait with his or her fingers crossed, for a fortnight or more, for getting crossed cheques or crisp notes for the sale proceeds of his or her securities. Another material development, which proved to be of immense relief to investors, was dematerialization. The Indian capital market is heading towards better efficiency and profitability of securities.

# 4.17

# Insurance Services and Law

*Diljeet Titus and Kanwalvir Kang, Titus & Co. Advocates*

The insurance sector in India since its liberalization has witnessed a sharp increase in the number of private players entering the field. At present, the government allows FDI (foreign direct investment) up to 26 per cent in the insurance sector. However, the insurance companies have sought an increase in the FDI limit to 49 per cent to enable their foreign joint venture partners to plough more money into the business. The raising of the equity cap will not only bring more funds but also help in expanding the industry. The government is considering the proposed FDI hike. In the meantime, India's insurance sector is being regulated and nurtured in order to reach its full potential and can thus play a role in nation building and capital mobilization. The legislation governing this sector is fast developing in order to address the increasing complexities and uncertainties of life and business transactions.

## Nature of insurance contract

In a contract of insurance, the insurer agrees to indemnify loss that would be sustained by the insured and is bound to pay money or provide its equivalent in the case of any uncertain event as per the contract. The four essential features of the contract of insurance are: (i) definition of risk; (ii) duration of risk; (iii) premium; and (iv) amount of insurance. The insurance policy is the exclusive record of the insurance contract.

## Types of insurance in India

The following are the significant types of insurance businesses in India.

## Life insurance

Life insurance is a contract that pledges payment of an amount to the person assured (or his or her nominee) on the occurence of the event which has been insured against.

Section 2(11) of the Indian Insurance Act, 1938, states that 'life insurance' activity comprises:

- any contract in which one party agrees to pay a given sum upon the occurrence of:
  - a particular event contingent upon the duration of human life (and includes contracts in which the payment of money is assured on death, except death solely by accident); or
  - any contingency dependent on the human life; and
- any contract which is subject to payment of premiums for a term dependent on human life.

The Life Insurance Corporation of India undertakes various kinds of contracts which vary in the nature of their terms and conditions. There may be insurance contracts providing for payment of insurance money in the event of death or there may be endowment contracts providing for payment in the event of survival of the assured for a particular term.

In a life insurance contract, an insured agrees to pay the insurer certain sums, called premiums, at specified times and in consideration thereof the insurer agrees to pay certain sums of money on certain conditions in a specified way, upon the occurrence of a particular event contingent upon the duration of human life.[1] The objective of a life insurance policy is to safeguard the interest of dependants of the insured in the event of premature death of the assured as a result of occurrence of any contingency.

## Marine insurance

Section 3 of the Indian Marine Insurance Act, 1963 defines marine insurance as 'an agreement wherein the insurer undertakes to indemnify the assured in the manner and to the extent agreed against maritime losses, that is to say the losses incidental to marine adventure'. Marine insurance consists of insurance of property against losses due to marine perils consequent on or incidental to the navigation of the sea. A ship which is engaged in the earning or acquisition of any freight, commission or other pecuniary benefit or a ship and cargo which has been offered as a security for a loan are endangered by maritime perils in the course of navigation of the sea is 'insurable property' by marine insurance.

[1] *LIC of India vs. Vishwanathan Verma, AIR 1995 SC 189.*

Marine insurance protects the pecuniary interest of the assured in the insured property by indemnifying him or her financially if it is lost by insured perils. Therefore, interest insured is the assured's interest in the insured property.

A marine voyage need not be confined to sea voyage as it can also be extended to cover land risks. As per Section 4(1) of the Indian Marine Insurance Act, 1963, a contract of marine insurance may protect the assured against loss on inland waters or on land risk incidental to any sea voyage.

The marine insurance market in India differs from that in London, which has been the biggest centre of marine insurance for centuries. Unlike the United Kingdom, there are no brokers in India. Insurance agents in India are not technically as qualified as brokers but merely introduce business and perform such other functions as may be assigned to them by the insurer. They act as agents to the insurer and are licensed by the Controller of Insurance to act as agents.

## Fire insurance

Section 2(6A) of the Insurance Act, 1938, defines a fire insurance contract as a contract:

- whose principal object is insurance against loss or damage occasioned by fire;
- where the extent of insurers liability is limited by the sum assured and not necessarily by the extent of loss or damage sustained by the insured;
- wherein the insurer is only liable for the liability undertaken under the contract and has no interest in the safety or destruction of the insured property.

Fire insurance in India is a personal contract between the insured and the insurer for the payment of money and is not associated with the subject matter of the insurance. The insurance policy does not transfer automatically to the new owner with the transfer of subject matter. Hence if the connection with the insured property ceases by being transferred to another person, the contract of insurance also comes to an end. However, the contract of fire insurance can be validly assigned to another only with the consent of the insurer.

## Motor insurance

In India, it is compulsory for every owner of the vehicle to insure the vehicle against third-party risks to enable the victims of accidents to receive the amount of their claims in an accident. A contract of motor insurance comes into existence when a person seeking insurance in respect of his or her motor vehicle enters into a contract with the insurer to indemnify him or her against loss or damage to the vehicle or against the legal liability he or she may incur to third parties in respect of death or bodily injury caused to them or damage to their property caused by the use of the vehicle.

Like other contracts of insurance, the parties to a motor insurance contract must make a full and true disclosure of all material facts in good faith and not make any misrepresentations.

### General insurance

Insuring anything other than human life may be called general insurance. In addition to the types of insurances discussed above, other general insurance includes burglary and theft insurance, aviation insurance, liability insurance, contractors' risk insurance, professional indemnity insurance, employers liability insurance and personal insurance such as accident and health insurance.

Most general insurance policies last for one year period. While some policies, like fire insurance for residences, are given for longer periods, insurance for goods transportation or for emergency medical treatment during foreign travel are for shorter periods.

### Reinsurance

Reinsurance is the insurance in whole or in part of the risk of liability which an insurer has undertaken under a contract of insurance. Reinsurance helps the primary insurers to accept risks that are normally beyond their capacity and also in maintaining the financial stability in the case of losses due to mass settlement cases in catastrophic events. This is a way of reducing the net losses the insurer may have to suffer. The GIC (General Insurance Company) is the major player in reinsurance in India.

## Predominant laws governing the insurance sector

### IA (Insurance Act), 1938

In India, apart from specific legislations that regulate the functioning of the insurance sector, the general regulatory framework is contained in the IA (Insurance Act), 1938, and the Insurance Rules, 1939. The IA, 1938, requires compulsory registration of the insurers, qualification and other requirements for such registration, renewal of registration, restriction on name of insurer requirement as to capital, its structuring and voting rights, etc. Every insurer in India is subject to the provisions of IA, 1938, in relation to any class of insurance business.

## LIC (Life Insurance Corporation Act), 1956

The LIC (Life Insurance Corporation Act), 1956, was enacted to provide for the nationalization of life insurance business in India by entrusting it in the hands of a corporation with an objective (i) to ensure absolute security to the policy holder in the matter of his or her life insurance protection; (ii) to spread the insurance much more widely, especially in the rural areas and (iii) for effective mobilization of the public money.

By the operation of this Act, the corporation steps into the shoes of the insurer doing controlled business, and all contracts, agreements and other instruments are fully effective by or against the corporation as in the case of the insurer himself or herself, any pending suit, appeal or other legal proceeding by or against the insurer does not abate but is continued by or on behalf of the corporation.

## PLIA (Public Liability Insurance Act), 1991

The PLIA, 1991, provides for compulsory public liability insurance for installations handling hazardous substances so that adequate relief can be provided to the victim (other than a workman) of hazardous substances. The relief is sought on the principle of no fault.

Section 3(1) of the PLIA, 1991, provides that where death or injury to any person (other than a workman) or damage to any property has resulted from an accident, the owner shall be liable to give relief for such death, injury or damage. Section 3(2) further provides that in any claim for relief the claimant shall not be required to plead and establish that the death, injury or damage in respect of which the claim has been made was due to any wrongful act, neglect or default of any person.

Therefore, the PLIA casts a duty on the owners of hazardous establishments to take out one or more insurance policies providing for a contract of insurance whereby he or she is insured against the liability to give relief under Section 3(1) of the PLIA.

With the growth of industrialization, the exposure to installations handling hazardous processes and operations have increased manifold, thereby increasing the risk of accidents leading to death or injury of the innocent public who may be in the vicinity of industrial activity. Hence it was felt essential to provide for compulsory public liability insurance for installations handling hazardous substances.

## IRDA (Insurance Regulatory and Development Authority Act), 1999

The IRDA, 1999, was enacted to protect the interests of holders in insurance policies, to regulate, promote and ensure orderly growth of the insurance and reinsurance business and to amend the IA, 1938, to bring it in conformity with the changing philosophy of liberalization and privatization of the insurance sector. Under the IRDA, 1999, private companies can now operate in India's insurance industry upon obtaining a licence from the Insurance Regulatory and Development Authority.

To have its licence application considered, a domestic private company must be registered in accordance with the Companies Act, 1956, and have approximately $20 million of investment capital. The specific licensing requirements that private Indian companies must fulfil are set out in the Registration of Indian Insurance Companies Regulations, 2000, published by the IRDA. With the nationalization of the insurance sector, the role of the controller of insurance, which was set up under the earlier insurance act, diminished considerably as the ownership of the insurance companies was in the hands of government itself. When it was proposed that the Indian insurance sector should be opened up for private participation, it was felt there is a need for strong, autonomous and independent insurance regulatory authority.

In addition, the IRDA requires every insurer operating in India to undertake a certain amount of business in rural areas for the first five financial years. The IRDA de-regulated the insurance sector in India and allowed the entry of private companies into the insurance sector.

## IMIA (Indian Marine Insurance Act), 1963

The need for IMIA, 1963, was felt after the considerable expansion of the Indian shipping industry after India's independence. Marine insurance being international in character, its laws in India have been influenced by foreign judicial interpretations, and IMIA was enacted by adopting most of the provisions of the English laws.

Marine insurance is not compulsory in law. But modern methods of financing trade has made it indispensable both by providing protection against loss by maritime perils and by enabling a larger volume of trade to be carried on more freely.

## MVA (Motor Vehicles Act), 1988

In terms of the MVA, 1988, motor vehicles are mandatorily required to be insured against third-party risk. The purpose of this insurance is that in the case of damage to person or property of third party due to the use of the motor vehicle, the insurance company which is the second party pays the claims which are preferred against the owner of the motor vehicle, the first party.

## PIA (Personal Injuries (Compensation Insurance) Act), 1963

The PIA, 1963, was enacted in order to provide for payment of compensation to certain classes of workers like workers in factories, mines, plantations and major ports for personal injuries in addition to the relief provided under the PIA (Emergency Provisions), 1962, supplemented by compensation under the PIA (Compensation Insurance) Act, 1963.

# Conclusion

The insurance sector in India has immense growth potential. Even today, a giant share of the Indian population (approximately 80 per cent) is not covered by life insurance, let alone health and non-life insurance policies. This clearly indicates the immense potential for insurance companies to grow their market in India.

# 4.18

# Commercial Agency

*Diljeet Titus and Durgesh Singh, Titus & Co. Advocates*

An agency signifies a relationship wherein one person has an authority to act on behalf of another occupying the position of principal, to create a legal relationship between him or her and third parties. In India, the ICA (Indian Contract Act, 1872) provides statutory provisions which govern rights and obligations of the principal and the agent. Section 182 of the ICA defines 'an agent' as a person employed to do any act for another or to represent another in dealings with third persons. An agent is a person who acts for and on behalf of the principal and under the latter's express or implied authority and his or her acts done within such authority are binding on his or her principal and for his or her such acts, the principal is liable to the party with whom the agent has dealings as such agent.

An agent has authority to do all acts and things that are expressly given to him or her as well as the implied authority to do all acts that are incidental to the main powers. Section 189 of the ICA provides that an agent also has powers to do all acts for the purpose of protecting the principal in an emergency as would be done by a person of prudence in his or her own case. An agency can be granted orally or through writing, and it can also be created through subsequent ratification of the acts done by one person for the other.

## Who can employ an agent?

The basic principle of agency is that the principal must be capable of doing in law what he or she wants his or her agent to do. Capacity to contract or to do any other act by means of an agent is co-extensive with the capacity of the principal himself or herself to make the contract or do the act which the agent is authorized to make or do.

An appointment of an agent by a minor is void; but the minor has been held to be bound by the acts of his or her guardian. The guardian may, however, appoint an agent for the minor. A minor is incapable because he or she does not have sufficient discretion to choose an agent to act for him or her. He or she is all too likely to choose a wrong person; and so the law declares him or her to be incapable of choosing an agent at all. The position of persons of unsound mind would be similar, and the principal must be of sound mind when appointing an agent.

## Who may be an agent?

An agent's competency to act or contract for his or her principal is not limited to his or her competency to contract for himself or herself. A person who has no capacity to contract on his or her own behalf is competent enough to contract for his or her principal so as to bind him or her. As between the principal and third persons, the act of an agent is looked upon as the act of the principal who authorized it.

A person acting as agent for one party may act for the other party, provided he or she acts within his or her obligations to the principal. This practice is, however, denounced, as it might lead to conflict of interest. Keeping this in mind the Law Commission of India has recommended that the relevant provisions of the ICA be suitably amended to specify that such an agent may not be personally bound to third persons in respect of contracts entered into by him or her on behalf of the principal.

## Duties of an agent

The provisions of the ICA require agents to perform certain duties contractually and statutorily owed to the principal. These are as follows:

(*a*) to conduct the business of the principal according to the directions given by the principal;

(*b*) to conduct the business of the agency with as much skill as is generally possessed by persons engaged in similar business and to act with reasonable diligence and to make compensation to the principal in respect of the direct consequences of his or her own neglect for want of skill or misconduct;

(*c*) to render proper accounts to his or her principal on demand;

(*d*) to use all reasonable diligence in communicating with the principal and seeking to obtain his or her instructions;

(*e*) to pay to his or her principal all sums received by doing anything on his or her account, though in the course of the agency business and without the previous consent of the principal, that is in the event of his or her doing so, he or she is liable to pay to the principal for the benefit that may have resulted from the transaction. It may be stated that it is not necessary to include these in an agency agreement as these duties are not subject to any contract.

## Rights of an agent

An agent is entitled to certain rights which are discussed briefly as follows:

(*a*) The agent has a right to certain monies in his or her hands held on account of the principal for the expenses incurred by him or her in the course of agency business.
(*b*) He or she has a lien on the goods of the principal for his or her dues.
(*c*) He or she has a right to adjust his or her commission or remuneration against the amount payable to the principal.

All these rights are, however, subject to a contract to the contrary and therefore different provisions can be made in the agreement of agency.

## Duties of the principal

The provisions of the ICA require the principal to perform certain duties contractually and statutorily owed to the agent and agreement of agency. These are as follows:

(*a*) The principal is bound to indemnify the agent against any consequences of lawful acts done by such agent in exercise of the authority conferred on him or her.
(*b*) The principal is bound to indemnify the agent against consequences of the acts done by the agent in good faith though it may cause injury to the third persons.
(*c*) The principal is bound to make compensation to the agent in respect of any injury caused to such agent by the principal's neglect or want of skill.

The duties of the principal are different from that of an agent in that these duties are not subject to a contract to the contrary and, therefore, they cannot be avoided by an agreement.

Other salient features of an agreement of agency are as follows:

(*a*) Contracts lawfully entered by an agent on behalf of the principal are binding on the principal.
(*b*) What is done by the agent within authority is binding but what is done beyond authority is not binding on the principal, but if both the acts cannot be separated, then both the acts are not binding on the principal.
(*c*) Notice to or information obtained by an agent in the course of business is a notice or information to the principal.
(*d*) A contract entered into by an agent cannot be specifically enforced by him or her nor is he or she personally bound by it unless the contract is

for sale or purchase of goods or from a merchant abroad or unless the principal is not disclosed by the agent or unless the principal cannot be sued.

(*e*) In the case of an undisclosed principal, the third party has the same right against the agent as he or she would have if the principal was disclosed. Similarly, in such a case a third party would not be bound by the contract if he or she could show that he or she would not have entered into the contract if he or she had known the principal.

(*f*) In the event of personal liability, both the agent and the principal would be liable.

(*g*) Even an act of fraud or misrepresentation done by an agent in the course of his or her agency business is binding on the principal.

These provisions are not subject to any contract to the contrary between the principal and the agent.

# Sub-agents

A sub-agent is a person employed by and acting under the control of the original agent in the agency business. An agent cannot lawfully employ another person to perform acts that he or she has expressly or impliedly undertaken to perform personally unless by ordinary custom of trade a sub-agent may or from the nature of the agency a sub-agent must be employed.

A sub-agent cannot be appointed ordinarily by the agent without the express or implied consent of the principal. When a sub-agent is appointed with the consent of the principal, he or she is, as regards the third persons, represented by the sub-agent also and is bound by and responsible for the acts of the sub-agent as if he or she were an agent ordinarily appointed by the principal. Otherwise it is the agent who is responsible to the principal for the acts of the sub-agent, and the sub-agent is responsible for his or her acts to the agent and not to the principal except in the case of fraud or willful wrong.

The principal is not responsible for the acts of the sub-agent if the sub-agent is appointed without his or her consent.

Sub-agents are generally of three types:

(*a*) those employed without the express or implied authority of the principal and by whose acts the principal is not bound;

(*b*) those employed with express or implied authority of the principal but between the sub-agent and the principal there is no privity of contract;

(*c*) those employed with the express authority of the principal and between the sub-agent and the principal there is a privity of contract and a direct relationship of principal and agent is accordingly established.

# Types of agency

An agency can be broadly categorized as follows:

(*a*) General: A general agent has the authority to act for his or her principal in all matters concerning trade or business.
(*b*) Special: A special agent has authority only to do some particular act for some special occasion or purpose which is not in the ordinary course of his or her business and profession (*Jacob vs. Morris [1902] 1 Ch 816*).

Most common types of agents are as discussed below:

- *Sole selling agent*: In case of a sole selling agent, the relationship between the principal and the sole selling agent is more or less that of a seller and buyer and, therefore, when a sole selling agent sells the goods to his or her buyer, the relationship between the sole selling agent and the buyer may be that of the vendor and purchaser unless the agency is disclosed.
- *Mercantile agent*: A mercantile agent is one having authority in the course of business to sell goods or consign goods for the purpose of sale or to buy goods and even to raise money on the security of goods. A mercantile agent is also called a commissioner agent.
- *Factor*: A factor is a mercantile agent who, in ordinary course of business, is entrusted with possession of the goods or with possession of documents of title to goods.
- *Broker*: He or she only brings about the transaction between the principal and the buyer or seller; the possession of the goods or document of title to goods is not given to him or her. He or she is, therefore, an agent, who in ordinary course of business is employed to make a contract for the purchase or sale of shares or goods. He or she has nothing more to do with the transaction between the parties and is not concerned with the actual fulfilment of the contract (*Purushotam Haridas vs. Amruth Ghee Co. Ltd. AIR 1961AP 143*).
- *Forwarding or clearing agent*: A forwarding agent, also called a shipping agent or clearing agent, acts as the agent of the principal, who wants to export goods outside the country or to clear the goods imported by the principal, and all the functions for exporting or clearing and taking possession of imported goods are done by this agent.
- *Estate agent*: An estate agent generally deals as intermediary in the transaction of sale and purchase of immoveable property or in the management of any property. An estate agent has ordinarily no authority to enter into, or sign on behalf of the vendor, but there may be circumstances for which this authority may be inferred (*Abdulla Ahmed vs. Animendra Kissen Mitter [1950] SCR 30, AIR 1950 SC 15*).
- *Auctioneer*: An auctioneer is in law an agent of the person whose property is to be sold by auction through him or her. He or she also becomes the

agent of the auction purchaser when the bid is struck down in his or her favour. An auctioneer is primarily an agent for the vendor to sell at an open sale. He or she may be agent for both the buyer and the seller.
- *Insurance agent*: An insurance agent is employed to negotiate and effect policies of insurance. An insurance agent normally acts for the company, and his or her authority may not extend beyond submissions of the proposals. An insurance broker on the other hand, is *prima facie* an agent of the assured, and not of the underwriter.
- *Commission agent*: Where the agent not only brings about a contract between his or her principal and the third party purchaser, but also his or her responsibility in the deal continues till the delivery of the goods and the payment of the price, and the completion in this sense alone entitles him or her to demand and earn his or her commission, he or she would be a commission agent [*Banwarilal & Co. vs. Sundaram spinning mills AIR 1979 NOC 22{MAD}*].
- *Partners*: Section 18 of the Indian Partnership Act 1932, provides that a partner is the agent of the firm for the purposes of the business of the firm. As a consequence of this general rule any act done by a partner on behalf of the firm will be *prima facie* binding on the firm, but not if done on his or her own account.
- Del credere *agent*: A *del credere* agent is an agent who, in consideration of an extra remuneration, guarantees the solvency of the parties with whom he or she brings the principal into contractual relations, and undertakes to indemnify the principal against any damage that may be caused by the party's failure to perform the contract. In *KV Periyamianna Marakkayar & Sons vs. Banians & Co [AIR 1926 Mad 544]*, it was stated that a *del credere* agent guarantees the performance of the contract in consideration of an extra consideration.

An agency agreement, falling under the general item category of Article 5 of the Indian Stamp Act, would not attract any specified *ad valorem* stamp duty and is treated like any other ordinary agreement. Registration of the agency agreement is also not a mandatory requirement.

# Conclusion

Doing business by way of engaging commercial agents is an effective way of pooling resources and expertise to carry forward the business. The principal can engage agents specializing in certain fields while concentrating its resources on the core competencies of its businesses.

# Part 5

# Business Culture

# 5.1

# People

*Purvi Sheth, Shilputsi Consultants*

The country is beginning to appear in the front ranks of emerging markets, leveraging potential and hidden strengths. It is a country known to be culturally complex and politically democratic, but it is now witnessing mammoth economic change.

Today, India is perceived to be one of the more exciting markets, not just because of the revenue potential it offers, thanks to its large population, but because of the capabilities it provides at all levels of business management.

India's true spirit lies in its people. The country itself fosters a relatively open society, personifying its rich historical background, sociological diversity and cultural peculiarities. There is no one single India.

## India – the metaphor for diversity

### The Indian population

As per the census figures of 2007, the population of India is about 1.13 billion. Of this, the urban population comprises only 0.3 billion. Hence, a large part of India remains semi-urban and rural.

Average life expectancy at birth in India is 65.4 years. It is believed that a large part of the Indian population is in its middle age.

The total number of working population in 2001 was 402 million. However, a large part of the Indian population remains engaged in primary agricultural activities. In recent years, there has been significant growth of the secondary and tertiary sectors.

Most youth in rural areas aspire to jobs in cities or semi-urban areas and move there for better prospects. Many men leave their families in villages and migrate to the cities in search of a lucrative means of making a living. In cities, both large and small, corporate India employs a large part of the urban working population. Besides, fields like medicine, education and even filmmaking are becoming more corporate.

## Language

Contrary to the popular belief, the national language is not 'Indian'. Hindi is the official national language and is written in *devanagari* script. India also speaks several other languages and dialects. Each state has its native language. However, 18 languages have been specified in the constitution – including Bengali, Gujarati, Hindi, Kannada, Malayalam, Marathi, Oriya, Punjabi, Sanskrit, Tamil, Telugu and Urdu.

The universal language in business and at the workplace is English. Hindi is spoken and at least understood in most parts of the country, although there is a much higher level of familiarity with it in the northern regions.

Peninsular India is mostly acquainted with English and very comfortable in the native languages of the states there.

The government uses English as a principal language of communication, especially with business. However, Hindi is used in correspondence as well as in formal communication.

The urban population understands multiple foreign accents and is familiar with terminology from different parts of the world. Most commonly understood phrases are from the United States and British English.

At the workplace in cities, English is the main language of communication. Educated professionals speak the language fluently. It might be interpreted as patronizing or condescending to ask a manager if they understand English. From recruitment interviews to stock markets to business news channels, English is the language that is normally used. Leading newspapers and magazines, both political and business, are in English.

Every region has a distinctive noticeable accent that permeates into spoken English there. People sometimes tend to slip into regional native languages or Hindi in their interactions. These lapses are often inadvertent and a manifestation of their comfort level with their 'mother tongue', though most people are sensitive to others present who do not understand the language.

## Education

In 2007, there were a total of approximately 152,048 higher secondary educational institutions, 10,377 general education institutions, 3,201 professional education institutions, 407 universities and 99 business schools. High-quality education is available in metropolitan cities, mini metros and state capitals .The education curriculum is affiliated to universities and can be at diverse levels of difficulty and standard.

Many people in the urban areas manage to graduate or reach post-graduation levels. Foreign education is also very desirable and affluent, middle-class Indians frequently travel abroad for higher studies. This is viewed as a step up in social as well as professional hierarchies.

In India, the average level of exposure to management techniques and modern theories of business is extremely high. Most leading international management institutes have either partnerships or associations with domestic training institutes or business houses in India, where they conduct management programmes.

Management graduates seek employment in 'global' and 'multinational' companies where prospects of global exposure, higher salaries and international postings are greatest. In recent times, the number of job offers with global postings for management students has seen a steady increase.

The popular bias continues to be in favour of technical, commercial and/or management streams. Social sciences and humanities subjects have gained acceptance in the recent past, and although there are several courses offered in those fields, well-known colleges and institutes focus on the most commercially oriented courses.

## Religion

The Indian constitution specifies India as a secular state and professes no single religion. All forms of religion and places of worship coexist. Some 80 per cent of the population follows Hinduism and, as per the 2001 census, Islam constitutes around 15 per cent of the total population, making it the largest minority.

Other religions like Buddhism, Christianity, Jainism, Sikhism and Zoroastrianism account for a good part of other minority populations. Religions like Judaism are represented in small proportions also. In general, India is, religion-wise, a tolerant country. In the workplace, minorities and Hindus work together and no overt biases or preferences occur as a general rule. Harassment on the basis of religion or bias due to faith is more or less unheard of in corporate India.

Devout people may prefer to pray on certain days in their workplace. This privacy is normally easily granted in a professional set-up. Places of worship like temples, mosques and churches can be found all over the country but some companies reserve small spaces dedicated for prayers on their premises.

Most managers are naturally sensitive to disparities in food habits, dressing styles, etc. of co-workers of a different creed. People are considerate and avoid inconveniences to colleagues whilst following any religious practices, for example fasting, on their work premises.

Company policies include holidays for festivals of various religions and equality and fairness is the backdrop for any concessions granted for religious reasons. Businesses should remain neutral on their stances of religion and faith, and it is advisable not to bring up religious differences and opinions in the professional environment.

# Gender

In 2004–2005, India had a ratio of 934 females per 1,000 males. Male life expectancy, however, is slightly lower than that for females. In 2001, the literacy rate of men was 75.3 per cent, whereas for women it was 53.7 per cent.

Some rural and underdeveloped areas of India still tend to take a negative view on gender equality and female emancipation. In certain regions, the male child is believed to be the perpetuator of the race as well as the future patriarch and income generator of the family.

Corporate India has seen several successful women rise to the top echelons of the organizational hierarchy in recent years. Today, women are represented across industries, sectors, geographies and management levels. Indian women are not only reaching leadership levels but are key decision-makers in boardrooms, both in India and internationally.

For several decades, women have been studying up to post-graduate levels and beyond. Fields like research, medicine, physics and biotechnology see many women rising to the top. In sectors like education, social services, arts and theatre, Indian women are also highly successful, both nationally and at the global level.

In India, women participate and engage in various economic activities and their presence or impact is taken very seriously. Female Indian entrepreneurs run companies both large and small, and several lead large global corporations. It is hard to generalize undercurrents of gender-related tensions, but it is common for men to have female superiors and be perceivably comfortable with it.

In urban and semi-urban areas, gender inequality in the workplace is rare and in some places absent in day-to-day functioning. Women are treated with respect and in the professional set-up some level of personal distance can be maintained, although workmates interact freely at all times. In India, women shake hands and dine with their male colleagues and often work till late hours into the night, especially in cities. Private space and freedom is enjoyed by both sexes and personal relationships and familial interaction between colleagues of both genders is very natural and casual.

In the semi-urban areas, the professional male–female relationships are restricted to being formal.

Today, Indian women are marrying outside their communities and even outside their religion. While some may wear traditional Indian clothes like the sari or salwar kameez, workplaces also see young women especially in Western business suits, skirts and trousers. In the corporate world, wearing of the veil is uncommon and hardly ever seen.

Indian urban society is transforming into a post-modernist liberal social system, and women are working outside the home and running households simultaneously, breaking the traditional notion of being a passive home-maker.

## The caste system and social structure

The caste system was once made up of four *varnas*. The highest caste was the *Brahmins*, who were privileged, whilst the lowest was the *Shudras*, the 'untouchables', who performed the most menial of tasks. Other castes were the warriors and traders. Castes were an outline for personal identity and formed the basis for social hierarchy. With time, this system became more rigid and abuse of power as well as cruelty to the lower castes plagued the system. It degenerated considerably and steps had to be taken in the independent Indian constitution to give all castes the same rights and duties and allow for certain concessions for the oppressed.

Today, practising the caste system or discriminating on the basis of caste is legally forbidden. In cities and urban areas, casteism is not practised anymore. Most people are even unaware of others' *varna* status, mingling with each other freely. It is considered impolite to ask a person's caste in social and professional situations.

In certain rural areas and interiors of the country, the caste system dominates the social system. Discrimination on the basis of caste continues there and the depressed caste is frequently ill-treated. Legislation and media focus in these instances have helped their decline, although the country is not rid of it entirely.

Since the system and its accompanying malaise have been deeply embedded in the Indian social structure, a positive discrimination policy was planned to help uplift the 'backward classes' who had not had the opportunity and right of entry to contemporary facilities. This meant the reservation of places in educational institutions for the historically under-favoured, since they have not had the good fortune of accessing modern education and other benefits of the developing nation. Several legislative initiatives have come about, including a proposal for employment quotas in the corporate world, but this bill is under contention.

## Business culture

Indian corporate culture has evolved over a period of time. The workplace today is the amalgamated culmination of Western influence on Indian ethos.

Most large global business conglomerates coexist with mammoth diversified Indian groups, as well as smaller entrepreneurial set-ups.

Every business and organization will have a unique culture that embraces Indian society and its norms, global practices and regional differences. There is not one homogeneous Indian management culture.

## Talent acquisition

The availability of skilled human resources across segments and sectors within the country, as well as talented Indians in different parts of the world that are willing to come back to their home country, supplies a unique skill conglomerate that represents India.

Most job seekers and aspirants at junior and mid-levels look for salary hikes and benefits of growth, learning and potential for future avenues. At senior levels the motivators, apart from high salaries, are stability and span of control. Indian managers usually look for international exposure and impact on the global business in jobs.

Indian managers make discerning choices in their employment. Today, with a number of sectors open to foreign investment as well as rewarding financial markets, professional managers are faced with many choices and demand a commensurate price for themselves.

Large talent pools are available across industries, functional specializations as well as leadership and supervisory levels. People with international education and experience are also widely available. They can be accessed through networks, industry associations, search consultants or even advertisements.

In interviews, while it is polite not to, it is not always considered highly intrusive to ask about family details or age. Résumés contain personal information like marital status and family details sometimes. Interviews are regarded as formal, the interaction taken seriously and most candidates are not shy. At middle and junior levels, extensive questioning may be required to understand the exact responsibilities and skill sets. For top management, the style is less formal and the probe is kept at a conversational pace and tone. It is common for women to be interviewed by men (or vice versa).

## Managing people

Indian managers view their workspace as a place that comes close to home. Relationships with superiors are formal, especially in semi-urban areas and certain traditional industries. Bosses are not usually called by their first names but are addressed as 'Mr' or 'Ms'.

Peer level interaction is more casual and people develop personal affinities, often involving families. The post-modern organizational set-up is different. Newer industries like IT (information technology) and ITES (IT-enabled services), with a younger workforce, are more casual and the supervisor is treated with respect but the interface is less formal.

Work relationships are identified by familial relationship formats. Superiors and bosses are thought of as the 'head of the family', whilst peers are regarded in the same way as siblings. Age is respected and revered.

Communication is generally direct. Empathy is required in interaction and body language is a good indicator of people's thoughts and feelings. Language propriety and decency is essential, especially in the presence of women. However, in liberal work environments, it is forgivable to use inappropriate language up to a point. Touching is considered a sign of intimacy and not acceptable until a high level of familiarity is established. Managers are motivated by affiliation and a sense of identification with the organization. Power, recognition and achievement are strong drivers for performance.

# 5.2

# Language and Communication

*Deepak Mahtani, Winning Communications Partnership Ltd.*

There is no doubt that the international language of commerce is English, and this is true in India as well.

However, as any visitor to India would have experienced, the English used in India is quite different from that used in the UK or the United States. It was George Bernard Shaw who remarked: 'The United States and the United Kingdom: two countries divided by a common language.'

English exists in India today because of British rule. One of the legacies left behind alongside the schools, the legislature, railroads and parliamentary structures, is the language of English. It is because of the English language and a combination of centuries of strong emphasis on mathematics and sciences that India is on the world stage in terms of IT skills and business process outsourcing (BPO).

Many businessmen and women quickly drop their guard once in India because so much seems to be in English – the signs, the street names and the billboards look very familiar and people in the streets of Mumbai or Bangalore speak English. This would not be the case if they were travelling to China or Japan or Brazil. It is important for visitors to realize that they should not drop their guard but rather keep their cultural sensitivities intact, in spite of appearances.

It is both true and false that all Indians speak English. With a population of over 1 billion, there are differing degrees of competence in English. India has the second largest number of English speakers in the world after the United States. Some 15 per cent, or 150 million people, speak English. Some of the graduates from the venerable Indian universities and colleges read and write English fluently. However, their spoken English and comprehension levels may vary greatly.

Others in various professions may have been abroad to the United States or Europe for a year or longer and would therefore have great fluency in the English language. Now with the proliferation of satellite and cable television, more and more Indians are being exposed to American English or British English, with popular serials and Hollywood blockbusters.

However, to assume that they speak English to the same level of fluency and accuracy of a native English speaker is to flirt with danger. Most people doing business with India quickly discover that language and understanding are the key to ensuring success in India.

As with many things in India, there is much diversity in the languages of India. Whilst there are 18 official languages recognized by the Indian constitution, there are over 1,600 minor languages and dialects, according to the 1991 census. Hindi is the national language and most Indians will learn Hindi plus the local language of their state. To this they add English, thereby becoming tri-lingual. Very few Indians learn to speak any other foreign languages, although some companies are today training their staff in some of the European and Chinese languages, given the growth of both their domestic economies as well as their international business.

Given the extremes in India, one also finds extremes in the English language. You will come across urban professionals, educated in some of the best institutions in India, who have become prolific writers, novelists, politicians and journalists. You will also regularly come across taxi drivers, waiters, receptionists and shop-owners who earn their daily keep through contact with tourists and visitors to India with limited vocabulary, little grammar but who take great pride in saying 'I speak English' with a wide smile.

In between these two often colliding extremes is what many call Indian English or 'Hinglish', a new adaptation to the language to suit their own culture. You may hear some interesting expressions such as 'prepone', which an Indian proudly told me quite plainly was the opposite of 'postpone'. He had a smile on his face when he said 'You English never came up with it but we Indians improve your language for you.'

Other expressions may be akin to 'old English' – that which we were accustomed to in the 1950s and 1960s. I recently received an email 'announcing the sad demise of my uncle' which I had to think twice to realize meant that his uncle passed away. Or on your first visit to India you might be asked 'What is your good name?', which simply means your family name (and does by no means indicate that your first name is bad!).

Some may refer to a group of women as 'of the fair sex'. 'Please do the needful' or 'please expedite' are some other common expressions.

There are still occasions, perhaps in an attempt to impress foreigners, when some Indians may speak in very flowery language. This can lead to interesting results. I was recently at a high-level business meeting where the host of a government delegation, realizing that the programme was running behind schedule and his own speech would add a further delay, began with: 'Ladies and gentlemen, I am sorry to cockroach on your time further'. At this some 50 or so delegates started muttering under their breath, looking at the floor for cockroaches! Of course, what he meant was 'encroach'.

Once you have become accustomed to these linguistic challenges, there come the more important and potentially more serious ones related to cross-cultural communication.

The obvious communication issues are accents, names and pronunciation. There are certain rules of common sense that help. Speak clearer not louder, and slower not faster (I tend to reduce my own speed by 20 per cent with a speaker of another culture as a habit). Asking them to repeat if you have not heard something, rather than saying 'I can't understand your accent' leads to a better relationship with your Indian counterparts. Also remember that they, too, have the same problem with many accents, names and pronunciation. Do not be surprised if an Indian slips into both the British and American pronunciation of tomato or potato in the same telephone call. He or she is constantly required to switch, depending on which client and geography he or she is working with at a moment's notice.

The first serious challenge is the fact that some cultures adopt a very direct style of language, whilst others have a more indirect one. The United States has a very direct style of communication. Americans say what they mean and mean what they say, with seemingly little regard as to how it is received. This may come over as very confrontational and aggressive to less direct cultures. Compared to the Americans, the British are not as direct, but to Indians, they still say it like it is, albeit perhaps in a more roundabout way.

India is, on the whole, a country that is less direct and less confrontational in terms of language and communication. This comes over as a lack of assertiveness or not being willing to respond in a concise or direct way.

Whilst it would not be a problem to say: 'You've messed this up' or 'This is shoddy and unprofessional' in the US or the UK, Indians on the whole will adopt a language that is less direct and confrontational, by saying 'We may have to do this again' or 'We should find a better way of doing this'.

Whilst a Westerner may simply say, 'I've got a problem', an Indian may, more often than not, say something along the lines of: 'Would you mind sparing 15 minutes for me?'

The second challenge is how the language fits the context. The same words, phrases and statements have different meanings in different contexts. I have been in numerous meetings with both Westerners and Indians present, both in India and overseas, where it becomes obvious that both parties are understanding very different things at the same meeting; for example 'that could be difficult' to an Indian means 'that's impossible' whereas to other nationalities it may simply mean that it would be a challenge.

Another example of misunderstanding could be with time frames. Time orientations across cultures are very different indeed, as any Swiss person working with a Spaniard will tell you, and vice versa. 'Short term' and 'long term' are phrases used quite regularly.

In most of Western Europe and the US, executives in the IT and finance industries were asked what time frame they would give for short term and long term. They viewed short term as weeks, months, or six months maximum. Long term was deemed as anything more than that.

Executives in India working in the same industries were asked the same question and replied that they saw short term as anything from six months to two years and long term as anything between from two to five years.

Surprisingly a Swedish company wanting to test run some products in three Indian cities instructed their Indian partners to hire 50 sales staff for a short-term trial period. The Swedes finished their short term in three months and decided to pull out, leaving the Indians with 150 sales staff for another three months with nothing to do!

It seems clear then that when it comes to language and communication, especially when one is dealing with time, deadlines and deliveries, it is essential to be very clear in specifying exact dates and times. The use of any time-bound phrases such as 'immediate', 'asap' and 'prompt' need to be qualified so there is a common understanding as to what these imply.

The third challenge is the simple use of 'yes' and 'no'.

I have trained thousands of Westerners in cultural awareness of Indians. Almost all, with very little exception, say that Indians generally do not say 'no'. It is true that many Indians find it very difficult to say no as it is too direct, disrupts harmony and is counterproductive to a good relationship. One piece of advice I give expatriates is to never ask a closed question – a question with a simple 'yes' or 'no' answer – as this can lead to a dead end. It is better to use open questions, so rather than asking: 'Will you be able to deliver by 15 June?', to which the answer will invariably be 'yes', take a more indirect approach and ask, 'When do you feel you will be able to deliver?'

Body language is also something to consider. The differences in international body language has been the subject of many specialist books over the years and the lack of understanding across cultures has possibly been the single largest cause of loss of contracts when doing business.

Visitors to India will notice that Indians have a typical shaking of the head action or 'the Indian nod'. This is not the 'yes nod' as seen in Western societies. It is a circular 'figure of eight' nod. Many take a group of Indians in a meeting or a training context smiling broadly, agreeing with everything you are saying and nodding in this way as a very positive sign of complete understanding and agreement. However, the Indian nod does not mean 'yes' or 'no', but simply 'I'm enjoying this conversation, a relationship is being built, so please carry on – I am listening.' Do not mistake this for agreement.

Due to the fact that the Indian language is more indirect, words often do not mean exactly what they should. Whilst it is relatively safe to trust verbal communication in the West, more attention needs to be paid to non-verbal communication in India. Often what is *not* said is as important as what *is* said. Sometimes one needs to ask two or three leading questions to get to the correct understanding and action. Some managers often say 'we need to read between the lines' when communicating with Indians.

It is said that humour is a great ice-breaker and I would tend to agree with this. However, humour has its own context and what sounds humorous in one culture does not necessary translate or assume the same context. I have been in many meetings when a joke made by a British colleague falls on deaf ears with the Americans, French and Germans. It is therefore no surprise that often Indians may not understand or respond to your humour. In some cases, it may even cause offence or they could assume you are laughing at them.

Tied into humour are idioms. The English language is full of idiomatic expressions. Again in their context, they are fully appreciated and understood. However, taken out of context, they could be interpreted more literally. Thus, often with Indians, when the English use expressions such as 'this will be the best thing since sliced bread', the Indians may be thinking 'Why are the English so hung up about their bread?' and 'Can we say "the best thing since *naan* or *chapatti*"'?

Another area of caution is that of sarcasm and cynicism. Again, in a particular cultural context this is understood, but many an Indian businessman has walked out of a meeting assured of a deal with their British counterparts when they said 'Now, that's an interesting idea!' in a tone of voice which in fact meant exactly the opposite.

Accents and pronunciation can be a source of frustration to get right, especially when on teleconference calls. The key to this is to ask them to repeat and spell names or other concepts that may not be clear, and remember it works both ways. Some Western accents are very strong and can even cause difficulty between the Welsh, Irish, Scottish and English.

Much of the communication tends to be more formal in India. This is due to the way language is taught and learnt, often very formally and by rote. Expect your Indian colleagues to call you by your last name or Mr Bob (Mr + first name) even if you have tried to insist to be on a first name basis. They will often do this to avoid over familiarity which would undermine their own status with their colleagues. The 'Indian' in them will find it very difficult.

Having outlined some of the key differences, here are a few solutions. Keep your language clean and simple – jargon free. Do not embellish your words – either spoken or written – any more than is necessary. Keep it simple, understandable and as far as possible foolproof, so no misunderstanding or misconception takes place. Confirm timescales with specific dates and times.

Above all, even if you get it wrong, remember that if you have a strong relationship with your Indian colleagues, it will be easier to overlook many of these differences.

# 5.3

# Management and Leadership Style

*Deepak Mahtani, Winning Communications Partnership Ltd.*

One of the key challenges for foreign companies and managers doing business in India is trying to understand Indian leadership and management styles. In some areas, especially in the technology sectors of IT oursourcing and software, the influence of Western multinationals operating within India have made some Indian companies mirror Western culture.

However, despite appearances, the majority of the workforce in India still operates under a more traditional Indian management structure. This is especially true of many of the family-owned and -run companies and is more noticeable the further one moves away from the big cities in India. Status, age, position and rank still continue to be important in terms of authority and respect as seen in the workplace. Decisions still tend to be made at the very top of the leadership chain.

It is interesting to read of the 2007 buy-out of Corus by Tata Steel, and this is fairly typical in terms of Indian management. Corus produces four times as much steel as Tata Steel, has a higher market value and turnover, and logic would say that Corus should be the buyer. However, Corus found in its negotiations that family-controlled firms such as Tata Steel were not willing to sell.

Authority levels in India may be different from Western experience and expectations. Even though someone in India might share the same title or position with you, his or her actual authority levels may be lower than yours in terms of signing off an agreement, passing on information and the like. It is therefore essential to ensure you know what your counterpart's authority actually allows him or her to do. Remember, do not be fooled by appearances.

In spite of the recent economic resurgence of India since 1991, some 80 per cent of all Indians have Hinduism as their core belief. As a result, many Indians still today operate with their age-old traditions. Although it has been outlawed by two successive governments, and many modern Indians in the big cities will quickly tell you it does not exist, one of the key beliefs

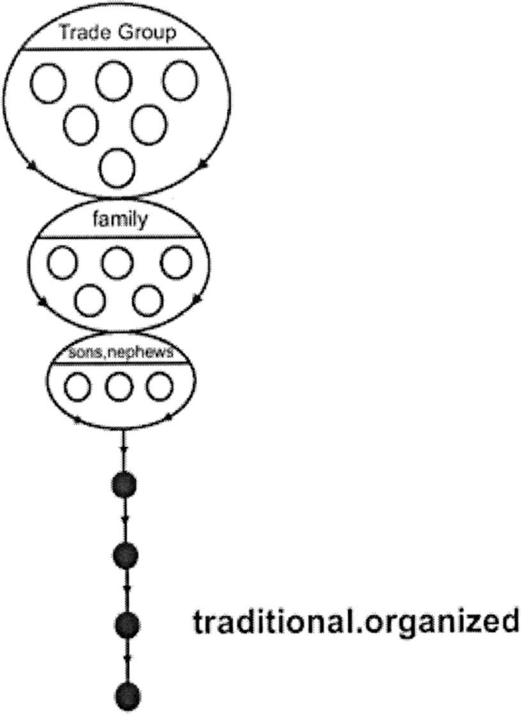


*Source:* Indian Leadership Style, Richard Lewis

Figure 1. The legacy of many Indian companies

in the caste system is that of status, which still pervades the mentality and mindsets of many Indian managers.

Whilst the system may have less of an influence that it did in the past, its impact is evident in the hierarchy found in India today.

From airport authorities to immigration officers to border controls, civil servants and even hotel staff, hierarchy still holds sway in India. Whilst John Smith may have created the concept of 'division of labour' for the West, Mahatma Gandhi once said: 'It is the strict adherence to the division of labour ordained by birth that has made Indians the shortest lived, most resourceless and most exploited nation on earth.' It is this hierarchy that leads to much of India's bureaucratic procedures and paperwork that no one seems to be able to escape.

Figure 1 illustrates the legacy many Indian companies have inherited and are still often struggling to move away from.

The characteristics of this organizational structure are:

- family members hold key positions;
- policy is dictated by trade groups;
- groups work together, develop close personal relations (through intermarriage) and come to each other's support in difficult times.

This then translates in a number of observable behaviour patterns:

- tight control at top;
- limited delegation;
- managers value status and power;
- staff await and expect direct, personal instructions;
- ability to cope with uncertainty;
- a fertile ground for creativity.

Even in the more cosmopolitan cities like Bangalore and Mumbai, beneath the facade of the billboards and young cinema-goers are age-old obligations and symbols of loyalty. As Daraius Ardeshir, managing director of Nestlé India, said whilst explaining the difficulties marketers face when looking behind the facade of Indian modernity, 'Indians are capable of living in several centuries at once. When I visit my father's house I still kneel and touch my forehead to his feet.'

In most Indian companies, everyone knows their place in society and in business. There is a strict adherence to hierarchical structures and a reverence for those in senior positions. This is sometimes demonstrated by junior staff standing to attention when their bosses or foreigners enter a room.

As someone who even appears senior, you will be afforded the best service in order to keep pleasing you, as is evidenced in the brief dialogue set out below, which seems to be a common experience of many.

## Dialogue: writing a report

| | |
|---|---|
| Ms Colson: | How is the evaluation going, Ram? |
| Ram: | It is finished, ma'am. We can start on the report anytime now. |
| Ms Colson: | Good. How long do you think it will take? |
| Ram: | Ma'am? |
| Ms Colson: | To write the report. |
| Ram: | I couldn't say, ma'am. |
| Ms Colson: | You don't know how long it will take? |
| Ram: | When would you like it, ma'am? |
| Ms Colson: | Well, I want to give you enough time to do a good job. |
| Ram: | You can be sure we will do a good job, ma'am. |

Craig Storti, *Cross-Cultural Dialogues: 74 brief encounters with cultural difference*, Intercultural Press, 1994

In Ram's culture, it is the boss's job to give direction and the employee's job to please the boss. It would be presumptuous of Ram to say how long the report will take, for that would be usurping Ms Colson's right as the boss to set deadlines. In any case, a good boss would know how long such a report should take and would specify accordingly. What is more, Ms Colson is paid a generous salary to make decisions like this and should not try to pass on the responsibility to Ram.

Ms Colson is starting out from the point of view that employees are the best judges of their work and will perform better with minimum interference. The boss's job is to orchestrate matters so the work can be done in the time the employee says he or she needs. In short, employees are given much more responsibility for their work. One study of authority patterns in organizations in India found that 85 per cent of subordinates surveyed believed they worked better under close supervision. It is hard to imagine many Westerners feeling the same way.

The cultural root of Ms Colson's attitude is probably that visceral reaction against rank, authority, and hierarchy in most of Europe and the US, with a bias for individualism and self-reliance. The ideal boss is still thought of as the one who gives workers their freedom and generally does not care what they do so long as they get the job done.

A German manager of a company I work with visited India for the first time a few years ago. He was surprised to see a person serving coffee and tea on every floor of the four-storey building. Assessing this as a waste of manpower, he then imported and installed a new coffee dispensing machine, serving lattes, cappuccinos and tea on every floor of their office building. A number emailed him to thank him for this investment. On his next visit there, he was shocked that the same four people who had been serving were standing by the machines, politely asking with a big smile 'What would you like, sir?', and mechanically pressing the buttons. He was told by the Indian manager that this was necessary, given the nature of Indian society, and to sack them would be to take away their livelihood.

Due to the hierarchy in India, there is always a need for a boss or several bosses and they demand – and sometimes do not deserve – respect from those working for them. The boss is always right, so many Indian workers or team members will not disagree or correct their superiors even if they know they are incorrect.

> In contrast to Western hierarchical relationships – which tend to be based on a fixed status and power relationship, governed by contractual agreements and an ideology of essential equality – Indian hierarchical relationships are oriented toward firmly internalized expectations in both superior and subordinate for reciprocity and mutual obligations in a more closely emotionally connected relationship.

Alan Roland, *In Search of Self in India and Japan*, Princeton University Press, 1988

Workers are generally told what to do and how it is to be done. This is one of the key criticisms of Westerners doing business in India.

Also significant is leadership style. In contrast to many Western cultures that have adopted a participative or empowering leadership, which stresses active participation, initiative, idea generation and a greater delegation of responsibility throughout the organization, Indian leadership style tends to be more directive. This is common to India and most of Asia. Directive leadership stresses the direction given by senior managers to those junior to them. It looks to the boss for instructions, knowledge, wisdom and strategy, and does not encourage much initiative or feedback.

One common refrain from many Westerners in India is that there are not too many chiefs, and not enough Indians, but rather there are too many managers but not enough leaders.

This, of course, is not the full picture as evidenced by the CEOs of some of the largest IT conglomerates in India today, such as Infosys and Wipro, to name but two. However, these would be the exception to the rule rather than the rule themselves.

> ... Private companies suffered from problems typical of government sector companies in India ... Salaries were low compared to non-government sector companies. The principal reward that people looked forward to was the acquisition of new titles and perquisites by promotion into higher grades. The company had many levels of managers so that people could be rewarded as they progressed upwards in their careers. Power to make decisions was related to rank. Decision making was encumbered by the plethora of levels that information had to flow through. The directors and general managers sat atop tall organizational pyramids. ... And thus, level-by-level, the pyramids built up. The pyramids were organized by functions with a 'functional' director, appointed directly by the government, on top. People within one pyramid did not work easily with people within others. ... [no] one could respond quickly to the changing needs of customers.

Arun Maira, *Shaping the Future:Aspirational Leadership in India & Beyond*, John Wiley & Sons, 2002

Unless India produces more leaders who are able to lead rather than follow, its economy and long-term growth will be undermined. However, it is encouraging to see that it has a growing number of excellent examples and role models.

One such example is that of Elattuvalapil Sreedharan, who has become a hero by doing the seemingly impossible. Much of the infrastructure in India suffers because of the old style of management where bribes and corruption, a hierarchy of rule and command created delays, which led to half-finished projects in roads, airports and railways. The 10-mile metro in Kolkata took some 22 years to build, with a budget revised 14 times. As managing director of the Delhi Metro Rail Corporation (DMRC), Mr Sreedharan built Phase One of Delhi's three-stage metro project last December – a total network of some 33 miles, strictly on budget and nearly three years ahead of schedule. This caused the Prime Minster Manmohan Singh to call Mr Sreedharan 'a role model for future generations.'

Another such person who has challenged traditional Indian management and leadership style is Sam Pitroda, by calling into question many of the stereotypes, and much of the bureaucracy, hierarchy, bribery and corruption to government level.

> India desperately needs to create technological leaderships at all levels. While the information technology entrepreneurs have been justifiably celebrated in the country, we need similar stories in other fields. It is heartening to know that some segments of India's politics and administration have begun to understand the importance of technology. They have also begun to understand that if they do not keep up with the pace, technology would make them redundant. In the 1980s when we introduced computerization of the railway reservation system, certain quarters of India's establishment reacted with unvarnished anger. They thought it spelled doom for hundreds of thousands of railway employees. Little did they realize that while technological intervention can be disruptive in the short term, in the long term its benefits far outweigh the loss.

Sam Pitroda, 'Technology, the great social leveller, ushering in change', *The Indian Express,* October 2005

These role models need to increase in number and impact for India to change. The example of the IT companies has given many Indians and the growing middle classes their 'big break'. A strong consumer culture is pervading through India, not only in the five big cities, but throughout India. This boost of belief in oneself and the 'I can make it' mentality is overtly tangible today.

There is every indication that a political will to change does exist. The president and the prime minister have seen how, in many ways, the private sector and industry has led the way to bring India into the market as a serious global player, something the government has been unable to do.

> I was studying different dimensions of knowledge society, how will it be different from the industrial economy. In the knowledge economy, the objective of a society changes from fulfilling the basic needs of all-round development to empowerment. The education system, instead of going by text book teaching, will be promoted by creative, interactive self learning – formal and

> informal – with focus on values, merit and quality. The workers, instead of being skilled or semi-skilled, will be knowledgeable, self-empowered and flexibly skilled. The type of work, instead of being structured and hardware-driven, will be less structured and software-driven. Management style will emphasize more on delegation rather than giving command. The impact on the environment and ecology will be strikingly less compared to the industrial economy. Finally, the economy will be knowledge-driven and not industry-driven.
>
> President Abdul Kalam, Inauguration of International Conference on Digital Libraries, 24 February 2004.

Whilst progress may be slow, India often does things very differently from other countries. As Yogesh Deveshwar, chairman of India's largest tobacco firm, ITC, said: 'We are building a cathedral. They see us chipping away at the stone, and wonder at such a wasteful activity.'

In conclusion, perhaps the tiger analogy often linked to Asia (Japan, Taiwan, Singapore, Thailand and South Korea) is less appropriate to describe India than an elephant – if someone is standing in front of one, they would do better to either sit astride or step aside.

# 5.4

# Business Interaction

*Deepak Mahtani, Winning Communications Partnership Ltd.*

Many a businessperson starting to do business with India is confronted with a number of challenges. The way business is conducted is different from what one would expect. Having done business with Japan or South Korea does not necessarily guarantee success when trying to do business in India.

The reason for this is that there are some key differences in the way Indians tackle business, based largely on the country's history and religion. Whilst many things are changing in terms of business culture, with more professionals and companies trying to adopt Western business culture, the majority of Indian business still lags behind.

India has a long tradition spanning over 7,000 years and its culture is engrained more deeply than many would care to admit or acknowledge. Will India ever change? In his book *India Unbound*, Gurcharan Das, former CEO of Proctor & Gamble, wrote: '... India is more likely to preserve its way of life and its civilization of diversity, tolerance, and spirituality against the onslaught of the global culture. If it does, then it is perhaps a wise elephant.'

And it is this cultural distinctiveness that makes India a challenging country in which to do business.

The key concept to grasp is that India does business through relationships. Extended family, arranged marriages, the relationships between family and business, the interdependence of culture, religion, work and life are only a few examples.

This legacy of the family is one of tradition. From independence in 1947 up until 1990, 80 per cent of India's output was controlled by 20 large conglomerates – mostly family-owned and managed businesses with names like Tata, Birla, Mahindra, Bajaj and others permeating every industry sector. These names are still around today. It is unlikely that this family-centric approach will decline in any major form for the foreseeable future.

It is estimated that family businesses make up some 70 per cent of the total market capitalization in India today and 75 per cent of total employment. Indians are born into groups (families, clans, castes, sub-castes and communities, be they social, cultural or religious). They live with a sense of 'belonging' to these specified groups, which give them both security and identity. They act as social security, marriage bureaus, money exchanges and job agencies, etc.

It is said that an Indian's greatest fear is to be left alone to fend for himself. This is, of course, very different from the Western individualistic culture.

It is within this social context and sense of relationship that business is conducted best. Many companies and indeed some of the largest in India today employing 20,000+ employees often appear as an 'extended family', with mutual respect and responsibilities being manifested at every level of the organization, between senior managers and middle managers, managers and employees, and colleagues and colleagues. This is one of the main reasons that relationships are critical in doing business in India.

Whilst much Western business is done in a task-oriented way, it would be wise for anyone trying to do business to focus more on personal relationships.

This involves knowing family history, company history and referring to it. Remembering family names, ages and job titles is very important. You may be surprised by what appears to be Indian curiosity when asked 'How much do you earn?' or 'What kind of house do you live in?' These are not intended to be probing questions, but purely aimed at building a relationship. The Indian mindset is 'if I can trust you as a person, I can trust you with my business.'

This is often why you may be invited for endless cups of tea or meals with your Indian hosts. Business deals may seem to take longer than you are used to. However, to an Indian, the view seems to be: 'if I know who I am working with, I can leave the business to take care of itself.'

Initial contacts or meetings often may take place over lunch or dinner, usually in a neutral place such as a restaurant or hotel lobby. If an Indian invites you to his or her home, it is a great honour and you should accept if you can.

## Contacts or referrals

Another key to unlocking success in India is working with contacts or referrals. Cold calling works to some limited extent in the Western business world. However, the rate of success of cold calling in India is next to nil. Instead, success is aided very much by who you know or who has recommended you. This is not to say that appointments are impossible to come by in India – people generally are too polite to refuse – but you may not see the right person at the right level for any decision or buy-in.

Using your local contact and going under his or her recommendation will save you much time and effort. They know the local customs, ways of doing business and can help you navigate an otherwise sometimes frustrating environment.

## Status and authority levels

It is very important to know who your counterparts in India are. What authority level(s) does he or she have to agree terms and conditions with, sign agreements with, etc. Many a Western businessperson has experienced a very positive meeting, with all the right signals and many promises, but then received no business at the end of the day.

The myriad of interrelationships and interpersonal contacts that people have mean that it is always preferable to go with a referee, someone who knows the local scene or is an agent. Even if it costs a few percentage points less in terms of profit margins, it does tend to save a great deal of time and sometimes endless meetings with a string of people.

Due to the importance attached to status and hierarchy, it is essential to get your own credentials right. Some businesspeople going to India make separate cards indicating their position, their qualifications and any letters after their name. Often a letter of recommendation from head office or a senior manager or CEO can suffice. This is especially so if the perception of your Indian counterpart is that they perceive you to be young and inexperienced in a culture where age and experience derived from years of service are still important. It is a rare occurrence that (apart from a handful of IT and finance companies) people in senior management are aged below 50 years.

Whilst much Indian business interaction in the office environment seems formal, the importance of an informal setting cannot be overlooked. It is often in informal settings (over a cup of tea or meal), that problems are raised, real decisions are made, and true and honest feedback on project deadlines and timetables is received.

## Negotiation – everything is negotiable

Another key to business interaction in India is understanding negotiation or what many Westerners call ‘haggling’. It is said that Indians have negotiation in their blood. They are a nation of traders and marketers. Every young Indian grows up with the concept that ‘everything is negotiable’. Sometimes children as young at five years old can be seen bartering for sweets. This practice continues throughout their lives.

Negotiation is a way of life and an Indian quickly learns that if one does not negotiate, he or she ends up the loser. Negotiation arises with rickshaw drivers, taxis, and shop owners. It is expected and is not restricted to price. Indians negotiate what table they sit at in a restaurant, which floor of a hotel they stay in, how far from the elevator they are located – the list goes on.

For the businessperson in India, the biggest frustration will be an aversion to negotiate and accepting things at face value. What you see is not necessarily what you get. Indians also negotiate time and deadlines. What begins as a time frame of four weeks will be negotiated to six or eight until gradually a common agreement.

Many foreign businesspeople say that the Indians are some of the hardest negotiators in the world and truly do 'drive a hard bargain'.

# Conflict

Due to the strong relational basis of society, conflict and conflict resolution are very different to what many Westerners are accustomed to. In many Western societies, conflict is a part of work and business. In fact, it is part of the creative cycle.

In India, however, Indians tend to avoid conflict at all possible cost, as it is seen as bringing shame and loss of face to an individual, a company or indeed an entire nation. Conflict is handled within the context of the relationship with an intention to preserve the relationship and the harmony within it.

This is best illustrated with two examples:

1. A French company I dealt with had a good relationship with their Indian partners, whose managing director was known to me. After a few years, however, things became difficult. The French managing director called on a Friday, telling me that his Indian counterpart had not returned his calls, did not see the importance of the deadline and as a result he was going to sue the Indian company. After calming him down, I told him that this is not how things are resolved in India. Having told him to give me the weekend, I spoke to the Indian MD, informed him of the French MD's anger and that urgent steps needed to be taken. We had a three-way telephone conference on the Monday talking warmly about the last seven years of work, how they worked well together, and into that context introduced the current problem. By the end of the discussion, having re-established the relationship, we managed to move on.
2. A colleague of mine who travels regularly to India recounted a story of being in a traffic jam in Bangalore. His private car was taking him and his two overseas guests from the hotel to Electronics City. In heavy traffic, his car hit the taxi in front. Already running 30 minutes late, the foreign guests were becoming impatient. The two drivers got out of their cars, inspected the damage, exchanged a few words and pointed in a direction. A few metres later, they turned off the main road and stopped off at a tea shack. By this time, the two guests were furious and demanded their host did something, but the Indian said: 'It will be sorted out.' A few minutes later, the two drivers walked back to the cars and my colleague's driver just put a few hundred rupees in the taxi driver's hands for the repairs and got back on the road. There were no lawsuits,

no insurance claims; conflicts were handled within the relationship, seeking, above all, to maintain harmony.

If at all possible, it is better to try to work out differences within the relationship and maintain harmony with colleagues. Do not instantly say: 'I'll take you to court' or 'You're breaking the contract.' These concepts of court and contract are very different in India.

Some of the key differences in Indian business interaction can be summed up as the following:

- Values
  - Success brings increased status.
  - Creativity is admired.
  - Attitude to experimentation is positive.
  - Honesty is not a major issue as a value, but is relative.
  - Fatalism is widespread.
  - Risk-taking is common and seen as positive.
  - Work ethic is strong.
- Relationships
  - Hierarchical system with its duties and obligations is accepted.
  - Boss must be humanistic.
  - Loyalty to a group is important.
  - Honour to both family and group is defended.
  - Family orientation is strong.
- Negotiating style
  - Authority is given (but may choose not to use it).
  - Negotiation is seen as a game of life.
  - Style is indirect.
  - Style is non-confrontational.

Keeping these factors in mind will enable your business interaction in India to bring successful results. Indians are often said to be some of the most hospitable and friendly people. You will not only engage in good, effective business but also develop some good friends who will challenge your own views and ideas and open your mind to new horizons. Perhaps this is the richness of India being able to assimilate the old and the new, the good and the bad, the rich and the poor. The extremes do not seem to contradict or clash as much in a country such as India.

# 5.5

# Human Resources Issues

*Devyani Vaishampayan, Global HR*

## Introduction

India is increasingly attractive not just as a growth market with a large number of new consumers but also as a source of talent. This is evident by a large number of 'offshored operators' and recent plans by multinationals like Cisco to set up their Global Technical Centres here. This chapter examines the key areas of HR (human resources) that any business needs to look at while planning entry or expansion into India and focuses on differences with respect to the West.

## Resource planning

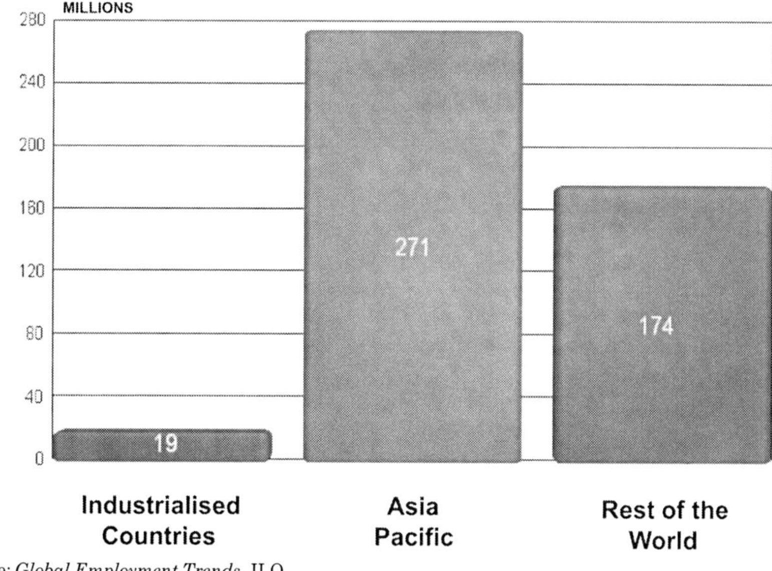


Source: *Global Employment Trends*, ILO

Figure 1. Workforce growth to 2010

According to an International Labour Organization (ILO) Global Employment Trends report, in 2010, 50 per cent of the new entrants to the global labour market will come from India and China. This means an estimated 135 million new workers will be available in India alone. In sharp contrast, the industrialized countries which comprise most of what we know as the Western economy (Europe and United States) will produce only 19 million of the labour supply. In theory, therefore, there should be no shortage of skills for any new business entering India. In reality, however, there is a huge talent shortage in the country. This is because most of the population still does not have the necessary education or vocational skills needed.

Even where professional skills exist on paper, the actual availability becomes limited due to the following factors.

## Limited suitability

A study by McKinsey (*The Emerging Global Labor Market,* McKinsey Global Institute, June 2005) shows that while India produces a large number of graduates, a number of them are unsuitable to work for a Western or multinational business for several reasons. The first is unfamiliarity with the English language, which is the language of business in India. The second is that the educational approach is very 'exam-oriented' as opposed to a 'project-oriented' one. This makes students strong on concepts/theory but unable to apply it when they start work. Finally, there is often a lack of 'cultural fit'. Western societies and organizations are based on a concept of 'equality' while 'status' still pervades the mindsets of many Indians and they find it difficult to adjust in an environment where 'hierarchy' does not dictate.

Figure 2 gives a relative comparison of the suitability of graduates across a number of emerging economies.

| | Countries | Engineer | Finance/accounting | Generalist |
|---|---|---|---|---|
| Eastern Europe | **Russia** | **10** | **20** | **10** |
| | Czech Republic | 50 | 40 | 20 |
| | Poland | 50 | 30 | 15 |
| | Hungary | 50 | 50 | 30 |
| Asia | **China** | **10** | **15** | **3** |
| | Philippines | 20 | 30 | 25 |
| | India | 25 | 15 | 10 |
| | Malaysia | 35 | 25 | 20 |
| Latin America | **Brazil** | **13** | **13** | **8** |
| | Mexico | 20 42* | 25 35* | 11 |

All suitability rates are empirically based on a total of 83 interviews with HR professionals working in each country

Source: The Emerging Global Labor Market by McKinsey Global Institute, 2005, which interviewed HR managers, HR agencies and heads of global resourcing centres.
"Of 100 graduates with the correct degree, how many could you employ if you had demand for all?"
* Mexico is the only country where interview results (higher number) were adjusted since interview base was thinner and risk of misunderstanding high.

Figure 2. Comparison of suitability across various countries

## Dispersion

In order to be realistic about the skills available, a second factor to take into account is the location of your business. Larger cities (Mumbai, Bangalore, Delhi, etc.) tend to have a larger proportion of qualified professionals along with the second tier cities (Pune, Ahmedabad, Chandigarh, etc.) while the third tier or rural areas are better suited for manufacturing. However, as compared to the other emerging economies, India fares very well as there is a larger number of graduates willing to relocate for the right job or living close to a major airport (see Figure 3).

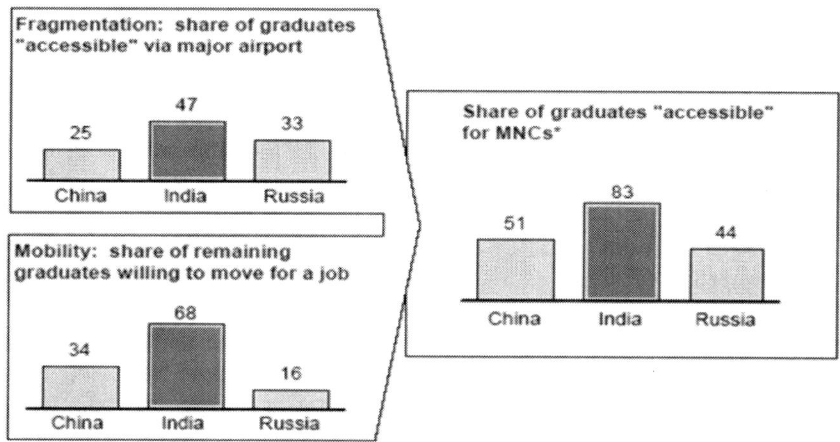


Source: *The Emerging Global Labor Market* by McKinsey Global Institute, 2005

Figure 3. Dispersion of labour force

Table 1. Key statistics on the available workforce in India

| | |
|---|---|
| % of total global workforce | 27% |
| Number of young professional graduates with up to seven years' work experience | 14 million |
| % of graduates qualified for work in MNCs | 15% |
| Mobility – % of graduates willing to move for a job | 68% |
| Fragmentation – % of graduates accessible via a major airport | 47% |
| Projected demand for qualified university graduates | Number of jobs in IT and BPO exports to increase from 700,000 in 2005 to 2.3 million by 2010. |
| Projected demand for international calibre managers | Number of middle managers in offshore services expanding by more than 20% a year. |

Source: *The Emerging Global Labor Market* by McKinsey Global Institute, 2005

In summary, due to its strong educational base, India has a large number of technical and professional graduates. According to Jeff Immelt, Chief Executive of General Electric, it is this combination of limitless demographics and a strong technical underpinning that makes India such a strong competitor in the talent market.

## Recruitment

Given the above it is necessary to design HR processes that are flexible and suited to local environments – in contrast to the 'headquartered' approach still employed in many multinationals. For example, a call centre in India typically puts applicants through a rigorous seven-stage screening process, because of the 'sifting' required to select from such a big pool of potentially qualified candidates, and then, because of the limited job opportunities within India, acceptance rates tend to be of the order of 90 per cent. A similar operation in the United States would have a two-stage process and an average acceptance rate of only 50 per cent.

A second factor to be careful of is the quality of the 'recruitment agency' used for recruitment efforts. Rapid growth over the last decade has spawned a large number of recruitment companies – many of whom may not have the capability to deliver optimal standards.

While a skill shortage exists at all levels, it is particularly acute in two areas. The first is mid-level managers in their 40s who have experience of both the industry or sector and managing in the 'new environment'. For example, in the oil and gas sector most of the managers come from ONGC (Oil and Natural Gas Corporation), which is the large national oil company. However, the culture and management style there can make them unsuitable for some of the Western oil companies. Technical people get promoted to project management in IT (information technology) firms but do not have the necessary skills to be able to interact with clients. The so-called 'finishing schools' have emerged in India to fill this gap, but it does not necessarily provide the solution.

Indian firms also have to work to find talented managers who can surmount problems associated with distributing their products and managing their supply chains. Infrastructure beyond the cities is not that strong yet.

A second area of shortage is managers with real international experience. Given the international growth experienced by many Indian organizations, there is a big need for managers who have had experience of working abroad.

## Compensation and benefits

This is one of the biggest areas of differences that any organization entering India should be prepared for. With salaries growing at a rate of 15–45 per cent, the market can be very uneven based on the level and industry you are looking at. Many companies now give senior executives the lifestyle they crave – apartments in posh localities, soft loans to buy homes, health care, club memberships and of course a lot of cash.

A study by ECA International shows that in 2007 India saw the highest pay hikes in the world. While the cost of living is going up too, real wages are keeping up, in spite of inflation.

Table 2. Real wage increases, 2007

| Country | Increase (%) |
|---|---|
| India | 7% |
| Indonesia | 6% |
| China | 6% |
| Philippines | 4% |
| Thailand | 4% |
| Russia | 3% |
| United States | 1.2% |

Source: ECA International

But these averages are being spiked by a small elite group of people – particularly the ones from the premier management schools. Prospective employers Goldman Sachs, BNP Paribas, Barclays Capital, Merrill Lynch, ABN Amro, UBS, JP Morgan and HSBC have made pre-placement offers to students this year, and their salaries are the same as those being offered to those from the top business schools in the United States. Salaries for the average employee have not shown the same levels of increase.

According to a recent survey by Hewitt Associates, for 2008, India is likely to top salary hikes in Asia for a fifth year. Real estate and energy companies were seen offering the biggest hikes of 25 per cent and 17.5 per cent, respectively. But the salary increases in India are expected to stabilize in the 9–10 per cent range by 2012.

## Unions

India has the distinction of developing one of the most comprehensive labour laws in the world. Under the Constitution, labour is a concurrent subject implying that both the central and state governments are empowered to enact laws. Over the course of five decades, India has enacted over 150 laws covering various aspects of a worker's life. Some of the important laws include:

- The Minimum Wages Act, 1948;
- The Payment of Wages Act, 1936;
- The Contract Labour [Regulation & Abolition] Act, 1970;

- The Inter-State Migrant Workmen [Regulation & Employment of Conditions of Services] Act, 1979;
- The Bonded Labour System [Abolition] Act, 1976;
- The Child Labour [Prohibition and Regulation] Act, 1986, etc.

The rights, privileges and protection provided by the law, however, are realized only marginally. In India, 93 per cent of the workforce operates in the 'informal economy' and the prevailing conditions have led to the development of duel labour market situations. The workers in the organized sector are fully protected through coverage by the labour laws, although they account for about 8 per cent of the workforce only. Incidentally, the majority of this workforce is employed in government owned establishments. The labour in the unorganized sector, accounting for over 92 per cent of the workforce, is deprived of the benefits accruable under the various laws, primarily due to the informal nature of employment. Consequently, they face exploitation of various kinds both at work and at home. Women workers are the worst sufferers of this exploitation. Further, it is in this sector that one observes the existence of child labour.

The Indian trade union movement has a multiplicity of unions, is politically influenced, has centralized decision making and personalized leadership and negligible gender representation. However, the rate of globalization is forcing change. Increasingly, independent and affiliated plant level unions are successfully competing with the recognized and rather ineffective affiliated unions to represent the workers at a particular plant. In the process, they are finding themselves more acceptable to workers and also to employers who find theirs demands and pattern of negotiation more reasonable and attuned to the existing situation in the organization/ enterprise.

## Development and employee engagement

Partly because of the high-service economy and partly because of the longer traditions of high levels of education in the country, management development in India is more sophisticated than in most countries. Given the issues mentioned above around resourcing, organizations need to budget at least 15 per cent more toward training. Training is usually focused around business and customers, leadership, management and product knowledge. The use of e-learning training courses is widespread – and not just for hard skills. IBM, for example, has developed a virtual career coach designed to help employees understand who they are, where and how they do their best work and the options available to them. This then feeds into their individual development plan.

Given the shortage of talent, it is imperative for employers to develop strong employee engagement as a differentiator and increase retention. This is creating a strong culture within organizations around 'focus on the employee'. HCL Technologies is a good case study of this. In an example of employee empowerment, anyone with a complaint or query can open a 'service ticket' – a request for action from one of HCL's internal service functions. So an employee who is concerned about a delayed visa application, say, will open a ticket with the in-house immigration service, while a colleague with a gripe about pay will contact the HR team. Crucially, only the person who opens a ticket can close – or re-open – it, and all support functions are assessed on their ability to resolve issues raised through this system and meet pre-agreed service levels. There is hard evidence that the 'employee first, customer second' philosophy, as it is called, is paying off. A couple of years ago, the employee attrition rate at HCL Technologies was more than 20 per cent, in line with the industry average in India. Today, it is well below that average, ranging from 12 to 14 per cent in India and from 7 to 8 per cent in Europe.

## Diversity management

This is a relatively new concept in Indian organizations and is predominantly seen in the multinationals. Three factors are driving the business case for this. The first is the increasing number of international firms establishing a base in India. The second is a genuine shortage of talent particularly in the service sector. And finally, changing demographics mean that there are more women entering the workforce.

However, the definition of 'diversity' can mean a few different things in India. Table 3 gives an overview of this comparison.

Table 3. Diversity differences

| Definition – West | Definition – India |
|---|---|
| Ethnicity | Caste |
| Gender | Ethno-linguistic (Place of birth) |
| Age | Gender |
| Disability | Religion |
| Sexual Orientation | |

Some hot issues around diversity that need particular attention are:

- Reservation: While caste-based reservation was introduced by the Indian government for all government jobs 60 years ago, its proportion has been rising steadily. At a rough estimate, almost 80 per cent of the jobs in government today are reserved for the scheduled castes and tribes. However, the government is now seriously considering introducing it in the private sector, which is alarming the business community.
- Generational differences: In India today, 50 per cent of the population is under the age of 25. Rapid economic growth is leading to changing

attitudes or aspirations and you have a new generation that is more media savvy and immersed in technology. They seek innovation in everything, are independent minded and want 'quality of life'. Employers need to respond strategically to this talent pool and energy.

- Increase in female employment: Women are becoming an increasing part of the workforce in India. This is due to several macro trends such as the shift from manufacturing to services, better education levels, increased productivity through machines for housework and the need for dual incomes to maintain changing lifestyle aspirations. Social attitudes towards marriage are changing and there are many more women choosing a career over marriage. However, senior management in most organizations is still predominantly male, leading to a lack of understanding in many instances.

## Conclusion

India is going through a rapid pace of growth – both economically and socially. Yet many of the so-called changes are very superficial and the appearance of modernity can lull an outsider into a false sense of understanding. It is important to understand these differences in order to manage issues related to 'people management' effectively.

# Part 6

# Appendices

# 6.1

# Sector Specific Guidelines for FDI

| S. No. | Sector/Activity | FDI Cap/Equity | Entry Route | Other Conditions | Relevant Press Note Issued by D/o IPP1Department of Industrial Policy & Promotion; www.dipp.gov.in |
|---|---|---|---|---|---|
| 1 | **Airports** | | | | |
| a | Greenfield projects | 100% | Automatic | Subject to sectoral regulations notified by the ministry of civil aviation (www.civilaviation.nic.in) | PN 4/2006 |
| b | Existing projects | 100% | FIPB beyond 74% | Subject to sectoral regulations notified by the ministry of civil aviation (www.civilaviation.nic.in) | PN 4/2006 |
| 2 | **Air transport services** | 49% FDI; 100% for NRI1NRI – non-resident Indian investment | Automatic | Subject to no direct or indirect participation by foreign airlines. Government of India Gazette Notification dated 2.11.2004 issued by the ministry of civil aviation (www.civilaviation.nic.in) | |
| 3 | **Alcohol** – distillation and brewing | 100% | Automatic | Subject to licence by appropriate authority | PN 4/2006 |
| 4 | **Asset reconstruction companies** | 49% (only FDI) | FIPB | Where any individual investment exceeds 10% of the equity, provisions of Section 3(3)(f) of Securitization and Reconstruction of Financial Assets and Enforcement of Security Interest Act, 2002 should be complied with (www.finmin.nic.in) | |

*(continued)*

| S. No. | Sector/Activity | FDI Cap/Equity | Entry Route | Other Conditions | Relevant Press Note Issued by D/o IPP1Department of Industrial Policy & Promotion; www.dipp.gov.in |
|---|---|---|---|---|---|
| 5 | **Atomic minerals** | 74% | FIPB | Subject to guidelines issued by the Dept of Atomic Energy vide Resolution No. 8/1(1)/97-PSU/1422 dated 6.10.98 | |
| 6 | **Banking** – private sector | 74% (FDI+FII) | Automatic | Subject to guidelines for setting up branches/ subsidiaries of foreign banks issued by RBI (www.rbi.org.in) | PN 2/2004 |
| 7 | **Broadcasting** | | | | |
| a | FM radio | FDI+FII investment up to 20% | FIPB | Subject to guidelines notified by the ministry of information & broadcasting (www.mib.nic.in) | PN 6/2005 |
| b | Cable network | 49% (FDI+FII) | FIPB | Subject to Cable Television Network Rules (1994) notified by the ministry of information & broadcasting (www.mib.nic.in) | |
| f | Up-linking a non-news and current affairs TV channel | 100% | FIPB | Subject to guidelines notified by the ministry of information & broadcasting (www.mib.nic.in) | PN 1/2006 |
| 8 | **Cigars and cigarettes** – manufacture | 100% | FIPB | Subject to industrial licence under the Industrial (Development & Regulation) Act, 1951 | PN 4/2006 |
| 9 | **Coal and lignite mining** for captive consumption by power projects, and iron and steel, cement production and other eligible activities permitted under the Coal Mines (Nationalization) Act, 1973 | 100% | Automatic | Subject to provisions of the Coal Mines (Nationalization) Act, 1973 (www.coal.nic.in) | PN 4/2006 |
| 10 | **Coffee and rubber processing and warehousing** | 100% | Automatic | | PN 4/2006 |

| | | | | | |
|---|---|---|---|---|---|
| 11 | **Construction development projects** – including housing, commercial premises, resorts, educational institutions, recreational facilities, city and regional level infrastructure, townships | 100% | Automatic | Subject to conditions notified vide PN 2/2005 including: a) minimum capitalization of $10 million for wholly owned subsidiaries and $5 million for joint ventures. The funds would have to be brought within six months of commencement of business of the company<br>b) minimum area to be developed under each project – 10 hectares in the case of the development of serviced housing plots; and a built-up area of 50,000 square metres in the case of a construction development project; and any of the above in the case of a combination project. [Note: For investment by NRIs, the conditions mentioned in PN 2/2005 are not applicable] | PN 2/2005; PN 2/2006 |
| 12 | **Courier services** for carrying packages, parcels and other items which do not come within the ambit of the Indian Post Office Act, 1898 | 100% | FIPB | Subject to existing laws and exclusion of activity relating to distribution of letters, which is exclusively reserved for the State (www.indiapost.gov.in) | PN 4/2001 |
| 13 | **Defence production** | 26% | FIPB | Subject to licensing under the Industries (Development & Regulation) Act, 1951, and guidelines on FDI in production of arms and ammunition | PN 4/2001; PN 2/2002 |
| 14 | **Floriculture, horticulture, development of seeds, animal husbandry, pisciculture, aquaculture, cultivation of vegetables, mushrooms under controlled conditions and services related to agro and allied sectors** | 100% | Automatic | | PN 4/2006 |
| 15 | **Hazardous chemicals** viz. hydrocyanic acid and its derivatives; phosgene and its derivatives; and isocyanates and diisocyanates of hydrocarbon | 100% | Automatic | Subject to industrial licence under the Industries (Development & Regulation) Act, 1951, and other sectoral regulations | PN 4/2006 |
| 16 | **Industrial explosives** – manufacture | 100% | Automatic | Subject to industrial licence under the Industries (Development & Regulation) Act, 1951, and regulations under the Explosives Act, 1898 | PN 4/2006 |

*(continued)*

| S. No. | Sector/Activity | FDI Cap/Equity | Entry Route | Other Conditions | Relevant Press Note Issued by D/o IPP1Department of Industrial Policy & Promotion; www.dipp.gov.in |
|---|---|---|---|---|---|
| 17 | **Insurance** | 26% | Automatic | Subject to licensing by the Insurance Regulatory & Development Authority (www.irdaindia.org) | PN 10/2000 |
| 18 | **Investing companies in infrastructure/services sector** (except telecom sector) | 49% | RIPB | Foreign investment in an investing company will not be counted towards sectoral cap in infrastructure/services sector provided the investment is up to 49% and the management of the company is in Indian hands | PN 2/2000; PN 5/2005 |
| 19 | **Mining** – covering exploration and mining of diamonds and precious stones; gold silver and minerals | 100% | Automatic | Subject to the Mines & Minerals (Development & Regulation) Act, 1957 (www.mines.nic.in) [PN 18/1998 and PN 1/2005 are not applicable for setting up 100% owned subsidiaries in so far as the mining sector is concerned, subject to a declaration from the applicant that he has no existing joint venture for the same area and/or the particular mineral] | PN 2/2000; PN 3/2005; PN 4/2006 |
| 20 | **Non-banking finance companies** – approved activities | | | | |

| | | | | | |
|---|---|---|---|---|---|
| i) | merchant banking | 100% | Automatic | Subject to: a) minimum capitalization norms for fund based NBFCs – $0.5 million to be brought up front for FDI up to 51%; $5 million to be brought up front for FDI above 51% and up to 75%; and $50 million out of which $7.5 million to be brought up front and the balance in 24 months for FDI beyond 75% and up to 100%<br>b) minimum capitalization norms for non-fund based NBFC activities – $0.5 million<br>c) foreign investors can set up 100% operating subsidiaries without the condition to disinvest a minimum of 25% of its equity to Indian entities subject to bringing in Under Secretary $50 million without any restriction on number of operating subsidiaries without bringing additional capital<br>d) joint venture operating NBFCs that have 75% or less than 75% foreign investment will also be allowed to set up subsidiaries for undertaking other NBFC activities subject to the subsidiaries also complying with the applicable minimum capital inflow<br>e) compliance with the guidelines of the RBI. | PN 2/2000; PN6/2000; PN 2/ 2001 |
| ii) | Underwriting | | | | |
| iii) | Portfolio management services | | | | |
| iv) | Investment advisory services | | | | |
| v) | Financial consultancy | | | | |
| vi) | Stock broking | | | | |
| vii) | Asset management | | | | |
| viii) | Venture capital | | | | |
| ix) | Custodial services | | | | |
| x) | Factoring | | | | |
| xi) | Credit reference agencies | | | | |
| xii) | Credit rating agencies | | | | |
| xiii) | Leasing and finance | | | | |
| xiv) | Housing finance | | | | |
| xv) | Forex broking | | | | |
| xvi) | Credit card business | | | | |
| xvii) | Money changing business | | | | |
| xviii) | Micro credit | | | | |
| xix) | Rural credit | | | | |

*(continued)*

| S. No. | Sector/Activity | FDI Cap/Equity | Entry Route | Other Conditions | Relevant Press Note Issued by D/o IPP1Department of Industrial Policy & Promotion; www.dipp.gov.in |
|---|---|---|---|---|---|
| 21 | **Petroleum and natural gas sector** | | | | |
| a | Other than refining and including market study and formulation; investment/financing; setting up infrastructure for marketing in petroleum and natural gas sector | 100% | Automatic | Subject to sectoral regulation issued by the ministry of petroleum and natural gas; and in the case of actual trading and marketing of petroleum products, divestment of 26% equity in favour of Indian partner/public within five years (www.petroleum.nic.in) | PN 1/2004; PN 4/2006 |
| b | Refining | 26% in the case of PSUs; 100% in the case of private companies | FIPB (in the case of PSUs); Automatic (in the case of private companies) | Subject to sectoral policy (www.petroleum.nic.in) | PN 2/2000 |
| 22 | **Print media** | | | | |
| a | Publishing of newspaper and periodicals dealing with news and current affairs | 26% | FIPB | Subject to guidelines notified by the ministry of information & broadcasting (www.mib.nic.in) | |
| b | Publishing of scientific magazines/specialty journals/ periodicals | 100% | FIPB | Subject to guidelines notified by the ministry of information & broadcasting (www.mib.nic.in) | PN 1/2004 |
| 23 | **Power** – including generation (except atomic energy), transmission, distribution and power trading | 100% | | Subject to provision of the Electricity Act, 2003 (www.powermin.nic.in) | PN 2/1998; PN 7/2000; PN 4/ 2006 |
| 24 | **Tea sector** – including tea plantation | 100% | | Subject to divestment of 26% equity in favour of Indian partner/Indian public within five years and prior approval of state government for change in land use | PN 6/2002 |
| 25 | **Telecommunication** | | | | |

| | | | | | |
|---|---|---|---|---|---|
| a | Basic and cellular, unified access services, national/ international long distance, V-Sat, public mobile radio trunked services (PMRTS), global mobile personal communications services (GMPCS) and other value-added telecom services | 74% (including FDI, FII, NRI, FCCBs, ADRs, GDRs, convertible preference shares, and proportionate foreign equity in Indian promoters/investing company) | Automatic up to 49%; FIPB beyond 49% | Subject to guidelines notified in PN 5/2005 | PN 5/2005 |
| b | ISP with gateways, radio-paging, end-to-end bandwidth | 74% | Automatic up to 49%; FIPB beyond 40% | Subject to licensing and security requirements notified by the Department of Telecommunications (www.dot.gov.in) | PN 4/2001 |
| c | ISP without gateway, infrastructure provider, providing dark fibre, electronic mail and voicemail | 100% | Automatic up to 49%; FIPB beyond 40% | Subject to the condition that such companies shall divest 26% of their equity in favour of the Indian public in five years, if these companies are listed in other parts of the world; also subject to licensing and security requirements where required (www.dot.gov.in) | PN 9/2000 |
| d | Manufacture of telecom equipment | 100% | Automatic | Subject to sectoral requirements (www.dot.gov.in) | PN 2/2000 |
| 26 | **Trading** | | | | |
| a | Wholesale/cash and carry trading | 100% | Automatic | Subject to guidelines for FDI in trading issued by the D/o IPP vice PN 3/2005 | PN 4/2006 |
| b | Trading for exports | 100% | Automatic | | |
| c | Trading of items sourced from small scale sector | 100% | FIPB | | |
| d | Test marketing of such items for which a company has approval for manufacture | 100% | FIPB | | |
| e | Single brand product retailing | 51% | FIPB | | |
| 27 | **Satellites** – establishment and operation | 74% | FIPB | Subject to sectoral guidelines issued by the Department of Space/ISRO (www.isro.org) | |
| 28 | **Special economic zones and free trade warehousing zones** – covering setting up of these zones and setting up units in the zones | 100% | Automatic | Subject to the Special Economic Zones Act, 2005, and foreign trade policy (www.sezindia.nic.in) | PN 9/2000; PN 2/2006; PN 4/ 2006 |

Source: Updates to these guidelines can be found at http://dipp.nic.in/manual/FDI_Manual_Latset.pdf (note that the spelling is "latset" in the address)

# 6.2

# Clearances and Approvals Information

| Subject matter | Concerned ministry/ government department | Website address |
|---|---|---|
| Industrial entrepreneur memorandum for delicensed industries | Department of Industrial Policy & Promotion | http://dipp.gov.in |
| Approval for industrial licence/carry-on-business licence | Department of Industrial Policy & Promotion | http://dipp.gov.in |
| Approval for technology transfer: | | |
| i) automatic route | Reserve Bank of India, | http://www.rbi.org.in |
| ii) government approval (PAB) | Department of Industrial Policy & Promotion | http://dipp.gov.in |
| Approval for financial collaboration: | | |
| i) automatic route | Reserve Bank of India | http://www.rbi.org.in |
| ii) government approval (FIPB) | Department of Economic Affairs | http://finmin.nic.in |
| Approval of industrial park: | | |
| i) automatic route | | |
| ii) non-automatic route (empowered committee) | Department of Industrial Policy & Promotion | http://dipp.gov.in |
| Registration as a company and certificate of commencement of business | Department of Company Affairs (Registrar of Companies) | http://dca.gov.in |
| Matters relating to FDI policy and its promotion and facilitation as also promotion and facilitation of investment by non-resident Indians (NRIs) | Department of Industrial Policy & Promotion | http://dipp.gov.in |
| Matters relating to foreign exchange | Reserve Bank of India | http://www.rbi.org.in |
| Matters relating to taxation | Department of Revenue, | http://finmin.nic.in |
| Matters relating to direct taxation | Central Board of Direct Taxes, | http:// incometaxindia.gov.in |
| Matters relating to excise and customs | Central Board of Excise and Customs | http://www.cbec.gov.in |
| Matters relating to industrial relations | Ministry of Labour | http://labour.nic.in |
| Import of goods | Directorate General of Foreign Trade | http://dgft.delhi.nic.in |
| Matters relating to environment and forest clearance | Ministry of Environment & Forests | http://envfor.nic.in |
| Overseas investment by Indians | Ministry of Overseas Indian Affairs | http://moia.gov.in/ |
| Allotment of land/shed in industrial areas, acquisition of land, change in land use, approval of building plan, release of water connection, etc. | Concerned Departments of State Governments | A link for website address of the state/UT is given at www.dipp.gov.in |

Source: Government of India, Ministry of Commerce

# 6.3

# Addresses for Filing Applications

| Sl.No. | Application | Address for filing |
|---|---|---|
| 1. | Industrial licence/COB licence | PR&C Section, SIA, Department of Industrial Policy & Promotion, Ministry of Commerce & Industry, Udyog Bhavan, New Delhi – 11 India |
| 2. | IEM | PR&C Section, SIA, Department of Industrial Policy & Promotion, Ministry of Commerce & Industry, Udyog Bhavan, New Delhi – 11 India |
| 3. | Monthly production returns | Jt. Director, Industrial Statistics Unit (ISU), Department of Industrial Policy & Promotion, Room No. 326, Udyog Bhavan, New Delhi – 11 India<br>Fax: 011-23014564<br>E-mail: vishu@ub.nic.in |
| 4. | FDI application with NRI investment & 100% EOU application and FDI in retail trading | PR&C Section, SIA, Department of Industrial Policy & Promotion, Ministry of Commerce & Industry, Udyog Bhavan, New Delhi – 11 India |
| 5. | Foreign technology agreement under government approval | Project Approval Board, SIA, Department of Industrial Policy & Promotion, Ministry of Commerce & Industry, Udyog Bhavan, New Delhi – 11 India |
| 6. | Approval for industrial park, model town/growth centre under government approval | PR&C Section, SIA, Department of Industrial Policy & Promotion, Ministry of Commerce & Industry, Udyog Bhavan, New Delhi – 11 India |
| 7. | FDI under automatic route | Regional Office concerned of Reserve Bank of India (addresses are available at RBI website) |
| 8. | FDI application under government route | FIPB Unit, Department of Economic Affairs, Ministry of Finance, North Block, New Delhi – 110001 India |
| 9. | Registration and incorporation of company | Registrar of Companies, Ministry of Company Affairs, B Block, 2nd floor, Paryavaran Bhavan, CGO complex, New Delhi – 110003 India |
| 10. | For setting up liaison/project/ branch office of a foreign company | Reserve Bank of India, Central Office, Foreign Investment Division, Shaheed Bhagat Singh Road, Mumbai – 400001 India |

Source: Government of India, Ministry of Commerce
Note: NRI – non-resident Indian

# 6.4

# State Statistics

| *State* | *Capital* | *Official Website* | *Official Language/s* | *Location Description* | *Area in Square Kms* | *Population (2001 census) in millions* | *Literacy Rate (2001) %* | *Gross State Domestic Product (GSDP) (2004/5, 2003/4*, 2002/3**) US$ bn* | *Per Capita US$pa* |
|---|---|---|---|---|---|---|---|---|---|
| Andhra Pradesh | Hyderabad | www.aponline.gov.in | Telugu, Urdu | Mid Eastern coast | 275068 | 76.20 | 61.11% | 44.54 | 509 |
| Arunachal Pradesh | Itanagar | http://arunachalpradesh.gov.in/ | English, Hindi | NE/Chines border | 83743 | 1.10 | 54.74% | 0.56 | 430 |
| Assam | Dispur | http://assamgovt.nic.in/ | Assamese; Bangla; Bodo; Karbi | S & E of Bhutan | 78483 | 26.70 | 64.28% | 9.57 | 300 |
| Bihar | Patna | http://gov.bih.nic.in/ | Hindi; Angika; Bhojpuri; Magahi; Maithili | SE of Nepal | 94164 | 83.00 | 47.53% | 12.56 | 127 |
| Chhattisgarh | | www.chhattisgarh.nic.in | Hindi; Chhattisgarhi | Inland from Kolkata | 135194 | 20.80 | 65.18% | 8.47* | 326* |
| Goa | Panaji | http://goagovt.nic.in/ | Konkani; Marathi | Middle of west coast | 3702 | 1.30 | 82.32% | 2.12* | 1290* |
| Gujarat | Gandhinagar | www.gujaratindia.com | Gujarati | Pakistan coastal border | 196024 | 50.70 | 69.97% | 39.48 | 623 |
| Haryana | Chandigarh | http://haryana.gov.in | Hindi; Punjabi | NW of Delhi | 44212 | 21.10 | 68.59% | 18.25 | 719 |
| Himachal Pradesh | Simla | http://himachal.nic.in/ | Hindi; Pahari | borders China/ Tibet | 55673 | 6.10 | 77.13% | 4.41 | 604 |
| Jammu and Kashmir | Summer: Srinagar Winter: Jammu | http://jammukashmir.nic.in/ | Kashmiri; Urdu | Borders Pakistan & China | 222236 | 10.10 | 54.46% | 4.59 | 356 |

| | | | | | | | | | |
|---|---|---|---|---|---|---|---|---|---|
| Jharkhand | Ranchi | www.jharkhand.gov.in | Hindi | West of Kolkata | 79700 | 26.90 | 54.13% | 6.05 | 286 |
| Karnataka | Bangalore | www.karnataka.gov.in | Kannada | west coast | 191791 | 52.80 | 67.04% | 32.66 | 526 |
| Kerala | Thiruvananthapuram (Trivanderum) | www.kerala.gov.in | Malayalam | SW tip | 38863 | 31.80 | 90.92% | 22.1 | 594 |
| Madhya Pradesh | Bhopal | www.mp.nic.in | Hindi | Central India | 308144 | 60.30 | 64.11% | 22.66 | 309 |
| Maharashtra | Mumbai | www.maharashtra.gov.in | Marathi | Mumbai and inland | 307713 | 96.90 | 77.27% | 81.77 | 707 |
| Manipur | Imphal | http://manipur.nic.in | Meitei | borders Myanmar | 22327 | 2.10 | 68.87% | 0.89 | 327 |
| Meghalaya | Shillong | http://meghalaya.nic.in | Garo; Khasi; English | north of Bangladesh | 22429 | 2.30 | 63.31% | 1.16 | 430 |
| Mizoram | Aizawl | http://mizoram.nic.in | Mizo; English | borders Myanmar | 21081 | 0.90 | 88.49% | .48** | 488** |
| Nagaland | Kohima | http://nagaland.nic.in | English | borders Myanmar | 16579 | 2.00 | 67.11% | 1.04** | 456** |
| Orissa | Bhubaneshwar | www.orissa.gov.in | Oriya | S of Kolkata | 155707 | 36.80 | 63.61% | 13.04 | 299 |
| Punjab | Chandigarh | http://punjabgovt.nic.in | Punjabi | borders Pakistan | 50362 | 24.40 | 69.95% | 19.43 | 675 |
| Rajasthan | Jaipur | www.rajasthan.gov.in | Hindi; Rajasthani | borders Pakistan & SW of Delhi | 342236 | 56.50 | 61.03% | 24.28 | 356 |
| Sikkim | Gangtok | http://sikkim.nic.in | Nepali | borders Nepal and Bhutan | 7096 | 0.54 | 69.68% | 0.34 | 530 |
| Tamil Nadu | Chennai | http://tn.nic.in | Tamil | SE tip | 130058 | 62.40 | 73.47% | 41.54 | 571 |
| Tripura | Agartala | http://tripura.nic.in | Bengali; Kokborok | E of Bangladesh | 10492 | 3.20 | 73.66% | 1.57* | 447* |
| Uttar Pradesh | Lucknow | www.upgov.nic.in | Hindi; Urdu | S of Nepal | 238566 | 166.20 | 57.36% | 51.82 | 252 |
| Uttarakhand | Dehradun | http://ua.nic.in | Hindi; Garwhali; Kumaoni | W of Nepal | 53566 | 8.50 | 72.28% | 4.44 | 432 |
| West Bengal | Kolkata | www.banglarmukh.com | Bengali | N of Kolkata | 88752 | 80.20 | 69.22% | 45.49 | 494 |

## Union Territories

| *State* | *Capital* | *Official Website* | *Official Language/s* | *Location Description* | *Area in Square Kms* | *Population (2001 census) in millions* | *Literacy Rate (2001) %* | *Gross State Domestic Product (GSDP) (2004/5, 2003/4*, 2002/3**) US$ bn* | *Per Capita US$pa* |
|---|---|---|---|---|---|---|---|---|---|
| Andaman & Nicobar | Port Blair | www.and.nic.in | Hindi; Bengali; Malayalam; Telugu; Punjabi; Tamil; Nicobarese; English | islands in Indian Ocean, c. 1200kms SE of Kolkata | 8249 | 0.36 | 81.18% | .25** | 623** |
| Chandigarh | Chandigarh | http://chandigarh.nic.in | Punjabi; Hindi | within Punjab | 144 | 0.90 | 81.76% | 1.13 | 1481 |
| Dadra and Nagar Haveli | Silvassa | http://dnh.nic.in | | N of Mumbai | 491 | 0.22 | 60.03% | n/a | n/a |
| Daman and Diu | Daman | | Gujarati | Enclaves on Arabian Sea coast | 122 | 0.16 | 81.09% | n/a | n/a |
| National Capital Territory Delhi (NCT) | Delhi | http://delhigovt.nic.in | English; Hindi; Punjabi; Urdu | | 1483 | 13.80 | 81.82% | 19.95 | 1186 |
| Lakshadweep | Kavaratti | http://lakshadweep.nic.in/ | Malayalam | islands off SW coast | 32 | 0.61 | 87.52% | n/a | n/a |
| Puducherry (formerly Pondicherry) | Pondicherry | http://pondicherry.nic.in | French; Tamil; Telugu; Malayalam | 4 previously French coastal enclaves of: Pondicherry and Karaikal (within Tamil Nadu), Mahe (within Kerala) and Yanam (within Andhara Pradesh) | 492 | 0.97 | 81.49% | 1.42 | 1232 |

Union Territories (UT) do not have local State governements but are ruled by central government through a governor.
Delhi and Puducherry have elected legislatures and are moving towards full Statehood.
Chandigarh is the capital of both the Punjab and Haryana States, but it is not under either jurisdication; it is administered by central government as a UT.
The National Capital Region is an informal term referring to the National Capital Territory Delhi plus the satellite towns of Faridabad, Gurgaon (both in Haryana State) and Noida and Ghaziabad in Uttar Pradesh.
Literacy source: www.srcindore.org/litstate.htm
GSDP source: http://mospi.nic.in/

# 6.5

# Indian Numbering System

Large numbers are counted in India in different units to Western countries.

10
100
1000
are dealt with in the normal Western way.

| | | | |
|---|---|---|---|
| 10,000 | = 1 lakh (or lac) | | |
| 10,00,000 | = 10 lakhs | = one (Western) million = | 1,000,000 |
| 1,00,00,000 | = 1 crore | = 10 (Western) million = | 10,000,000 |

Note that the number has the same amount of zeros, it is just that the commas break it up in a different manner.

# 6.6

# Useful Websites

## Government and State Operated Websites

For states official websites see 6.4.

| | |
|---|---|
| National Portal of India | http://india.gov.in |
| National Portal of India - Business pages | http://india.gov.in/business.php |
| Government of India Directory | http://goidirectory.nic.in |
| Ministry of Commerce & Industry | |
| Department of Commerce | http://commerce.nic.in/ |
| Department of Industrial Policy & Production (DIPP) | http://dipp.nic.in |
| Secretariat for Industrial Assistance (SIA) | http://siadipp.nic.in/sia/default.htm |
| Ministry of Finance | http://finmin.nic.in |
| Ministry of Corporate Affairs | http://mca.gov.in |
| Ministry of Statistics and Programme Implementation | http://mospi.nic.in |
| Reserve Bank of India (RBI, the Central Bank) | www.rbi.org.in |
| Clearing Corporation of India (CCIL) | www.ccilindia.com |
| Securities and Exchange Board of India (SEBI) | www.sebi.gov.in |
| National Council on Educational Research & Training | http://ncert.nic.in |
| Literacy Database State Resource for Adult Education | http://www.srcindore.org/litstate.htm |
| India Trade Promotion Organisation | www.indiatradefair.com |
| Pharmacy Council of India | www.pci.nic.in |
| Press Council of India | http://presscouncil.nic.in |

## Business and Trade Organizations

| | |
|---|---|
| Confederation of Indian Industry | www.ciionline.org |
| Federation of Indian Chambers of Commerce and Industry | www.ficci.com |
| India Brand Equity Foundation (IBEF) | www.ibef.org |
| Institute of Marketing and Management | www.immindia.com |
| Market Research Society of India | www.mrsi-india.com |
| Institute of Chartered Accountants of India | www.icai.org |
| NASSCOM (IT, Software & BPO association) | www.nasscom.org |
| Indian Banks' Association | www.iba.org.in |

## Bi-lateral Trade Organizations

| | |
|---|---|
| Contact details for Joint Business Councils and Chambers without websites can be found at | http://commerce.nic.in/ Bi_Chambers%20_Trade.pdf |
| India-China Chamber of Commerce & Industry | www.indiachinachamber.com |
| Indo-African Chamber of Commerce & Industries | www.indoafrican.org |
| Indo-Australian Chamber of Commerce | www.indoaustchamber.com |
| UK India Business Council | www.ibpn.co.uk |
| Indo-German Chamber of Commerce | www.indo-german.com |
| Indo-Italian Chamber of Commerce | www.indiaitaly.com |
| Indo-Japan Chamber of Commerce & Industry | www.ijcci.com |
| Singapore Indian Chamber of Commerce & Industry | www.sicci.com |
| US India Business Council | www.usibc.com |
| Council of EU Chambers of Commerce in India | www.euindiachambers.com |

## Miscellaneous

### *Newspapers*

| | |
|---|---|
| *Business Standard* | www.business-standard.com |
| *The Economic Times* | www.economictimes.com |
| *Financial Express* | www.financialexpress.com |
| *The Hindu* (Madras based national newspaper) | www.hinduonnet.com |
| *The Hindustan Times* (Delhi based national newspaper) | www.hindustantimes.com |
| *India Daily* (Expat focused) | www.indiadaily.com |
| *Indian Express* (Delhi based national newspaper) | www.indianexpress.com |
| *Times of India* (Delhi based national newspaper) | www.timesofindia.com |

### *Major Commercial Banks*

| | |
|---|---|
| State Bank of India | www.statebankofindia.com |
| SBI Commercial and International Bank | www.sbici.com |
| Standard Chartered | www.standardchartered.com |
| Export-Import Bank of India | www.eximbankindia.com |
| HSBC India | www.hsbc.co.in |
| List of all Indian banks websites | www.rbi.org.in/scripts/banklinks.aspx |

### *Other*

| | |
|---|---|
| National Centre for Trade Information | www.ncti-india.com |
| Global Supply GS1 | www.gs1india.org |
| National Small Industries Corporation | www.nsic.co.in |

| | |
|---|---|
| Office of Development Commissioner, ministry of micro, small & medium enterprise | www.laghu-udyog.com |
| Jobs in India | www.naukri.com |
| Official Tourism Portal (Ministry of Tourism) | www.incredibleindia.org |

## International

| | |
|---|---|
| World Bank | www.worldbank.org |
| IMF | www.imf.org |
| World Association of Investment Promotion Agencies | www.waipa.org |
| Coface | www.coface.com |
| CIA Factbook | www.cia.gov/cia/publications/factbook/index.html |
| GMB Publishing | www.globalmarketbriefings.com |
| GMB Research | www.gmbresearch.com |
| International Executive Development Programmes | www.iedp.info |

# 6.7

# Contributors' Contact Details

Confederation of Indian Industry Institute of Logistics
98/1 Velachery main road
Guindy
Chennai 600032
India
Tel.: +91 44 42 44 4555 Ext. 566
Fax: +91 44 42 44 4510
Email: cil@ciionline.org
Website: www.ciilogistics.com

DTZ Debenham Tie Leung
2A Paharpur Software Technology Park
21 Nehru Place Greens
New Delhi 110019
India
Tel.: +91 11 2620 7108-114
Fax: +91 11 2620 7575
Mobile: +91 98715 07801
Email: vivek.dahiya@dtz.com
Website: http://www.dtz.com

Global HR
Tel.: +44 (0)77 956 51143
Email: dvaishampayan@yahoo.co.uk

Global Marketing Network
103 High Street
Wrestlingworth
BEDS, SG19 2EJ
United Kingdom
Tel.: +44 (0)1767 631 809
Email: Darrell.kofkin@gmnhome.com
Website: www.gmnhome.com

C. Jayanthi
46, Shivalik Apartments
Alaknanda, Pocket-A
New Delhi 110019
India
Tel.: +91 98 1067 2403
c/o The Financial Express
B 14A, Qutab Institutional Area
New Delhi 110016
India
Tel.: +91 11 2603 0883
Email: Jchandrasekharan@gmail.com

KPMG India
Marketing & Communications
Block No. 4B
DLF Corporate Park, DLF City
Phase III
Gurgaon
Haryana 122002
India
Tel.: +91 0124 307 4000 / 254 9191
Fax: +91 0124 2549101 / 254 9102
Website: www.in.kpmg.com

Management Development Institute
Mehrauli Road
Gurgaon 122001
Haryana
India
Tel.: + 91 124 234 9831-36, 401 3050-59
Fax: +91 124 234 1189
Mobile: +91 98104 02639 (Dr. Amit Kapoor)
Email: dramitkapoor@gmail.com; asay@mdi.ac.in
Website: www.mdi.ac.in

Roderick Millar
GMB Publishing Ltd.
Hereford House
23-24 Smithfield Street
London EC1A 9LF
United Kingdom
Tel.: +44 (0)203 031 2900
Fax: +44 (0)207 248 9333
Email: rmillar@gmbpublishing.com
Website: www.globalmarketbriefings.com

NASSCOM (National Association of Software and Service Companies)
International Youth Centre
Teen Murti Marg
Chanakyapuri
New Delhi 110021
India
Tel.: +91 11 2301 0199
Fax: +91 11 2301 5452
Email: Rajdeep@nasscom.in/info@nasscom.in
Website: www.nasscom.in

Shilputsi Consultants
Mumbai
India
Tel.: +91 22 243 79611
Fax: +91 22 243 62909
Email: purvi@shilputsi.com
Website: www.shilputsi.com

Synovate Business Consulting
2nd Floor, AML Centre I
8 Mahal Industrial Estate
Off Mahakali Caves Road
Andheri (East)
Mumbai 400093
India
Tel.: +91 22 4091 8000
Mobile: +91 98676 97194
Email: karthik.ramamurthy@synovate.com
Website: www.synovate.com

Titus & Co. Advocates
Titus House
R-4, Greater Kailash-I
New Delhi 110048
India
Tel.: +91 11 2628 0100, 2647 0700, 2647 5800
Fax: +91 11 2648 0300, 2648 9950
Email: dtitus@titus-india.com; titus@titus-india.com

Winning Communications Partnership Ltd.
P.O. Box 43
Sutton
Surrey
SM2 5WL
United Kingdom

Tel.: +44 (0)208 770 9717
Fax: +44 (0)208 770 9747
Email: mahtanid@aol.com
Website: www.winningcommunications.com

# Index

References in italic indicate figures or tables

LaVergne, TN USA
04 June 2010
184971LV00003B/1/P